Managerial
Dilemmas

Managerial Dilemmas

Exploiting Paradox for Strategic Leadership

John Storey
Graeme Salaman

A John Wiley & Sons, Ltd., Publication

Published in 2009 by   John Wiley & Sons Ltd, The Atrium, Southern Gate, Chichester,
West Sussex PO19 8SQ, England
Telephone (+44) 1243 779777

Email (for orders and customer service enquiries): cs-books@wiley.co.uk
Visit our Home Page on www.wiley.com

Other Wiley Editorial Offices

John Wiley & Sons Inc., 111 River Street, Hoboken, NJ 07030, USA

Jossey-Bass, 989 Market Street, San Francisco, CA 94103-1741, USA

Wiley-VCH Verlag GmbH, Boschstr. 12, D-69469 Weinheim, Germany

John Wiley & Sons Australia Ltd, 42 McDougall Street, Milton, Queensland 4064, Australia

John Wiley & Sons (Asia) Pte Ltd, 2 Clementi Loop #02-01, Jin Xing Distripark, Singapore 129809

John Wiley & Sons Canada Ltd, 6045 Freemont Blvd. Mississauga, Ontario, L5R 4J3 Canada

Wiley also publishes its books in a variety of electronic formats. Some content that appears in print may
not be available in electronic books.

Library of Congress Cataloging-in-Publication Data

Storey, John, 1947–
    Managerial dilemmas : exploiting paradox for strategic leadership / John Storey, Graeme Salaman.
        p.   cm.
    Includes bibliographical references and index.
    ISBN 978-1-4051-6027-8 (cloth)
    1. Leadership.   2. Organizational behavior.   3. Strategic planning.   4. Decision making.
I. Salaman, Graeme.   II. Title.
    HD57.7.S758 2009
    658.4'092–dc22

                                                                        2009007435

British Library Cataloguing in Publication Data

A catalogue record for this book is available from the British Library

ISBN 978-1-4051-6027-8

Typeset in 11 on 15 Goudy by SNP Best-set Typesetter Ltd., Hong Kong
Printed and bound in Great Britain by TJ International Ltd, Padstow, Cornwall

Dedication

This book is dedicated to Anne, Rebecca and David, Rena, Sophie and Alexandra.

Contents

Preface

This book is no ordinary textbook on management. We do not seek to cover, summarize and comment upon the vast literatures on the various key managerial themes covered in this volume. Our aim is rather different, namely, to pursue a central theme and a core tension in managerial work and managerial decision making: managerial dilemmas and paradoxes. Our purpose is to speak to practising managers and advanced students of management so that they can reflect more deeply than is normally encouraged, upon certain underlying currents running through management practice. The book is especially written with the needs of MBA students in mind and for those taking courses in Organizational Behaviour and Strategic Management in particular.

We seek to respond to the challenge presented by Chris Argyris (1999: 92):

> If paradoxes are an important phenomenon for administrators ... why is it that the prominent theories of administration or organization do not have them as a central focus? What would it require to craft theories where paradox has a prime role?

Duality is a constant strand in management thinking and in thinking about management and organizations. Organizations are thought of as mechanistic or organic, as centralized or decentralized, formal or informal, differentiated and integrated, stable and changing and so on. Business strategies likewise, are typically thought of in terms such as low cost or premium, strategies as deliberate or emergent, strategies as fit versus strategies as stretch and diversified or focused strategies. Human resource strategies are conceived of as high trust or low trust. These common ways of depicting management and organizational work as modes of decision making leads us on further to the idea that managers face numerous dilemmas. 'Dilemmas' suggest a set of either/or choices. Conventional wisdom suggests that adept managers find the answer by clever alignment of opportunity, choice and situational context – plus a dash of anticipation of change. In so far as many managerial and organizational issues and problems are not so easily resolvable this leads on to the notion of paradox. 'Paradox' exists when seemingly divergent principles or pulls co-exist – that is they are held in tension simultaneously. To this extent, a paradox is the opposite of a dilemma – the idea in the former is that no absolute either/or choice needs to be made or should be made. There is a further point. The ongoing tensions within the paradoxes provide the impetus for change; any approximation to equilibrium has to be managed. Paradoxical forces therefore provide a dynamism which is exciting, promising and positive, and yet also potentially threatening, discomforting and negative.

We suggest that, in an age of uncertainty, dilemmas and paradoxes are especially evident and prevalent. The ultimate responsibility of leadership is to make sense of these and to handle them in a competent manner. This, we argue, demands a new *mode* of leadership. The management of dilemma and paradox is, we contend, the essence of leadership today.

Charles Dickens famously illustrated the nature of paradox when describing the time leading up to the French Revolution in his novel *The Tale of Two Cities*:

> It was the epoch of belief, it was the epoch of incredulity, it was the season of Light, it was the season of Darkness, it was the spring of hope, it was the winter of despair.

The word paradox derives from the Greek 'paradoxos' – with 'para' denoting against or over and 'doxos' meaning contrary to received wisdom or common sense (Thompson 1988: 131). It is used today to refer to instances where meanings appear to be contradictory and yet where there is also a sense that there is a hidden truth entwined within the opposites.

We are by no means the first to note the power of paradox. Many others have gone before us on this quest. For example, Charles Handy noted 'we have to learn to use the paradoxes – to balance contradictions and incon-sistencies – as an invitation to find a better way' (Handy 1994: 13). Before him, Marx and Weber, Gouldner and many other social scientists also placed dialectic, contradiction and paradox at the heart of their philo-sophies. Thus, the purpose of this book is not to promote a new idea but rather to rediscover its import and its applications under contemporary conditions so that we can gain new insights.

We draw upon two decades of our collaborative research projects and consultancy in these interrelated aspects of management: strategy, knowl-edge, innovation, organizational forms, performance management and control. During these decades as authors we have worked both together and separately on these themes. Many of the projects were funded by the Eco-nomic & Social Science Research Council and by the Engineering & Physi-cal Sciences Research Council and more recently by the NHS National Institute for Health Research and the Service Deliver Organization. Other work was funded by corporate clients including Astra Zeneca, John Lewis, Nortel, Waitrose, Rolls Royce, Ernst & Young, Morgan Stanley and UPS. The work was conducted mainly in the UK but also in the US, Japan, Germany, India and Ethiopia.

As noted, early social scientists placed contradiction and paradox at the heart of their work. But in the latter part of the twentieth century with the rise of management science many of the early lessons were lost. Management writings of the industrial age emphasized order and appeared to recommend the elimination of and resolution of tensions and paradoxes. Contemporary challenges, we suggest, demand a rediscovery of some classic ideas. Our aim is to illustrate the application of such ideas.

We are grateful to the numerous managers and directors with whom we have worked. Most have to remain anonymous as that was part of our con-tracting arrangements with them but others we can name. In the later stages of the work we benefited from conversations with Sanjeeb Chaudhuri, Managing Director of Retail Banking for CitiBank – Europe, Middle East and Africa; Andreas Raffel, Executive Vice Chairman of NM Rothschild & Sons, formerly CEO of Rothschild GmbH; Maurice Dunster Organizational Development Director of JLP; David Day, European Chief Executive of Lightspeed Research – a WPP business; Andy Street, Managing Director of John Lewis and Mark Price, Managing Director of Waitrose.

List of case organizations

Age Concern
Allianz Insurance Group
Astra Zeneca PLC
Barclays Bank
BBC, The
Boots Company PLC
Citigroup
Creda-Hotpoint GDA
DHL
EasyJet
Eni Lasmo Oil PLC
Ernst & Young
Fujitsu
GEC
Hewlett-Packard
ISS UK Carlisle
John Lewis Partnership
KV Automation
Land Command (Army)
LloydsTSB
Luton and Dunstable NHS
    Foundation Trust

Milton Keynes Council
MITIE
Morgan Stanley
NatWest Bank
Nortel
Northampton NHS Trust
Oxfam
Pfizer
Premier Foods
Psion Dacom
Rentokil Initial
Rolls Royce
Sonatest
Tensator
University College London
    Hospitals NHS Foundation Trust
Waitrose
Whitbybird Engineers
Willis Insurance Group

About the authors

John Storey (Ph.D., University of Lancaster) is Professor of Management at the Open University Business School. He is Chairman of the Involvement & Participation Association (IPA) and Non-Executive Director on the Land Command Civilian Personnel Management Board. He is an Elected Fellow of the British Academy of Management, a Fellow of the Higher Education Academy and a member of the UK Government's Leadership & Management Panel. He was formerly Principal Research Fellow, Warwick University Business School and Chair of Strategic HRM at the University of Loughborough. He was Editor of the *Human Resource Management Journal* 1994–2000. He has led a number of major research-council funded studies. The ESRC, the EPSRC and the NHS have funded his projects on the management of innovation, the evolution of business knowledge, strategic human resource management, leadership, board effectiveness, governance and supply chain management. He has written and/or edited 20 books with leading publishers including Blackwell, Edward Elgar, Gower, Wiley, Routledge and Sage. His books include: *Developments in the Management of Human Resources*, (Blackwell); *The Management of Innovation* (Edward Elgar) *Leadership in Organizations* (Routledge) and *Managers of Innovation* (Blackwell). His latest book is: John Storey, Dave Ulrich and Patrick Wright (2009) *Companion to Strategic HRM*, London/New York, Routledge. He has extensive consultancy experience at senior management and board level. His most recent consultancy work includes board level work with John Lewis, Waitrose, the NHS and the Army. He has published around 100 articles in leading journals.

Graeme Salaman (Ph.D., Cambridge University) Graduated from the University of Leicester with a first class degree in Social Sciences, he took a Ph.D. in Organizational Sociology from the University of Cambridge. After two years at the Institute of Industrial Psychology he joined the Open University. He has written over 60 books and articles in his research areas. Most recent publications include *Strategy and Capability* (with David Asch) Blackwell, 2003; *Strategic Human Resource Management*, Blackwell, 1996; *Organizations*, Routledge, 2000; *Decision-Making*, Sage, 2000 and *The Managers of Innovation*, (with John Storey) Blackwell, 2004. Other recent work includes an analysis of current approaches to leadership and a critique of the Learning Organization thesis in *Human Relations* and an analysis of the Management of Innovation (with John Storey) in *The Journal of Management Studies*.

He currently holds (with John Storey) a research grant from the Economic Social Research Council for a study of Knowledge Management. He is a joint grant holder (with John Storey) from the NHS/SDO for a three-year study in 'Comparative Governance and Comparative Effectiveness'. He is an associate of Ashridge Consulting. He has worked as a consultant or trainer for a number of organizations. Current or recent clients include: Allianz Cornhill, DHL, Willis, John Lewis Partnership, Ernst & Young, Sun MicroSystems, British Oxygen, PowerGen, Morgan Stanley, Rolls Royce and The Post Office. He has worked for a number of years as a consultant to the Government of Ethiopia. In that country he is currently working for the Minister of Information – Bereket Simon – on improving the strategy and capability of the Government's media and information management systems.

Part 1
INTRODUCTION

1

Exploiting dilemmas and paradoxes through a new mode of leadership

A century ago, Andrew Carnegie had this advice: 'Concentrate your energies, your thoughts, and your capital. The wise man puts all his eggs in one basket and watches the basket.' But of course the risk, then and now, is that no matter how attentive and focused you are, the basket you're watching is simply the wrong one.

(Moyer 2008)

Knowing which 'basket' to watch and how to design, manage and watch it is a crucial set of skills for managers and leaders. It is our contention in this book that the myriad tasks of and demands on management can be reduced to five core essentials and that these broadly can be sequenced as follows. First, managers are charged with setting a sense of direction (for example, having an answer to the question 'what business are we in?'); second, they are charged with shaping and structuring the array of capabilities and resources at their disposal into some shape and form; third, they are charged with maintaining and improving performance; fourth, they are expected to additionally enable innovation; fifth, they are expected to be able to adapt each and all of the above to meet changes in the environment of the organization such as changing customer and market demands. This set of core managerial roles is a combination of strategic and organizational capabilities. They do not easily fit within any single discipline or function. Moreover, we argue they are not easily reducible to a set of rational rules. On the contrary, the thesis of this book is that when taken separately and together these tasks and activities are subject to multiple dilemmas and paradoxes which defy conventional prescriptions and rules. Such a contention flies in the face of most current management thinking.

In general, managers and management theorists in the mainstream business and management literature over the past 25 years have taken, we maintain, a wrong turning. Guidance, lessons and prescriptions have become increasingly emphatic, increasingly 'rational' and increasingly misleading. Early social theorists as divergent as Weber, March, Simon, Gouldner and Merton recognized the dysfunctionalities and therefore dangers of order and of formal 'rationality' and tried to draw attention to the contradictions and paradoxes inherent in organizations and society. However, over the years, these insights often seem to have been lost. The emphasis gradually, but insistently, shifted to order and tidiness. Hence, the early insights have been neglected as formal rationality asserted its dominance during the high industrial and late industrial age. However, now this 'industrial' model is under stress. The old rules and strictures no longer seem to make sense. New projects, reforms and reorganizations are launched at an increasingly rapid rate and fail to meet expectations just as frequently. In response, 'chaos theory', 'dynamic capability', the 'learning organization' and a number of other such counter movements offer variable glimpses of this truth.

This tension has been accentuated in recent times because of rapid strides in communication technology and global competition – these forces expose the rational model to greater strain and reveal its deficiencies. For example, Prahalad and Krishnan (2008) show how, in the new business paradigm, products and services are at times inseparable, hardware and software merge, and consumption by users is part of production. Because of the intensity and speed of change, managers have increasingly been exposed to different cycles of reorganization and they find colleagues harder to convince with the latest idea. Multiple initiatives are launched. Projects multiply and their proliferation demands that they be consolidated into 'programmes' and placed within 'Programme Offices'. However, the tensions between initiatives and priorities still tend to remain. There is growing awareness that the underlying problem is one of multiple logics and inescapable tensions (Eisenstat 2008).

Ideas such as devolved 'strategic business units', 'empowerment' or 'teamwork', which appear eminently logical when considered in isolation, reveal themselves to be problematical when considered alongside competing logics. Studies of management decision making increasingly reveal organizational problems to be *inherently* multi-dimensional. Managerial decisions on the core issues of strategy, organizational form, managing performance, innovating and changing all involve tensions, dilemmas and paradoxes. Managing these tensions becomes the core competency of top managers under the new order. Ideas and solutions can rebound. For example, one of the most successful corporate growth stories of the past few decades has been that of Hewlett-Packard. That success was usually explained in part at least by reference to the code of values and practices known as 'The HP Way'. When we interviewed one of the senior most UK-based HP Directors in 1999 he made this point:

> The 'HP Way' is central to who we are. It's not just a slogan or a list on a pocket-sized laminated card. It is very much a values-based organization, we try hard to value commitment for example and we value loyalty in both directions.

However, following a de-merger and a series of financial problems, a few years later the 'HP Way' was an idea used by employees to castigate a new management team whom they judged had 'betrayed' that promise. This is a pattern we have found in many other values-based organizations in recent years.

Organizations and management are under increasing pressure to meet multiple, often inconsistent, demands. Increasing technological change, global competition and workforce diversity reveal and intensify paradox. These kinds of disruptions expose tensions within organizations. For example, rising commodity prices or new international competitors raise new questions about sustainability, competitive advantage and core capabilities. Ambiguity fosters multiple, often conflicting interpretations of phenomena. David Day, European Chief executive of Lightspeed, a company within the global WPP Group, gave us an example:

> In today's climate, many large companies – not just WPP – with large complex systems, increasingly look across at businesses that are entrepreneurial, energetic and innovative and say to themselves 'We would like to acquire one of those'. They bring it in and fit it into the financial systems of the broader organization. The founders tend to remain for a while and so the business never really gets integrated, they say 'Don't touch us, we'll deliver'. Then the founders tend to leave and all of a sudden you are left with something which doesn't deliver any more. That is very common, as the founders, the

entrepreneurs who created the company, decide to leave and the spirit of the business goes with them.

Sometimes, trade-offs are required; at other times and in other circumstances they can be avoided. Seductive prescriptions often turn out to be oversimplified depictions. When we refer in this book to 'managerial dilemmas' therefore, we want to move beyond simplistic conceptualizations and to explore instead the rich territories of paradox, complexity, ambiguity and temporality.

Let us take an example from Hewlett-Packard. One of the UK-based Directors explained to us:

> If you get a complex system and you add rules to it, it gets more complex. You see if you try to control complexity with structure, it gets worse. So, what HP has is a number of simple rules which are very powerful in the way that they drive things. One of those rules is: 'You must come in under on expenses and over on quota. …' Um, and if you don't, then the men in grey suits arrive fairly soon. So, it's fiscally fairly tight. And, the moment you're going near breaching the simple rules the red flags start waving. Thus, in this way we seek to be both tight and loose.

Toyota provides another example. Conventionally, it is thought that there is a necessary trade-off between productivity and innovation. This is reflected in Abernathy's work on *The Productivity Dilemma* (Abernathy 1978). However, Toyota's phenomenal record in productivity gains *at the same time* as its impressive achievements in innovation have cast doubts on earlier conventional thinking (Liker and Hoseus 2008; MacDuffie 2008; Osono, Shimizu *et al.* 2008). As these studies reveal, there are a number of 'radical contradictions' at the heart of the Toyota method.

Abernathy's analysis of the productivity versus innovation dilemma is important for a further reason. The fundamental lesson to be drawn from his work (supported in meticulous detail by data stretching over decades in the American automobile industry) is that when managers mishandle this dilemma they jeopardize whole firms and indeed whole industries.

Contrast this with the results of recent investigations behind the success of Toyota. Toyota's unorthodox manufacturing system has enabled it to 'make the planet's best automobiles at the lowest cost and to develop new products quickly' (Osono *et al.* 2008: 96). Between 1980 and 2006 its revenue grew 13-fold – an annual growth rate of 10.1%, and between

1997–2001 it opened 31 new plants around the world (Osono *et al.* 2008): 191–2. Moreover, its system has been widely emulated not only by the world's leading automobile companies and manufacturing forms, but also by organizations in service industries such as hospitals. Detailed study of the Toyota Corporation has revealed that the key to its success is its subtle handling of – and indeed promotion of – contradictions. As Osono and colleagues observe: 'The company succeeds we believe because it creates contradictions and paradoxes in many aspects of organizational life' (2008: 98). In many areas it deliberately fosters contradictory viewpoints and challenges its managers and employees to find answers which transcend differences rather than settle for compromises. Examples of its paradoxical nature include: it takes big leaps yet is patient and moves slowly; it grows steadily and yet maintains a state of never-satisfied and indeed even a degree of paranoia; it has outstandingly efficient operations and yet seems to use employees time wastefully (for example including large number of people in meetings at which they often do not directly participate); it is frugal and yet spends heavily is selected areas; it maintains a strict hierarchy and yet prompts employees to challenge.

In order to foster these 'contradictions' Toyota combines both *forces of expansion* with complementary *forces of integration*. Its forces of expansion include the setting of highly stretching and near-impossible goals. Second, there is a huge emphasis on experimentation – most notably, Toyota encourages all employees to search for improvements by highlighting mistakes and failures. Third, despite its huge emphasis on efficiency and a standardized system, it also promotes and encourages local customization. These forces of expansion are complemented by forces of integration: the values of the founders are held in high esteem, these values are inculcated; the company is loathe to make any redundancies even in times of economic downturn and even when this policy costs money; Toyota also invests in communication across the board. Thus, the forces of expansion are balanced by the forces of integration in a manner which allows a restless forward momentum.

In these and other ways, Toyota exemplifies the contemporary manifestation of managing with paradox. It can be seen to represent a living embodiment of a post-modern, knowledge-based, manufacturing company. It seems to have rejected the logics of the industrial age and through its constant experimentation with contradictory forces made a 'successful transition to the post-industrial, knowledge age' (Osono *et al.* 2008: xii). Toyota actively embraced and cultivated contradictions and management through paradox. In their extensive six-year study of Toyota across numerous countries, Osono, Takeuchi and colleagues found that the company 'actually thrives on paradoxes; it harnesses opposing propositions to energize itself' (2008: xii).

Consider some examples of the contradictions: it thinks and acts both globally and locally – it has a Global Knowledge Centre and yet goes to extraordinary lengths to learn from and adapt to local cultures and settings. It combines hard and soft modes of management. It strives for short-term efficiency and associated incremental wins while also striving for long-term step-change gains. It cultivates frugality yet is willing to spend large sums on selected projects. It cultivates stability and yet also a mindset of paranoia. It is characterized by bureaucracy and hierarchy yet fosters a spirit of dissent. It maintains both simple and complex modes of communication. It sets very hard-to-achieve goals yet emphasizes the need for a strong sense of reality. It expects small scale experimentation *and* occasional audacious leaps.

The company is constantly restless. Tellingly, the Toyota President, Kaysuaki Watanabe, said: 'The two things I fear most are arrogance and contentment' (Osono *et al.* 2008: 214). He also observed:

> We need to create a routine in which tacit knowledge and explicit knowledge can spiral upwards effectively. That requires human effort. We humans should go all out to create a solid educational routine that enables the knowledge level to spiral up ... and to do it globally' (Osono *et al.* 2008: 229).

The contradictions at play propel Toyota to a state of instability and disequilibrium while allowing it simultaneously to exploit hard-won routines. In this manner the platform of performance is moved ever higher in a spiral fashion.

In so far as the business and organizational environment is increasingly dynamic, with shorter product life cycles, technological shifts, changing fashions and new entrants, it can be argued that a crucial competitive advantage and indeed condition for survival will increasingly be the capability to manage paradox. One such paradox at the geopolitical level is that of China, the fastest growing economy of recent times and forecast soon to be the largest, which has developed an economy more capitalist than many western countries while maintaining a communist political regime.

One example of the apparent increase in paradox for corporations can be found in the shift in recent years from a simple competitive model of business to a more complex cooperative and collaborative approach. Organizations began to build collaborative relations and strategic alliances with competitors as well as with suppliers and customers. The coexistence of cooperation and competition brings advantages and tensions (Child and Faulkner 1998; De Wit and Meyer 1999). For example, Unisys and Oracle are working on several initiatives in financial services, outsourcing, the public sector and enterprise computing. They remain competitors and yet, on a global basis, they have developed a strategic 'systems integrator' partnership. In financial services, they combine Unisys's expertise in payments with Oracle's database capabilities.

There is also a fundamental paradox at the very heart of business strategy itself. Strategies that have the greatest chance of success, it has been noted provocatively, also have the greatest probability of failure. The paradox arises because companies base their strategies on specific beliefs or ideas about the future (this is a theme we explore in depth in Chapter 3). However, the future is uncertain and strategies succeed because of luck. It sometimes happens that companies do make what proves to be the right choice on that occasion. If they are less lucky, the same commitments prove to be the wrong ones – and enterprises fail (Raynor 2007).

Often, the management of paradoxes and dilemmas is left to the individual manager. For example, in one of our case companies (Marconi plc – a telecommunications switching-gear designer and manufacturer with a very chequered history) one of the directors who was overseeing a wide range of product groups made this observation about how they handled the demands of efficiency and learning/innovation:

> I mean, there is a very delicate balance to be struck, because obviously we want a culture where meeting deadlines and quality standards is absolutely paramount. But it also has to be a culture where, when things going wrong, they are looked at in a positive light. Everybody's striving very hard to meet targets but failure is looked at from the point of view of well … you know it's looked at as an opportunity, it's not a slagging-off that I have to hand out, you know you're not going to try and criticize people and come down heavy. What you're looking at is the way forward from the problem and looking at the way out. I mean, I think this is particularly important, if you've got a team of people, this is how we manage this – if you've got a team of people designing a particular thing like an ASIC [an application specific integrated circuit]

... well there have been incidents where, well, although we're fairly good at getting ASICS right first time, occasionally ASICS have not worked. If you get the team together after that happens and give them all a bollocking the chances of solving the problem are significantly reduced.

Notable in this case was the wide variety of practice across the company. In some parts, the manager and the subculture was very much efficiency-focused (in some situations some engineers even said it was based on management by fear) in other parts of the company, a very different style of management prevailed. Hence, it would be difficult to claim any corporate-wide approach of the Toyota kind.

In the light of these tensions and of the emergent promising practices, the purpose of this book is to analyse in some depth the true nature of the managerial dilemmas and paradoxes that lurk within each of these and indeed many other areas of organizational life. However, underpinning these phenomena is our long-standing interest in understanding managers' use of theory. During the course of a couple of decades we have conducted a series of studies of managerial action and cognition. These have been funded by the Economic & Social Science Research Council (ESRC), the Engineering & Physical Sciences Research Council (EPSRC) and the NHS. In this book we seek to focus in on the theme of dilemmas and paradoxes as this has been a recurring issue across multiple empirical studies. Hence, at many points throughout the book we allow managers to speak directly for themselves. In this way their own use of theory-in-practice is revealed.

A great deal of management is about making choices or at least getting ready to make choices. Much of management education has encouraged divergent thinking with familiar categories such as Theory X or Theory Y, transactional versus transformational leadership, and so on. The choices facing practising managers are real enough: they range from the big choices such as, at the policy level, in health services 'should we introduce some elements of the market into health and if so where and to what extent?', through corporate level choices such as 'what market are we in or should we be in?' and down to the smaller, team-management level, choices such as 'should I grant that request for a few hours leave in order for that individual to attend to some personal business?' Rarely is there one 'right' correct and enduring answer. Answers which tend in one direction (e.g. tight control) or in another (e.g. indulgence and compassion) may lead to outcomes which eventually require a course correction.

In part, the need for course correction stems from changes in circumstances; but another reason can be that an overplayed strength becomes a weakness. The implication of either is that capable managers must learn to handle competing rationales – in other words to learn to manage with paradox.

There are a few main responses typically made to what we term the 'common dilemmas'. One tendency adopted by some management teams is to try to stick to 'best practice' – i.e. to find a presumed enduring formula and to cling to it. A second, very different approach is to be adaptable – and to embark on a continual search for adaptability. This is the conventional, rational management approach – to analyse the environment and its changing messages and to respond to these patterns of contingencies with a temporary fit. However, there is a third approach – and this is the one we explore most of all in this book – and this involves seeking not to choose one 'solution' but to seek to exploit the paradoxical nature of many decision choices and to seek a blend of elements which retains the options in tension rather than opting for one in preference to another.

For example, traditionally managers have been told to focus on key products and, through appropriate accounting techniques, ensure that every product is paying its way, pruning products that do not. However, with increasing uncertainty the opposite case can be made: firms may be advised to opt for a wider portfolio approach. Unpredictability about which product will be a success can be an argument for maintaining a wide array of products – and then reaping the benefit across a wider front. Bharat Anand gives the example of Star TV in India which increased its prime-time viewer share from less than 5% to more than 80% in one year because its single hit show, *KaunBanega Crorepati* helped all its productions become more popular. Likewise, the Apple iPod generated higher sales than any of its other products (Anand 2008).

As change becomes ever faster and more far-reaching – as with the examples above such as product life cycles shortening – so too do the 'answers' become even more temporary and thus the nature of the dilemmas have to be faced more frequently.

Meanings of dilemmas and paradox

In conventional everyday use, the terms 'dilemma', 'contradiction' and 'paradox' are often deployed more or less interchangeably. However, more analytically it is possible to draw some important distinctions. For example, as Cameron and Quinn (1988: 2) point out, a dilemma is more of an either-or situation where one alternative has to be selected. However, the essence of the idea of paradox is the precise opposite of this. The whole point of paradox is that no either-or choice needs to be made or should be made. Indeed, the key to the idea is that two apparent contradictory notions are held and worked with *simultaneously*. The value to be derived from paradoxical thinking stems from this duality.

We accept this analytical distinction. However, in practice there is some considerable overlap in managers' experience of dilemma and paradox because both constructs are conceptual and interpretative rather than objective and categorical. We see the interplay between dilemma and paradox as a fluid and dynamic one. These may not be absolute categories but rather ways of seeing. The initial experience of discomfort and tension may be very similar. It is the mode of resolution which differs.

The exploitation of paradox

The power of paradoxical thinking – and we see it as a capability which can be learned, fostered and developed – is that it promotes and utilizes creative thinking which transcends old familiar ways of thinking. By balancing out the patterns of thought and action, leaders and managers can learn to exploit the strengths of seemingly antithetical ideas so that a blend of alternative value-adding attributes can be enjoyed.

Managerial practice has probably always involved a handling of dilemma and paradox. However, early attempts to conceptualize the nature of management and attempts to codify practice, as in the works of the classical management writers, tended to suppress and hide the uncertainties and ambiguities. Later work also in 'management science' and strategy tended to portray management as an exercise in logical, linear planning and thinking. However, more recently, with the sheer pace and extent of disruptive changes both externally and internally, managers have come to be suspicious of, and discontented with, simple one-dimensional solutions. The global nature of competition, the pace of technological change and the number of disruptive and discontinuous events means that managers and management researchers have to confront dilemma and paradox in a more forthright manner. This book is built on the premise that there is merit in highlighting the prevalence and nature of dilemma and paradox and in seeking to examine this phenomenon in detail. We envisage this book as an extended essay on the theory and practice of organizational dilemmas and paradox. The various chapters focus on different examples of dilemma/paradox and through these domains, and the live examples they contain, we seek to surface and examine their nature and value.

We are not of course the first to point up the importance of managerial dilemmas and paradoxes. Hence, in Chapter 2 we review the key works upon which we build our analysis. In brief, here we can note that dilemmas and paradoxes are to a large extent the result of socially constructed ways of seeing. They are tied to polarized conceptions and our claim is that by getting behind these either/or constructions it can be possible to realize the more liberating possibilities that are richer and more complex. This is a journey into knowledge and the framing and reframing of knowledge.

Dilemmas derive from perceived polarities – but these may disguise the opportunity to exploit simultaneity. Leaders and managers can learn how to exploit the tensions between seemingly conflicting priorities and use the energy to transcend the fixation on dualities. This entails *working with rather than against* the dilemmas and paradoxes which in turn means overcoming learned reactions and responses. It means finding advantage in the seemingly 'opposing' options and seeking to harness their logics into a new, higher level, form. In effect, this requires a willingness to subject conventional thinking and stances to self-critique. It may mean shifting the interpretation of the problem from fixing the presenting symptoms to a deeper review of the underlying forces and issues which gave rise to the problem in the first place. The skill to be developed is one of reframing and reconceptualizing. This means increasing one's awareness of more complicated repertoires that are a closer reflection of complex organizational realities.

For example, Quinn (1988: 3) suggests that:

The people who come to be masters of management do not see their work environment only in structured, analytical, ways. Instead, they also have the capacity to see it as a complex, dynamic system that is constantly evolving.

In order to interact effectively with it they employ a variety of different perspectives or frames.

In other words, accomplished managers of dilemmas and paradoxes have a special capability to deal with complexity and uncertainty in a creative way. They can deploy multiple 'frames'. In advocating the recognition and utilization of dilemma and paradox we are not suggesting that the solution can be found in simple compromise.

Throughout the book we seek to explore the nature of managerial dilemmas and paradoxes, the types and the various ways in which dilemmas and paradoxes can not only be confronted but also utilized to positive advantage.

Types

There are different forms and types of dilemmas and paradoxes. First, there are what Weber termed the 'paradoxes of unintended consequences'. This essentially refers to the way in which means can and often do subvert ends. Or, to put this another way: how human action and choice lead to outcomes which were not planned and can even be in opposition to the expected and desired outcomes. Some scholars of Weber suggest that this idea is central to his whole canon of political and social thinking. It is recognizable, for example, in his analyses of bureaucracy, religion, political action and charisma. With regard to bureaucracy, he notes how means become ends and the 'iron cage' of bureaucracy comes to dominate and to displace the original set of purposes. With regard to religion, one of Weber's most famous works on the link between the Protestant work ethic and the rise of capitalism is indeed focused on the irony that the original commitment to asceticism and hard work tends to lead to the accumulation of wealth and the subversion of the original ideals. Likewise, in his study of politics as a vocation and his analyses of types of power and authority, Weber observes how the charismatic form of leadership and of authority is ultimately doomed to failure as it becomes routinized.

Thus, in these varied ways, the first form of dilemma and paradox is that human intent and agency is often subverted by the law of unintended consequences.

A second form of dilemma and paradox relates rather more to ways of seeing and perceptions. This, as we shall see – and indeed as we will explore in more depth in each of the subsequent chapters on managerial dilemmas – has both positive and negative aspects. This second mode concerns the frames of reference which managers (and of course others) use in order to make sense of the world. The argument here is that the external world is inherently a highly complex phenomenon or set of phenomena and is ultimately incomprehensible in any complete sense.

Thus, in order to avoid paralysis, managers and others collect enough information which will 'suffice' to make enough sense in order to make decisions. To help make judgements about what constitutes sufficient information, managers construct and draw upon models of the world. The observed outcomes of these actions and decisions should provide a 'reality check'. In practice, it has been noted (e.g. March and Olsen 1976) that managers tend to cleave to a view of the world which reconfirms existing understandings and frames. Hence, selective perception is used to focus on information and data which assist with the confirmation of existing frames, whereas data and information that tend to challenge, disconfirm and potentially disrupt the existing frame tend to be deselected. Indeed, March and Olsen suggest that managers actively seek out information which will confirm their prevailing representations of reality. The process becomes self-referential. When the signals from the environment becoming overwhelmingly at odds with the preconceived frame then a 'reframing' may be triggered.

A perspective which combines the features of the above two types of dilemma and paradox is the analysis which appears to stand conventional wisdom about management improvement and much of management consultancy advice on its head. Normally, management advisers and educators contend that managers need better decision-making tools and better information. The two combined, it is assumed, will lead to more rational decisions. However, one leading Swedish academic (Brunsson 1985) argues that an over-concentration on decision-rationality can actually impede action. This paradox stems from the distinction between decision and action. Action requires more than decision, it also requires expectation, motivation and commitment. The more radical the change, the more a drive stemming from some ideology or belief pattern is required. Managers can obsess about the decision process and neglect the action focus. Using a number of case studies including a study of a large investment decision by a Swedish steel company, he shows how 'irrational decision making' (i.e. a process departing from the conventional norms) led to better action outcomes.

So far, we have suggested that there are two main types of dilemma and paradox – the first being the paradox of unintended consequences which proceed outside the individual and indeed group subjectivities, while the second type is inherently entwined within human subjectivity and the way humans construct frames of reference in order to make sense of the world.

Now, cutting across both of these types is a series of dilemmas and paradoxes which relate to types of business and organizational decision making. So, these are not types of dilemma in the generic sense noted above but are rather forms which are specific to business organizations and work organizations. We suggest that in the field of business there are essentially six of these (see Figure 1.1 below). The first relates to dilemmas and paradoxes in the domain of business strategy, the second to dilemmas and paradoxes in the domain of decisions about organizational structuring, the third to dilemmas and paradoxes inherent in performance management and control, the fourth concerns dilemmas about innovation, the fifth is concerned with the realm of underlying frames of management knowledge and the sixth and final one concerns change management. Below we sketch each of these and then each is examined and illustrated with case material in turn and in this sequence in the subsequent chapters.

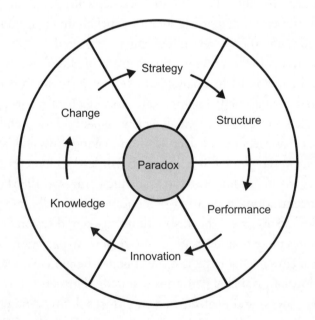

Figure 1.1 The six paradoxes.

Dilemma/paradox 1: strategy and business models

We begin with a very basic and fundamental dilemma and paradox: what is enterprising activity for? The conventional answer is that business organizations are driven by a rational-instrumental logic and this in turn is often articulated as survival and profit. However, increasingly in recent years, there has been growing attention to other issues and goals such as sustainability and corporate social responsibility. The idea of a triple bottom line expresses the multiplicity of objectives and the attempt to balance them. Acknowledgment of Corporate Social Responsibility (CSR) and corporate citizenship starts to raise many issues of dilemma and paradox involving, for example, engagement with multiple stakeholders (and questions around which ones to accept as legitimate and which to seek to marginalize) and the relative priority accorded to the ensuring multiple objectives.

Another way to approach this question is to ask what founders of organizations are trying to achieve. What do they want? When asked this question, entrepreneurs often claim their drive is 'to make money'. However, there is often another motivation: the drive to create and lead an organization. Research by Wasserman (2008) published in the *Harvard Business Review* shows that 'the surprising thing is that trying to maximize one, imperils the achievement of the other. Entrepreneurs face a choice, at every step, between making money and managing their ventures. Those who don't figure out which is more important to them often end up neither wealthy nor powerful'. He found that the faster that founder-CEOs lead their companies to the point where they need outside funds and new management skills, the quicker they lose that control. Success makes founders less qualified to lead the company and changes the power structure so they are more vulnerable. His research revealed that a founder who gives up more equity to attract investors and managers builds a more valuable company than one who parts with less equity – and the founder ends up with a more valuable slice, too.

On the other hand, in order to attract investors and skilled executives, entrepreneurs have to give up control over most decision making (Wasserman 2008):

> This fundamental tension yields being 'rich' versus being 'king' tradeoffs. The 'rich' options enable the company to become more valuable but sideline the founder by taking away the CEO position and control over major decisions. The 'king' choices allow the founder to retain control of decision making by

staying CEO and maintaining control over the board – but often only by building a less valuable company. For founders, a 'rich' choice isn't necessarily better than a 'king' choice, or vice versa; what matters is how well each decision fits with their reason for starting the company.

Or, a paradoxical solution to a business model dilemma may be deceptively simple adjustment to the product offering. For example, Citibank's credit card business is built on the principle of revolving credit. However, in some emerging markets they found resistance from customers who found this an alien concept and who were instead wedded to the more traditional concept of instalment credit. Faced with this dilemma of two types of product Citibank devised a card which carries the potential to offer both kinds of credit on the same card. A telephone call can be used to set-up an 'automatic loan on the phone'. Customers recognize this as within their familiar comfort zone as an instalment loan which is paid off but it also builds a familiarity with the credit card mode of operating.

A particular type of paradoxical thinking with regard to business strategy is instanced by those cases where firms decide to 'share' part of their market in order to take advantage of a business opportunity that might otherwise require exceptional marketing effort. For example, T-Mobile, a mobile phone network operator, has agreed with IKEA to offer its customers a low-cost mobile phone service. This turns IKEA into a mobile virtual network operator (MVNO). The arrangement echoes the similar deal T-Mobile has with the Virgin brand. Dilemmas and paradoxes relating to business models are scrutinized in this book in Chapter 3 using detailed case analyses.

Dilemma/paradox 2: organizational structuring

Organizations per se – i.e. the very phenomenon of 'organization' as a thing or accomplishment and the process of organizing are inherently paradoxical. Organizations are comprised of independent and creative individuals and yet the attempt is made to mould them into something other than this – a more unitary phenomenon based on predictability, order and control (Clegg et al. 2002). Hence, the paradox specifically is: 'how does the freedom of individual subjectivity accommodate the strictures of organization? How does the structure of organization envelop the freedom of individual subjectivity?' (Clegg et al. 2002: 483–4). The same point has been expressed more dramatically by Bouchikhi (1998: 224) who defined organizations as 'social spaces continuously torn by members in multiple and contradictory directions'. This suggests that organizations are inherently unstable. Yet, attempts to stabilize them through the imposition of greater control, risks stultifying the creative energy and commitment upon which organizational viability depends. This is a classic managerial dilemma.

Dilemmas and paradoxes relating to organizational design and redesign are examined and exemplified in Chapter 4.

Dilemma/paradox 3: performance and control

An inherent part of the management role is usually some attempt to influence the performance of individuals, teams and of course the whole organization. This can be done in numerous ways and the attempts often contain their own contradictions and paradoxes. In the attempt to control managerially an organization, a number of different things can go wrong. For example, managers may get drawn into a vicious circle. If there is a perception that employees could deliver higher performance there may be a strong temptation to try to secure this through increased direction and control. However, the imposition of more control may provoke a negative reaction. This in turn may further convince the manager that more control is needed. This can spiral: tighter and tighter controls result in greater degrees of resistance and an eventual loss of control. The paradox here is that more controls can result in less actual control. These kinds of dilemmas are explored in detail in Chapter 5.

Dilemma/paradox 4: innovation dilemmas

One of the most well-recognized and indeed classic dilemmas is the tension between managing for today versus planning for tomorrow. In other words, the pressure on organizational leaders to deliver efficiencies and results from the current business model and the current product and service offerings is set against the need to prepare to supplant these 'answers' by looking for new ones to meet changing times and circumstances. This type of paradox and dilemma revolves around the exploitation of a given combination of resources in order to yield optimal efficiency versus the need to prepare for the future by innovation and making other forms of change. This dilemma has been expressed in various ways – most notably in the succinct contrast between 'exploitation' and 'exploration'.

The dilemma becomes all the more acute when the issue of radical rather then 'mere' incremental innovation is contemplated. For example, the Chairman and CEO of Hewlett-Packard observed: 'We have to be willing to cannibalize what we are doing today in order to ensure our leadership in the future. It's counter to human nature but you have to kill your business while it's still working' (cited by Leonard-Barton 1992: 29).

Various ways to handle this kind of dilemma have been posited: for example, the construction of 'buffered contexts' (protected zones that offer a separate environment for explorative project teams); alternation between different organizational designs; 'rhythmically switching' between more organic and more mechanistic structures; loosely-coupled organizations; or experimental units completely separated from exploiting units. A paradoxical solution would look to ambidextrous or dual organizational forms – organizational architectures that build in both tight and loose coupling simultaneously.

The issues surrounding these tensions are explored and illustrated in Chapter 6.

Dilemma/paradox 5: managers' knowledge

This domain lies at a deeper level – it involves the knowledge and assumptions which underpin thinking about strategizing, structuring, performance management and innovation. This area is therefore concerned centrally with how managers 'frame' and 'reframe' problems and opportunities. The ways in which underlying knowledge is both tacit as well as explicit forms a key theme of Chapter 7.

Dilemma/paradox 6: organizational change

This is our final realm of dilemma and paradox. The start point for analyzing this paradox is the observation that 'The perplexing paradox in managing core capabilities is that they are core rigidities' (Leonard-Barton p. 30). In other words, a firm's advantages and strengths are simultaneously also its disadvantages and vulnerability.

When organizations become successful they become better and better at doing what they already do while increasingly failing to learn how to do other things. They may learn to increase their exploitative capacities but this tends to limit their ability to explore both their own creativity and the environment for new opportunities. Conversely, companies who overplay the opposite strength – i.e. are competent at exploring – are apt to fall into exactly the same trap. They become better at finding new opportunities but worse at learning how to do anything else, including exploiting those opportunities to their advantage. They spread their resources too thin over an increasing number of opportunities.

The six paradoxes identified above are each examined and illustrated in turn in the six chapters forming Part 2 of this book.

The role of leadership

We refer a great deal in this book to 'managers'. In fact, our main focus is upon the senior leadership team. There is a long-standing debate about the possible distinctions between leadership and management and it is not one we intend to revisit here. We are concerned with the senior group. It will be our argument in this book that this group can perform more effectively when they adopt a particular approach to leadership – one which exploits the power of paradox. We now sketch out this point in the following paragraphs before seeking to demonstrate it throughout the rest of the book.

This book is about dilemmas and paradoxes in organizations, with attention to four aspects in particular. First, how they arise (as integral to organizational structures, processes and dynamics); second, the forms they take; third, the ways managers and leaders typically respond to them; and fourth, the more creative ways in which they could respond to them.

However, while our subject is paradox our concern is the implications for leadership. While the book is *about* paradox it is *for* leaders. While our interest in organizational paradox is informed by academic research and writing, and is we believe all the richer for this literature, its concern is essentially practical: to initiate a debate about, and make some proposals for, how organizational paradoxes can be better handled.

The responsibility for handling paradox, we suggest, is ultimately a responsibility of leadership. The essential function of leaders, notes Senge (2007), is to define organizational realities. If they do this in a simplified, exaggerated, polarized and caricatured manner, believing (because they have read the hagiographic leadership biographies) that leaders are distinguished by their conviction, their certainty, their commitment to the chosen path and their ability to drive their purposes despite apathy and resistance, then they risk confusing their model of the world for the real world. They risk overlooking the pervasive and powerful paradoxes that surround them and which can easily divert or block their best endeavours. Organizational paradoxes cannot be wished away. We advocate a sense of leadership which augments commitment with recognition of doubt, which allows the possibility of rethinking how problems and solutions are framed, rejecting starkly posed polarities, seeking to achieve not zero-sum thinking but win-win – achieving balance between the pervasive polarities: big/small; innovation/production; centralized/decentralized; and control/trust.

If paradox is integral to organization, and if paradox means that apparently sensible, rational means can produce unanticipated and contrary outcomes (so that for example, actions taken to control or limit undesired behaviours actually generate an increase in these behaviours) then it is important to analyse how leaders can better handle paradoxes so that not only their negative possibilities are trimmed but also their beneficial qualities are encouraged.

For this to occur, leaders must lead paradoxically: eschewing the conventional indicators of leadership behaviour. One of the Board Directors we interviewed for this book saw this clearly: 'The old command and control structure in business that we had … required that people at the centre were omniscient, omnipresent and omnipotent and none of us are that "omni" anymore'. In this company, executives defined their leadership role as critics of the establishment, as enemies of conservatism, not as representatives of guardians of the organization's past but as prepared to dismantle that organization in order to ensure it remained able to innovate.

The key responsibilities of leaders are to ensure the formulation of intelligent and successful objectives and strategies and to ensure that the organization is capable of achieving these specified objectives – to ensure organizational capability. However, in fact, both these responsibilities involve capabilities of different types: after all, the ability of an executive team to develop intelligent strategy depends on the constitution, membership, dynamics, processes and relationships of the senior team (and ensuring these work well is a responsibility of leadership). And it also requires that the top team is capable of being aware of and able to be reflective about the knowledge it contains and the assumptions members hold. It also requires that the team is able to explore and interrogate (rather than simply express, disagree or fight over) differences in knowledge and assumptions. This too is a form of organizational capability.

When it comes to trying to implement strategy through organizational action, this too requires the appropriate ('aligned') organizational capacity which will vary depending on the ends that are selected. Finally, when trying to ensure that individual employees contribute appropriately to the attainment of the selected organizational and/or unit goals, a management and performance management system will be required.

These are the constituents of organizational capability – the ability to develop strategy, the ability to achieve strategy and to manage the organization and its employees so as to maximize their contribution to selected goals. This is, of course, our simplified overview picture. The core chapters in the book aim to show how every one of these components of organizational capacity building is highly problematic and characterized by paradox. So, the book can be seen as an analysis of the paradoxes that surround the achievement of executive responsibilities – the achievement of strategic and organizational capability – and how this requires a new, post-heroic form of leadership where the need to gain commitment through one firmly chosen option at the expense of rejected others, is qualified by a recognition that in many cases problems that are posed in terms of choices between available and polarized options are themselves problematic, and that the best response to paradox is not to deny or solve it, but to exploit it and thus to lead paradoxically.

Conclusions

In this introductory chapter, we have argued that one way for practising managers to respond to the sense of scepticism which can be the consequence of a series of failed reforms and transformations is to recognize that see-sawing between polarities on a whole range of common management problems is not necessarily the best or only way to proceed.

We have further suggested that leaders and managers of organizations can expect to face continually – at least at regular intervals – alternative pulls between a relatively common set of choices. These relate, for example, to familiar dilemmas such as whether to compete on price or on quality, whether to centralize or decentralize, whether to outsource or bring services in-house, whether to focus on the drive for efficiency (current exploitation of resources) or whether to explore and search for new opportunities and to innovate, and so on. We have argued that rather than oscillate between these polarities, an alternative path is to go beneath the surface dilemma and to actively search out and even embrace the inherent nature of the presenting dilemma or paradox and, by reaching a deeper level of understanding, to exploit its potential.

We have also argued that dilemmas and paradoxes are not simply things that need to be handled, or coped with, as if they were purely external phenomena. We have suggested that the successful handling of many common dilemmas reflects a certain state of mind – and state of organizations. We seek to show in this book how leaders and managers can learn to positively welcome and indeed exploit dilemma and paradox.

Managing through paradox should ideally be neither a compromise nor a split between competing tensions. Rather, it seeks to be aware of both and to utilize the strength of both. Change and pluralism are spurred on by these paradoxical tensions and reinforcing cycles. Because of this, conceptions of change as smooth, linear and planned vanish. Themes that are logical in isolation become contradictory when applied in tandem.

Harmony and discord come together. As do innovation and efficiency, control and flexibility, collaboration and competition, old and new. On its own, formal, rational logic cannot deal adequately with paradox. Managing dilemma and paradox emerges as an opportunity to explore the tensions at the boundary that reveal themselves in terms of mixed messages and contradictions.

As a result, managers may counteract their tendency to over rationalize and over synthesize by simultaneously holding and even exploring opposing views. The challenge for managers of organizations lies in learning how to manage the tensions or dualities between traditional and new forms of organizing, a process demanding the arbitration of continuity and change. This duality of coexisting tensions creates an edge of chaos, not a bland halfway point between one extreme and the other. The management of this duality hinges on exploring the tension in a creative way.

We can summarize the essential strands of our argument in the following points. We argue that organizations are characterized by a number of inherent and intrinsic features which generate paradox. Paradoxes occur when attempts to achieve an end fail to achieve the expected 'rational' outcome but instead create a different or opposite effect or set of effects. Of course the expressions 'expected' or 'rational' themselves require a referent especially since, in a sense, those 'rational means' that generate an unexpected (or paradoxical) end could be seen as not having been truly 'rational' in the first place (if by rational we mean that the means successfully achieves the desired end). In fact, as Max Weber pointed out, rationality can refer not only to the selection of effective ends but also the selection of what is commonly regarded as the effective means – a distinction which is critical to the understanding of organizational paradox.

This is because paradox arises in organizations when actions produce outcomes which are radically different from or even the opposite of the outcomes that are (quite reasonably) expected and desired. Paradox is a key, systemic and inherent feature of organization and of organizational dynamics. Paradox is, as Durkheim argued, 'normal' – that is, it is an expected feature of the modern organization.

We argue that paradox is a *systemic feature of social organizations*. It is not accidental or incidental: it is a result of the essential nature of organizations. If paradox is recognized as a systemic feature of organizations and not as some incidental, aberrant, phenomenon then leaders may come to recognize the importance of adopting a more considered response to it; and this is one of the arguments of the book. The roots of paradox lie in the essential nature and features of organization. Organizations are essentially complex, contradictory; characterized by conflict, tensions, choices/options around goals and means; characterized by contradiction, requiring for success the solution of a range of different even opposed problems and outcomes (for example, how to motivate and control staff, how to be accomplished at operations and at innovation and so on); and most important of all, are prone to a phenomenon whereby management actions produce unanticipated consequences – sometimes consequences that are diametrically opposed to the desired outcomes. These features are the terrain on which paradox grows and flourishes.

A key part of our argument is that it is not the fact of paradox as a key feature of organizations that matters, *but how leaders and managers respond to it*. Our thesis is not simply or solely that organizational paradoxes exist and are important but that how these paradoxes are addressed and 'solved', exacerbated or avoided by managers is an important factor in their success and the success of their organizations.

We recognize that conventional management approaches to paradox are not surprising but are understandable. Management response is characterized by tendencies which encourage polarized, black/white; good/bad thinking. We argue that this tendency is not accidental or incidental but an outcome of a central management dilemma: how to generate managers' commitment to a recommended option (by stressing – indeed over-stressing – the benefits at the cost of the rejected option). However, the appeal of this mode of thinking may have other foundations. It may be a product of a distinctively Western form of rationality applied to organizational issues, of the need for consistency, clarity and neatness. Certainly, it is remarkably prevalent and stands in sharp contrast to the approach to paradox which is recommended here which is, in brief, to encourage managers not to select one polarity over another, indeed not even to see the options as polarities. The relationship between apparently polarized options may not be one or the other but both, that paradoxes may not need to be (may not be open to being) solved but to be enjoyed; that paradoxes may not be phenomena to avoid or solve but to celebrate and exploit: that leaders and managers may even be able to have their cake and eat it.

Finally, the book explores new ways of responding to organizational paradox. And this is the main focus of the book. We argue that leaders and managers may adopt a range of approaches to organizational paradox. For example, when a high control approach to work design begins to generate negative returns (poor quality, lack of flexibility, staff problems, etc.) the manager 'solves' these problems by further tightening and increasing control). Using a second approach, managers faced with paradox may seek to 'solve' it by avoiding it. For example, one attempt to resolve the problems inherent in the management of people and resources might be sought through outsourcing. In this way other organizations handle the problems and paradoxes of management. Similarly, managers may decide to outsource the supply chain to a logistics company. These solutions 'solve' the paradoxes of staff management or supply chain management by avoiding them. However, by so doing they may well generate new paradoxes – new, unanticipated effects.

Organization of the book

In the next chapter, we review the existing literature on dilemma and paradox. Then, in Part 2 of the book we devote a sequence of six chapters to the six dilemmas and paradoxes identified above. That journey starts with an analysis of top managers' understanding of business strategy. Here, we draw upon our research to explore managers' understanding of business models – the assumptions and convictions which underpin managers' commitment to various conceptions of what the business should do and what it should be like to be able to do it. This has been a neglected area of research and discussion. This first theme also embraces analysis of the tension between exploitation of current resources and market position versus exploration (innovation) into new products and services and new markets which may undermine the existing business.

Hence, as Figure 1.1 illustrated earlier, the journey through the chapters of the book starts with aspects of strategy, moves through themes related to organizational form and capability, explores the paradoxical aspects of attempts to manage performance, then tackles the demand for innovation and finishes with the management of change. Each of these dilemmas and paradoxes is analysed separately in the following chapters. The purpose in each case is to demonstrate how managing with paradox can be beneficial and that it is *a capability that can be learned and developed.*

2

The nature of dilemma and paradox

In the previous chapter, we argued that, in the main, management theory and management teaching over many decades had veered towards an approach which assumed an underlying rationality. The analyses and pre-scriptions tended either to suggest a 'best solution' or a set of analytical tools which enabled managers to find the 'best fit' for their situation in relation to a known set of contingencies. We further suggested that the earlier analyses which had pointed to issues of contradiction and conflict had been increasingly neglected. In this chapter we revisit those earlier contributions and we widen the search for more recent treatments of these issues in the existing literature. Much good work has already been done and we want to highlight it and use it to inform our empirical work and analysis.

Dilemma and paradox

Chris Argyris makes a useful distinction between what he terms 'logical paradoxes' and 'world paradoxes' (Argyris 1999). The former refers to the philosophical word games and the science of reasoning exemplified by state-ments such as 'I am lying'. The conundrum and the contradiction are inher-ent in the statement itself. However, Argyris is more concerned – as we are – with the second form of paradox: the behavioural paradoxes. These are of a different kind. Indeed, Argyris has undertaken valuable consultancy work over many decades based on his realization that these kinds of paradox are traceable to the contrivances of managers. During his many attempts to help managerial teams work through a range of problems he observed that frequently the source of these problems was traceable to the 'defensive routines' routinely practised by managers. He says: 'defensive routines are created to bypass embarrassment or threat to individuals or systems ... in order for them to work, the individuals acting as agents for the systems must act as if they are not bypassing' (pp. 96–7).

One important form of this is the distinction between 'espoused theory' and 'theory-in-use'. Espoused theory refers to what managers *say* – it is the declared stance, the statement of 'policy'. On the other hand, theory-in-use is the policy that is revealed through repeated behaviours. Faced with these two forms, organizational members may thus receive mixed messages and they may also find that any discrepancy – even contradiction – between the espoused and the actual is off limits for discussion; it may literally be undiscussable. We have been very much influenced by Argyris's insights relating to such situations and we have, in the past, been fortunate enough to have found ourselves working with organizations where Argyris was engaged as a consultant.

The level of self-deception by top teams often goes very deep. Argyris reports incidents where executive teams appeal for his help in thinking through their problems which they purport to objectify as outside of their intentions. However, Argyris develops a theory of action which traces paradox to duplicitous behaviours and 'trickery'. His theory of action includes the attempts to deny personal responsibility for creating and maintaining paradoxes. His work is based on an attempt to build an adequate theory which would help understand how and why managers seek to 'protect inconsistencies' while also providing them with new sets of skills to help them reduce their resort to such defensive routines.

Social scientists who want to be able to work through such paradoxes, says Argyris, require theories which enable them 'not to take for granted the bypass activities which are taken for granted' within the systems themselves.

Thus, from Argyris's work we learn that organizational paradoxes are different from logical paradoxes. We also learn that organizational paradoxes are in a sense purposely created because actors (managers) seek defensive routines to protect themselves and their units from threat or embarrassment. They then conspire, in highly skilful ways, to protect and preserve the sources of these organizational paradoxes. Not only do certain issues become undiscussable, in addition, the 'bypass activities' adopted become part of the taken-for-granted in organizational routines and culture.

Experiencing dilemma and paradox

Other researchers of dilemma and paradox, usually with a more psychological orientation, suggest that paradoxes are experienced as cognitive states in tension and that these tensions prompt some attempt at resolution. These efforts may result in a recommitment to the status quo which therefore resists change (a defensive reaction), or a swing to one or other of the two 'sides'. We argue, along with others, that there is a third position – and this involves a rethinking which accepts complicated interrelationships. Adoption of this third approach requires insight, exemplification and practice.

Ford and Backoff (1988) define a paradox as 'some thing that is constructed by individuals when oppositional tendencies are brought into recognizable proximity through reflection or interaction' (1988: 89). Hence, these constructions can derive from individual construction and reflection or from social interaction. The definition also implies that paradox can be dissipated through *reframing* – that is, through a reconceptualization of a situation. This perspective prompts us to attend closely to the investigation of managerial 'logics'.

Such a reconceptualization can be seen in the thinking of John Chambers, Chief Executive of Cisco:

> In my view, the days of being vertically integrated and having everything within your control will never return. The entire leadership team, including me, had to invent a different way to operate. It was hard for me at first to learn to be collaborative. The minute I'd get into a meeting, I'd listen for about 10 minutes while the team discussed a problem. I knew what the answer was, and eventually I'd say, 'All right, here's what we're going to do.' But when I learned to let go and give the team the time to come to the right conclusion, I found they made just as good decisions, or even better – and, just as important, they were even more invested in the decision and thus executed with greater speed and commitment. I had to develop the patience to let the group think.

The dialogue to be analysed can either be naturally-occurring conversations of a kind which can be observed, or conversations with a researcher which provoke reflections. Hence, in this book we make extensive use of directors and managers talking – both with each other and with us. We cite extensively their attempts to make sense through their talking about the many dilemmas they face.

It has been suggested that the tendency to resort to polarized modes of thinking reflects a leaning towards formal logic. An aspect of formal logic is a tendency to think and talk in either/or terms. Things or positions are often defined in terms of what they are not: e.g. love versus hate, black versus white, wet versus dry. Researchers use these dialogical devices in instruments such as repertory grids. Organizational analysts perpetuate this mode of thinking with its major categories – centralized/decentralized; differentiation/integration; organic/mechanistic; change/stability.

Managers often extend this thinking by attributing and locating arguments and stances with references to particular individuals. Thus, strategic options become tied in with political position taking. This can lead to the formation of cliques.

This is just one of the potential defensive reactions to the anxiety induced by dilemma and paradox. However, there are many other ways in which individuals commonly seek to deal with this mode of discomfort. For example, subjects may indulge in 'projection' – the transfer of conflicting feelings and attributes onto others. Alternatively, people may resort to 'repression' – a form of denial which is used to try to avoid thinking about the tensions. Another way in which subjects may seek to cope psychologically is through 'regression'. This involves a reversion to past understandings which are imagined to be associated with security. 'Reaction formation' entails an excessive attachment to a practice or stance which is thought to be opposite to the threatening one. 'Ambivalence' signals a compromise which seeks refuge in a 'lukewarm' reaction to ameliorate the tension of extremes (Vince and Broussine 1996).

A further individual response to dilemmas and paradoxes is noted by Kets de Vries (De Vries 1995) who explores how the apparent 'irrational elements' of organizational and work life are suppressed by attending to the rituals and routines of 'normal' everyday conventional management. From his psychoanalytic perspective, he traces many of the non-rational aspects and paradoxes to the psychodynamic forces at work in human interactions and organizational behaviour.

The organizational level

In the section above the focus of analysis was upon individuals and their responses to paradox, but there is also literature which focuses on organizational behaviour. Quinn (1988) argues that, to be effective, organizations need to exhibit contradictory attributes simultaneously. For example, they need to be *both* controlling and flexible, to have *both* internal and external focus, to manage for today *and* to prepare for tomorrow. Quinn in a study of leadership (cited in Cameron and Quinn 1988: 12) found that the most effective leaders exhibited apparently contradictory styles and behaviours. Significantly, Quinn also claims that most leadership studies miss this because they are designed from the outset through their theoretical frameworks to discount such a possibility.

It is possible, theoretically at least, to distinguish between alternative choices (i.e. either/or choices) on the one hand and dilemmas on the other. The either/or choices may sometimes be resolved by close attention to the context. However, dilemmas may not be amenable to such a fit. The Chinese notion of yin and yang indicates the duality dilemma – this is different from western contingency theory. Managing with dilemmas thus means going beyond the idea of 'fit'. Dilemma theory seeks to avoid pendulum swings and to be more in tune with ongoing dynamics (Cameron and Quinn 1988). The idea is to seek to avoid maximizing along any dimension. Organizations they say need both agreement and disagreement. Managers, by implication, need to design organizations that have attributes in tension such as aspects of centralization and decentralization; an internal and an external foci (Hedburg *et al.* 1976; Miller 1992).

The duality of coexisting tensions '*creates an edge of chaos*, not a bland halfway point between one extreme and the other. The management of this duality hinges on exploring the tension in a creative way that captures both extremes, thereby capitalizing on the inherent pluralism within the duality' (Eisenhardt 2000: 703 emphasis added).

However, dual choices can lead to vicious circles. There is a serious danger of managers zig-zagging between extremes as they try to make course-corrections. This tendency has been well-noted by Hampden-Turner (1990a, 1990b). To be capable of successfully handling 'both' rather than 'either/or', requires some form of ambidexterity. Ambidextrous organizations allow

apparently inconsistent tendencies to coexist. For example, take the emphasis on process management techniques and process improvement using techniques such as TQM, BPR and Six Sigma. These process and quality
improvement approaches can reduce costs and provide reliable services
to customers. Independent auditing through ISO 9000 ensures consistent
follow-through of documented processes. However, while this approach
can certainly deliver improvements to existing products and customers,
the same values and techniques can unfortunately impede variation and
innovation.

The results can be counter-intuitive and counter-productive. It has been
noted that winners of the Baldridge Award and similar other awards which
signal strong adherence to process-improvement values and behaviours,
often tend to suffer subsequent poor financial performance out-turns
(Sterman *et al*. 1997; Benner and Tushman 2003). The reason is that the
clarity of focus which is a merit also carries within it a fatal flaw. It is both
a strength and a weakness. A firm's competitiveness over time requires both
a capability to conduct current processes in an efficient manner but also
requires the development of new capabilities and thus, by definition, a
departure from the current suite of routines and capabilities.

Ambidextrous organizations build on both tight and loose coupling simultaneously. That is they manage both process-efficient exploitation units and
more loosely managed exploration units. These 'contrasting, inconsistent
units must be physically and culturally separated from one another, have
different measurements and incentives and have distinctive managerial
teams' (Benner and Tushman 2003: 247). Management of these different
units organizations needs to be 'consistently inconsistent' as they strive to
be both focused on the long term and the short term, to be both centralized
and decentralized, tightly-focused on process and efficiency by driving out
variation through conformance to written process rules, and yet loose enough
to promote variation in the discovery units. Variation-decreasing units
(process-focused production and service units), it is argued, need to be
decoupled at least to some degree from variation-seeking units.

However, there may be exceptions. An alternative way to achieve dual
objectives such as high exploitation and high exploration may be to pursue
a 'punctuated equilibrium' strategy. This would mean devoting some periods
of time to a concentrated emphasis on one and then switching for a while
to a concentrated emphasis on the other. These options again indicate a

further managerial dilemma. If the organizational unit is considered as a relatively unified whole system, then the punctuated equilibrium approach may be sensible; if however the organization is framed as a number of loosely coupled units then it is possible to pursue process efficiency (exploitation) and radical innovation (exploration) simultaneously (Gupta, Smith *et al.* 2006).

A further organizational-level paradox is the 'paradox of control'. This operates as follows: if a manager fears the loss of even partial control, he or she may increase the degree and range of controlling mechanisms. These, in turn, may be perceived by the subordinates as forms of mistrust and instruments of oppression, hence, they trigger the very resistance that was feared; the evidence of increased resistance prompts the controller to impose even tighter controls which in turn may lead to stiffer resistance and so the vicious circle is progressed.

A virtuous circle, on the other hand, may be initiated through a degree of trust in the value of the exercise of autonomy by individuals and/or teams; this may encourage creative and willing use of freedom which in turn may trigger further trust which is again rewarded with commitment and discretionary effort.

Visualizing dilemmas

A useful way to think about managerial dilemmas is to view them as a series of alternatives and to map them. The figures below illustrate some of the key forms. These representations can help indicate the range of dualities and pluralities. Dualities are the most fundamental. They derive from distinctions which in turn are inherent in the way we make sense of something. The very act of reality construction normally involves drawing distinctions. To 'say something is "A" is to draw a distinction between that which is "A" and that which is "not A" ... things are put *in relation* to other things' (Ford and Backoff 1988: 86). Any definition or understanding entails constructing such distinctions. And distinctions give rise to dualities. They stem from human and social construction and they provide the potential for action.

In Figure 2.1 the traditional stark choices between centralization and decentralization is depicted.

The polar opposites could of course also be regarded as gradations along the line – i.e. as a continuum.

Figure 2.1 Polar opposites.

In Figure 2.2 the dilemmas are depicted as dual dilemmas offering multiple possibilities.

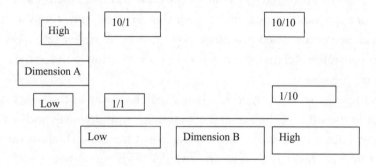

Figure 2.2 Two dimensional dilemmas.

In Figure 2.3 there are three dimensions.

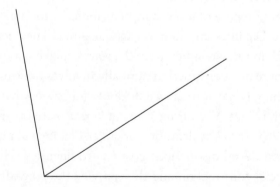

Figure 2.3 Three dimensional dilemmas.

In Figure 2.4 we show cross cutting dilemmas which allow the identification of four types of response.

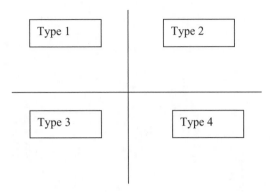

Figure 2.4 A two by two typology.

In Figure 2.5 we show how multiple dilemmas can allow a profile of choices to be revealed.

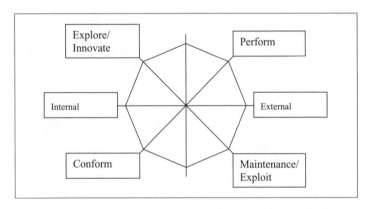

Figure 2.5 Profiles.

These multiple dilemmas may sometimes be created purposely. For example, the NHS reforms created a system where managers are challenged to build and maintain a 'commercial focus' and at the same time a 'patient focus' and also a 'political focus'. The three foci are it seems designed to *maintain* ongoing tension between these different pulls on managerial time, resources and attention.

Finally, in Figure 2.6 the 'competing values framework' of Cameron and Quinn (1988: 11) shows how simultaneous opposites can be used by managers in pursuit of organizational effectiveness. The six dimensions with 12 poles are regarded by the researchers as a fairly comprehensive representation of effectiveness indicators. They have each been subjected to statistical testing. The model displays the patterns of paradox and the authors claim that research on the model has confirmed that managers of effective organizations pursue these competing values *simultaneously*.

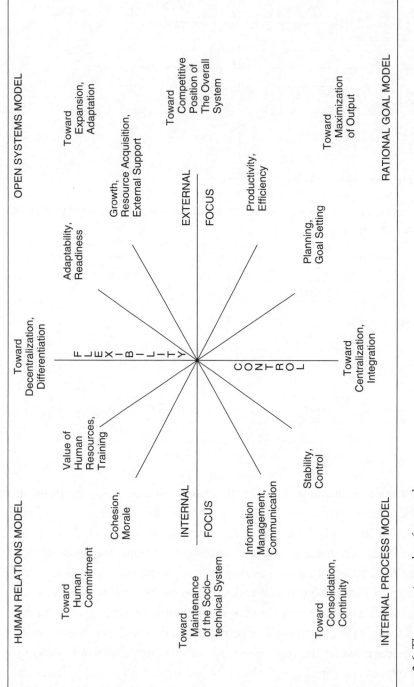

Figure 2.6 The competing values framework.
Source: Paradox and Transformation, edited by Robert E. Quinn and Kim S. Cameron.
Copyright © 1988 by Ballinger Publishing Company. Reproduced by permission of HarperCollins Publishers.

The subjectivity of dilemma and paradox

Dilemma and paradox are essentially human constructions. They are ways of seeing. As noted by Ford and Backoff (1988: 89) a paradox is something 'that is constructed by individuals when oppositional tendencies are brought into recognizable proximity through reflection or interaction'.

Tensions and co-existing opposites which allow the exploitation of synergistic tendencies rather than emphasizing the conflicting or incompatible aspects have been noted in various pieces of research. It has been argued that organizations should consciously make an effort *to become* dualistic entities and to attain and maintain this as a capability. However, the effort required to maintain such a juxtaposition of opposing forces should not be underestimated. As Graetz and Smith (2007: 2) note:

> From a duality perspective, continuity and change represent an overarching meta-duality, fundamental to building healthy organizations ... [r]ather than favouring one extreme over the other, a duality-sensitive mindset recognizes the merits of both sides of the duality continuum and is able to meet simultaneous challenges. These include balancing short-term and long-term imperatives, differentiation and integration, external and internal orientation, flexibility and efficiency, and dependence and independence.

Thus, paradoxical thinking and framing can be a useful skill in handling the dual requirements of continuity and change. Likewise, it can also highlight the value in recognizing the relationship between formal plans and situated improvisation (Orlikowski 1996). The nature of these kinds of skills and the way in which such a capability can be developed, forms the subject of the discussion throughout this book and they are illustrated in the case study chapters.

Comprehending paradox requires a guiding framework and an identification of the essential characteristics. Graetz and Smith (2007) note five main characteristics of 'duality' – these authors are concerned mainly with the dual aspects of stability – inducing aspects of organizing and the more flexible aspects of new forms; however, the same characteristics can have application beyond this restricted frame. The first characteristic, simultaneity, is crucial – the tensions and dilemmas arise because of the simultaneous pull of competing principles and forces. Without the recourse to paradoxical thinking these forces and principles may be viewed as simple contradictions and an attempt made to 'solve' the problem by electing for one or the other. However, a dualities-sensitive approach does not seek to remove, resolve or eliminate contradiction, but rather seeks to derive benefit from the latent complementarities. The second characteristic, the relational, is a natural accompaniment – it emphasizes the interdependent nature of the tensions and eschews the either/or mode of thought. The third characteristic, minimal thresholds, is a further corollary. If the dualities are to be sustained, then at least a certain minimum presence of both apparently competing elements will need to be kept in play. The fourth attribute, dynamism, refers to the energy required to manage simultaneously the competing principles and the energy and traction which can in turn be generated by so doing. Finally, the fifth characteristic, improvisation, points to the active, adaptable interplay between dual poles using bi-directional feedback.

A further skill required for managing with paradox which can be found in the literature is based on the idea of 'dynamic capabilities'. A firm's ability to compete over time may lie in its ability both to integrate and build upon its current competences while developing simultaneously fundamentally new capabilities (Teece, Pisano et al. 1997; Eisenhardt and Martin 2000). Because competences are hard to develop and the rates of environmental change are substantial, Benner and Tushman (2003: 251) argue that 'dynamic capabilities are not rooted in sequential attention or rhythmic pacing' (e.g. Brown and Eisenhardt 1998) but, rather, in 'exploiting and exploring simultaneously'.

Exploiting dilemmas and paradoxes

So, from the literature we can learn that in order to take advantage of and to exploit dilemmas and paradoxes their potential must be utilized. This usually requires a rethink of past patterns of thinking. It requires creative responses and a new approach to change. It means welcoming tensions and exploring their potential. This may allow new levels of understanding and insight and open up exciting new possibilities.

An example of the exploitation of paradox in management is the idea of Just-in-Time manufacturing, as we noted in the previous chapter. JIT competes with the conventional western idea of trade-offs; instead, quality, low-cost, service and efficiency are deemed to be mutually-reinforcing rather than opposing values requiring trade-off. For example, JIT prompts new, creative ways to interact with suppliers. In the health service in the UK a number or organizations are likewise declaring their aim to have as their target *zero*-instances of avoidable harm to patients. The paradox of pursuing 'ultimate goals' is seen as a key element of JIT (Eisenhardt and Westcott 1988).

Critical to making sense of the myriad developments is the ability to relate parts to the whole and vice versa: a movement, back and forth, between the whole conceived through the parts that actualize and comprise it, and the parts conceived through the whole that consists of and is made up of them. Running alongside that it is the theme of dilemmas and how to manage them.

In order to manage a dilemma the answer is not necessarily 'balance'. Choices still have to be made which lean more towards one end of a dimension rather than another. However, it does mean attending to the merits of both ends of the spectrum. The ends need to be held in tension with each other: Pascale refers to managing 'on the edge' – using conflict (Pascale 1991).

Dilemmas such as 'efficiency versus innovation', 'integration versus differentiation', 'control versus freedom', 'centralization versus decentralization' and 'competition versus cooperation' have been noted by various organizational analysts (Evans and Doz 1992; Child and McGrath 2001; Evans, Pucik *et al.* 2002). However, it is also argued that when these competing tensions are pursued *in concert*, they can be a powerful force for creativity and adaptation (Galunic and Eisenhardt 2001).

Other research has found that traditional and 'new' organizational practices are in fact rather more compatible than normally represented and that they are capable of being handled as complementary rather than opposing forces (Palmer, Benveniste *et al.* 2007). The practical implication is that the synergistic relationship between old and new work practices should be recognized and managers should be cautioned against eschewing established business principles when caught-up in the enthusiasm for a new fashion. The relational, interdependent characteristics of dualities illustrate that organizational forms are not independent of the other organizational practices they house. In addition, dualities themselves are not independent but are often related to other dualities (Pettigrew and Fenton 2000).

The practice of paradoxical management is revealed by a number of empirical studies which indicate that while innovative forms of organizing

are emerging within organizations, hierarchy and other traditional organizational practices are not necessarily discarded (O'Reilly and Tushman
2004; Palmer, Benveniste et al. 2007). These studies suggest that high-
performing organizations are adopting dual forms of organizing in which the
controllability advantages associated with traditional forms of organizing
work to complement and support the responsiveness attributes of new forms
of organizing (O'Reilly and Tushman 2004). Attributes such as speed, flexibility and responsiveness, for example, are of little value if there is no
guiding purpose, order or structure (Ashkenas et al. 1995).

Given this complexity, organizations never achieve a state of balanced
equilibrium, which highlights the important role that duality characteristics
such as dynamism and improvisation can play in arbitrating continuity
and change. For example, organizations might adopt bureaucratic line-
management structures for reporting and performance management, and
new forms of organizing for projects and informal connections. New
forms of organizing can overlay formal structures. In other words, it may be
possible to use traditional approaches to monitor, direct and coordinate
business operations, while adopting new approaches for explorative and
collaborative activities that might involve cross-functional, team-based
workgroups.

The movement between these sets of activities needs to remain dynamic
so that they can be changed in response to contextual pressures. 'Tacit
interactions', as Beardsley, Johnson et al. (2006) observed, offer a method
for loosely-coupled connections through less formal lines of authority. New
members can join teams formed by tacit interaction on the basis of interest,
collaboration and inspiration.

In summary, a dualities approach offers a framework for exploring phenomena that can be confusing but understandable, and predictable yet
surprising. It recognizes that the competing challenges of organizing forms
such as global/local, autonomy/control, flexibility/efficiency, centralization/
decentralization and order/disorder do not necessarily have to be resolved
either way. Each has a part to play, although how and where this is realized
along the duality continuum is likely to be shaped by the environmental
context and management systems and technologies. The central organizing
challenge is therefore the ability to develop systems that thrive on paradox,
providing both efficiency and innovation along with a centralized vision and
decentralized power (Child and McGrath 2001).

Managing paradoxes

Managing paradox means capturing its enlightening potential. Tapping the power of paradox is difficult, however, because escaping reinforcing cycles requires seemingly counterintuitive reactions (Cameron and Quinn 1988). Paradox management entails exploring, rather than suppressing, tensions. Vince and Broussine (1996: 4) make the point that persisting with an examination of paradox allows the uncovering of the linkages between opposing forces and allows access to the meanings behind the apparent contradictions.

Four main ways of responding to and handling paradoxes have been noted (Lewis 2000). The first of these ways is to accept instances of paradox and to learn to live with them rather than seek to resolve them. Acceptance helps organizational members avoid what might prove to be destructive and unproductive debates and encourages a clear focus on the job to be done. However, there are costs attached to this stance, failing to engage with them may lead to loss of insight that could derive from interrogating conflicting perspectives.

A second response to paradox is to adopt an analytical approach. This entails for example, distinguishing between different levels of analysis or different time periods and thus seeking to find the conditions under which one side of a statement is more generally upheld. In a managerial practice context this analytical approach may mean seeking to use paradox by confronting it. Discussing inconsistencies and tensions may allow a group to construct a more accommodating and informed understanding (e.g. Vince and Broussine 1996). As we noted when discussing Argyris earlier, however, managers conspire frequently to obscure and prevent such open examination of the underlying paradoxes.

A third response is in one sense, the converse of the analytical approach. This is to remove the paradoxical elements by accepting 'normal use' of language. Wittgenstein's response to the puzzling and troubling statement 'I always lie' was to defuse its illogicalities by suggesting it becomes less troubling when its normal use is emphasized (cited by Van de Ven and Poole 1988: 22). This implies that the listener fills in the normal meaning based on his or her learned and accomplished practice as a member of a give–community.

A fourth way of handling paradox is to seek to transcend its instances by actively modulating the inherent tensions. Many writers have pointed to the way that jazz bands learn to improvise by subtle modulations of group order and individual creativity. Likewise, Murninghan and Conlon (1991) found that members of successful string quartets are very much aware of the tensions in the way they work including the desire for personal expression and autonomy and yet also strong group leadership.

The literature thus suggests that exploiting paradox means benefiting from the creative insights which can derive from reframing. Reframing entails an 'unfreezing' – a reinterpretation of a situation in a new way. There would thus seem to be a promising link with creativity. In pursuit of this Bartunek (1988: 142) constructs a model which follows the cyclical trial and error character of creativity. Hence, 'stages' of emergent understanding are checked and validated – sometimes looping back to an earlier stage until things 'make sense'. One aspect of this is the way leadership and management as a process can be seen as a *meaning-making activity*.

To return to the phenomenon noted at the outset of this book – the tendency for solutions and fads and fashions to come around seemingly ever faster, this is explained by Bartunek: 'One reason that many business fads are fads is that many organizational members never develop their own understanding of, and responses to, particular organizational problems and solutions; they are simply told to adopt some particular perspective' (1988: 150). In other words, the reframing work has been too superficial; if meaningful reframing is to occur and paradox truly exploited, then the various stages must be completed (including frame testing) and not simply one or two stages such as relabeling and awareness building. The linearity of these stages should not, however, be over done; reinterpretations and new understandings are normally characterized by flows rather than by sequenced stages (Kimberley 1988). When this is done effectively, utilizing paradox through reframing, we are told, can be used as an effective driver of organizational change and transformation.

Conclusions

This chapter has reviewed the literature on how managers respond to the paradoxical nature of organizations. Paradox is the word used to describe the situation where a means generates an end which is the opposite of what was expected and intended. To define a situation as paradoxical therefore assumes the manager has used a polarized way of understanding the situation

– by defining the options available in terms of moralized opposites. The various authors whose work is reviewed in this chapter suggest generally that managers should not seek to solve paradox by emphasizing one option over another (which is sooner or later self-defeating). They suggest that to truly exploit dilemmas and paradox would require new ways of thinking – ways which permit an escape from the constraints of binary, polarized categories. This would require new, creative responses; it means welcoming tensions and exploring their potential.

The authors whose work is presented here offer frameworks for exploring phenomena by recognizing that the competing challenges of dichotomized polarities such as large/small, new/old, global/ local, autonomy/control, flexibility/efficiency, centralization/decentralization and order/disorder do not necessarily have to be resolved by allocating a privileged position to one at the expense of the other. Each option may have a part to play, each may have benefits. Why not seek to have both?

The central challenge is therefore to be able to think beyond polarities and to develop approaches and systems that thrive on paradox. The aim as Lewis puts it is 'to journey beyond reinforcing cycles, dramatically rethinking past perceptions and practices' (2000: 763). The task then, according to this range of authors who have investigated paradox, is to encourage managers to reframe, to rethink and to break out of learned and routinized ways of managing and of thinking about managing.

This book will show that it is not easy to escape from the new iron cage – the cage created by the seductive and appealing tendency to define organizational issues in polarized terms (the reasons for the appeal of this way of thinking are discussed in the following chapter); suffice to say here that it arises from the priorities of management decision making. And exploiting the power of paradox by moving beyond it is also difficult because the reinforcing cycles require counterintuitive reactions. If doing what is expected achieves an opposite response to what one expected then maybe doing what isn't expected will produce the desired response. Critchley and Casey (1989) argued some years ago that managers (and organizations) sometimes get 'stuck'. By this they mean that they find themselves unable to solve a major issue or set of issues. Their available strategies don't work: they seem unable, despite what they think are their best efforts to solve a persistent and serious problem. The answer, suggest Critchley and Casey, lies not in the problem but in the way it is defined by the group. The problem is *how managers define* 'the problem'. The defining and the (presumed) solution are at the root of the problem.

From this study of the literature we learn that 'paradox management' entails exploring and even generating (rather than suppressing) tensions. It means surfacing underlying assumptions; it means making the familiar strange and the strange familiar. It means redefining (sometimes very radically) the links between opposing (polarized) forces and the assumptions that give meaning to the apparent polarities. Ultimately, this does nothing less than to redefine the nature and responsibilities of management. It means moving management from prevailing definitions based on rationality, linear thinking planning and control, to a new approach based on coping, reframing and solving problems without necessarily 'resolving' them. It may also mean, as Chris Argyris pointed out, that our interventions as researcher-consultants must be robust and wise enough not to be deflected by the taken-for-granted bypass activities that powerful organizational players indulge in as part of their defensive routines. Unless this level of understanding is reached, any apparent and easily accepted solutions that win ready approval will be prone to being undermined by the undiagnosed defensive routines which created the paradoxes in the first place.

So, in these first two chapters we have set the scene by describing the nature of organizational dilemmas and paradoxes. We have summarized the existing literature in order to clarify what is already known about these phenomena. In the six chapters which comprise Part 2 we draw upon intensive case study and consultancy work in a number of organizations in order to delve more deeply into the issues identified. We begin with an analysis of how senior managers craft their business strategies and business models under conditions of uncertainty.

Part 2

THE SIX DILEMMAS AND PARADOXES

In this second part of the book there are six chapters. Each of these attends, in sequence, to the core functions of management which were identified in the first chapter, namely: Strategic decision making, Structuring, Performance monitoring and improvement, Managing innovation, Knowledge and Change. Each of these is examined and illustrated through the lens of dilemma and paradox.

3

Dilemmas and paradoxes of strategy

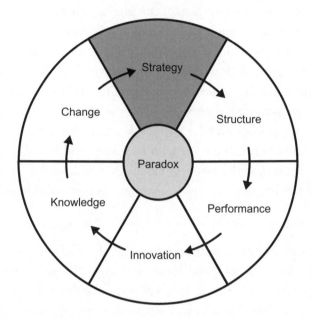

Figure 3.1 The six paradoxes: strategy.

This chapter addresses the first of the six paradoxes (relating to strategy and business models) identified in Figure 3.1. We begin with two short case examples.

The Executive Board of a Housing Association arranged an Away Day to discuss their strategy for the next five years. They completed some scenario planning prior to the event and, with the aid of a professional external facilitator, they came away satisfied that they had done a thorough, dispassionate, analytical job. Within a year, the Executive Board, after some hesitation, came to the reluctant conclusion that the new business model was no better – indeed was significantly inferior – to the one they had used previously. They replaced the Chief Executive and gave the new one permission to reinvent and rediscover the old model albeit using some new terminology.

A highly successful medium-sized retail chain held its annual senior managers forum in a very up market conference centre. The Chief Executive awarded prizes to the more outstanding branch managers. His subsequent speech assessed the opportunities and threats and set out the need for change and the direction of change. The delegates listened politely, discussed the issues in syndicates, reported back and went on their ways, content with their work. Over the next 12 months no change of strategy was evident and the business began to lose market share. The executive team failed to engage with the issues and by their day-to-day behaviour reaffirmed the business model that had worked so well. Two years later the business was taken over and many of the branches were closed.

Recent debates on business strategy have revolved around two main competing principles: (1) Find, and locate within, a distinctive market space; (2) Exploit your organizational resources and capabilities. In this chapter we examine this strategic dilemma and seek to show and demonstrate constructive ways forward by exploiting the paradoxes inherent in these choices.

Strategy and capability

The relationship between organizational capability – 'capability' as a set of organizational arrangements, processes and resources – and organizational direction and purpose is, in principle, simple. Since the demise of the 'one size fits all' ethos of the early twentieth century (the 'size' in question being the ubiquitous organizational form which dominated management thinking and organizational applications) observers, managers and academics have noted that the essence of the relationship between organization and purpose is 'contingency'. In other words, the central idea is to find alignment and 'fit'. Different types of organization are required for different types of organizational purpose. All organizations must have answers to a core strategic question: what goods and services with what features will we offer to what customers at what prices? Or, more simply, why should customers choose our products/services? However, developing answers to these questions, although crucial, is not enough: it is also necessary to ensure that there is an organization to hand which is capable of the design and delivery of the products and services to the agreed specification (cost, quality and innovation) and the agreed price at an adequate margin. Arriving at this organizational capability is itself a design issue. It usually means confronting many dilemmas and paradoxes.

The alignment between organizational structures, cultures, processes and competences (the main constituents of organizational capability) and organizational intentions can of course work two ways; organizations can be built (or after a change of strategy, rebuilt) to support strategic aspirations, or strategies can be built around distinctive organizational strengths.

However, whichever way the relationship works, the key to organizational success, we are assured, depends on the neatness and the quality of the *alignment* between strategy and capability; and of course there is a great deal of sense in this recommendation.

However, like many things which are true in the area of organizational analysis there is a risk that this is true but trivial. To say that in successful organizations the organizational *means* must fit the organizational *ends*, simply means that when organizations succeed, their various internal arrangements must have been the ones required to make sure the organization succeeds. This may be so except in very exceptional short-term market circumstances where an organization producing desired products and services can succeed regardless of its internal arrangements because demand is so high and competition so low.

So, to preach the necessity of 'aligned' organizational arrangements doesn't get us very far. The much more important (and complex) questions are: what actual arrangements are required for designated strategic objectives? What factors obstruct the identification or the installation of the necessary (aligned) organizational arrangements? Why do organizations persist with internal arrangements which do not support the achievement of objectives? Or, in the search for 'alignment' what sorts of structures and processes best fit the selected strategic direction and objectives?

Inevitably, in practice the desired alignment is difficult to achieve, and in practice the relationships between strategies (and strategy-making) and organizational structures, processes, cultures and competences are more complex and prone to paradox than the sensible but empirically problematic exhortations which emphasize the benefits of 'fit' for organizational performance. And this complexity is the subject matter of this chapter.

There are many reasons for complexity in these areas. Organizational solutions may resolve some problems but generate others. One of the key arguments of this book is that organizational dilemmas cannot always be resolved. There are a number of reasons for this. Some problems are integral to the basic nature of organizations. Another is that not all organizational problems are solvable. For example, inherent internal conflicts generally reflect different and opposed priorities which are generated by organizational structures and hierarchy. So, structures which are devised to support organizational efficiencies by focusing employees' attention, specifying areas of activity and tasks and measuring performance, also generate barriers to cross-divisional communication and collaboration and establish sectional priorities and loyalties: these are direct consequences of their existence.

Organizational forms are designed to focus and circumscribe the activities of staff – to particular activities or regions or products – but by so doing organizational structures create boundaries and so create problems of coordination and integration (divisions, after all, divide). So, specialization is required for efficiency but inherently creates problems of communication and cooperation between divisions. Similarly, any method of control of staff (high trust/low trust) inherently raises further problems. Low trust control exacerbates the need for further control (for low trust control discourages employee involvement) and high trust raises the possibility that forms of variability may arise which were unanticipated by managers.

And this is possibly why, although organizational change is frequently presented by consultants and executives as dramatic, revolutionary events, in reality, change is not only a normal state of organizations, but often change is simply a repetition of earlier change (sometimes with a new name). So, 'reforms are facilitated not by learning but by forgetfulness … forgetfulness also helps people accept reforms. Reforms focus interest on the future rather than the present. Forgetfulness also ensures that experience will not interfere with reform: it prevents the past from disturbing the future' (Brunsson and Olsen 2002: 41).

And it is some of these paradoxes which surround the achievement of fit that are discussed in this chapter via the exploration of two organizations as they struggle to adapt strategies and structures (and the links between them) to the demands of the knowledge economy.

Of course it is not unexpected that the achievement of fit should be problematic; indeed it is to be expected, for three reasons:

(1) There are no (or very few) clear, agreed, tested and validated principles, theories and models of organization.

(2) Managers are surrounded by exhortations and prescriptions from powerful and pervasive authorities which insist that there *are* clear agreed and tested models of organization.

(3) Whereas, in theory, strategies and structures are supposed to support each other, in practice they can have less positive or even obstructive effects. This is so not simply in the sense that structures and strategies which do not 'fit' will undermine the achievement of desired strategic objectives (a common, indeed normal occurrence), but in a more insidious sense. Structures can undermine the ability of key decision makers to recognize the need for strategic change and the need to formulate or to implement new strategies.

The focus in this chapter is overwhelmingly on the third problematic, but the first two also require some development.

Business and organizational models

'There are no (or very few) clear, agreed, tested and validated principles, theories and models of organization'. This of course is an over statement. There are some obvious simple rule-of-thumb propositions about appropriate structures. In some circumstances it is possible to recognize where organizational structures and processes are supportive of a given strategy – for example (and this is the easiest case) in circumstances where an organization is pursuing a low cost strategy and therefore all decisions on structures and processes must be determined by the application of the single simple test: 'cut costs!'. However, in cases of strategies of differentiation based on quality or innovation, it is not so easy to identify the core elements and principles of the appropriate organizational structures and processes. As other chapters in this book testify, it is not unequivocally clear how to design an organization to encourage innovation (otherwise it would be achieved more frequently and there would be less need for constant government exhortations about the importance of innovation). It is not (always) the importance of innovation that is the issue but the means of achieving it. Similarly with the achievement of quality: what organizational arrangements are best suited to achieving this? If employee commitment is critical to quality (or other goals) then how can this best be achieved; and how can the simultaneous priorities of encouraging employee commitment (often through high trust/empowerment work design strategies) and the need for high levels of monitoring of quality, be balanced?

Yet managers are surrounded by prescriptions from powerful authorities who insist that there *are* clear, agreed and tested models of organizing. Models of the relationship between organizational structures and organizational outcomes are often informed by general and ready-made rules and models about appropriate organizational form emanating from pervasive and powerful norms. So, the relationship between strategies and structures is complicated by the existence of powerful and appealing exhortations and analyses about how organizations work and about the best means of achieving improved organizational performance. Managers, when thinking about their organizations and how to redesign them, are under two types of pressure. They have to choose the right thing to do and they have to get it done (Brunsson and Olsen 2002: 116). In order to get it done they need to develop commitment, develop enthusiasm and enable colleagues to overcome intellectual, social or physical barriers. This problem was faced by the retail CEO noted at the commencement of this chapter. To succeed in this regard, managers need to 'construct mutual commitments', 'endorse proposed actions' and 'express confidence' in success. Since managers are concerned to achieve commitment and to solve (or clarify and reduce) the uncertainties that are inherent in issues of organizational design they tend to be prone to emphasize the importance of achieving what Brunsson (1985) calls *action rationality*. Action rationality means gaining commitment to proposed action (as opposed to decision rationality which stresses the element of systematic decision making) and requires simplifying the decision-making process, reducing the options to be considered, avoiding uncertainty and polarizing the choices available.

So, for proposals for organizational design to be attractive, they are frequently characterized by a number of features which appeal to managers with a need to gain enthusiasm and support: simplicity and clarity; an emphasis on principles rather than detail; and theories rather than perceptions. They are normative in that they represent attempts to bring order into a chaotic reality and they are one-sided in that they invoke a single set of consistent values and perceptions of the world. They stress certainty, predictability, conviction and commitment and are attractive as a result – despite the fact (or possibly because of the fact) that the world to which these proposals will be applied is one where complexity, uncertainty and ambiguity dominate.

Accounts of the nature of organizations and explanations of their dynamics and principles, and accounts of how they should be managed and structured, have always been the object of analysis. Just as it has been argued that the character and competences of the manager have been defined and constituted by different authoritative paradigms, each being superseded by the next, so the character of the organization and how it should be structured and managed has been a constant focus of authoritative speculation.

Possibly because of the ambiguity and uncertainty that is associated inherently with issues and decisions arising from the various and contested principles of organizational design, and because of the importance of these issues for organizational success and personal wealth, these have always been the focus of claims to have identified the fundamental principles and secrets of the business organization. Management consultants, the modern day alchemists, claim to have unlocked the secrets of business success and to have found the answers to the dilemmas. In practice, we see their primary role as offering reassurance.

The result is a plethora of changing (if in a somewhat circular manner) prescriptions for organizational design and redesign. This in itself is testament not only to the as yet unresolved issues of organizational design, but also to the inherently irresolvable nature of many key organizational design issues (paradoxes associated with core issues of organizational design). These issues, which constitute the subject matter of this book, have traditionally been framed in terms of binary pairs: tight/loose; bureaucratic/flexible; high trust/ high control; make/buy, etc. The reliance on such formulations may have contributed to the difficulties associated with resolving them: both polarities may have limitations as well as strengths. Paul du Gay has noted that a striking feature of current proposals for organizational change is their strongly 'epochalist' character (Du Gay 2003: 664). He observes:

By 'epochalist' I refer to the use of a periodizing schema in which a logic of dichotomization … establishes the available terms of debate in advance, either for or against epochal accounts seek to encapsulate the *Zeitgeist* in some kind of overarching societal designation; that we live in a postmodern society, a modern society, an information society, a rationalised society, a risk society … Such epochal … theories tend to set up their co-ordinates in advance, leaving no 'way out' from their terms of reference.

There is a bias towards overdramatic dichotomization 'that establishes the available terms of debate and critique in advance, in highly simplified terms, either for or against, and offers no escape from its own categorical impera-tives' (Du Gay 2003: 664). These sense-making schemas (such as 'postmod-ern society', the 'knowledge economy', etc.) define the situation they address (organizations and how they must change) in terms of sharply defined, polar-ized (and morally evaluated) dichotomies.

Such taxonomies of organization with their starkly opposed and moralized poles define away the rejected pole, making it largely indefensible – the taxonomies 'rule in' and by the same token they 'rule out'. Such taxonomies carry considerable intuitive appeal, offering 'an easily graspable narrative'. However, their core assumption – that they offer universal and invariable recipes of managerial procedures which provide answers to all organizational problems – is usually found to be simplistic and ill founded.

Strategy and organizational design

Managers are not only under pressure to accept the appealing blandishments of organizational analysts offering enticing accounts of how to understand and change their organizations, they are also under pressure to offer their own accounts of their organization, accounts which should stress 'unity, coherence, consistency action and control' (Brunsson and Olsen 2002: 34). In reality, organizations usually do not live up to these descriptions. However, the fact that managers describe their organizations in idealized terms adds to the authority of the definitions and descriptions.

One of the odd features of the exhortations aimed at executives about how to design and manage organizations is the degree of power and legiti-macy they claim. There may be a link between the inherent ambiguity of organizations – their inherent complexity and their paradoxical quality –

and the appeal of the exhortations and prescriptions of management writers and consultants and the prevailing discourses of organizations. Managers are practical people concerned with achieving practical outcomes. Research into how managers think and behave, stresses the bias towards 'action' in their work patterns. They are not usually tolerant of ambiguity, despite their inhabiting a world which is, we claim in this book, inherently problematic, uncertain and paradoxical. The solution to the anxieties generated by this dissonance – seeking certainty in an inherently uncertain predicament – could be to embrace readily the prescriptions of those who offer advice.

Whatever the reasons, there is little doubt that much organizational design or redesign is driven by powerful prevailing notions of what modern organizations should look like – how they should be structured and managed, the principles that should underpin their key relationships, the preferred 'solutions' to basic organization dilemmas. So, the link between strategies and structures is made complex and problematic. Managers are under pressure to design effective organizations and under pressure to demonstrate that as a feature of their stewardship of the organization they have accepted and incorporated prevalent pervasive and powerful conceptions of how modern effective organizations should be organized and structured. Some of these may be enshrined in dominant expectations from a variety of agencies which audit or survey organizational arrangements – for example accrediting agencies, quality assurance agencies, etc. Others may simply be part of pervasive and dominant regimes of truth, that is, discourses portraying available and pervasive views about how organizations should be managed and structured which, although they may vary in time and space, are nevertheless taken as received truths during their periods of dominance.

However, another reason for the paradoxical and complex relationship between strategies and structures is that in various ways strategies and structures carry implications for each other. The old adage suggests that structures follow (or should follow) strategies. However, structures also limit strategies and strategies create pressures on structures. We know, for example, that organizational structures (departments, levels, subunits, etc.) have implications both for the ability of the senior team to develop strategies and for the organization to achieve what the strategies require.

The connection between organizational structures and the capacity of the senior team to develop new strategies or even to recognize the need to develop new strategies has been identified and explored by a number of organizational researchers. Wilensky (1967) for example, shows the numerous ways in which organizational structures – levels and divisions – have implications for the quality and quantity of information that reaches the top team. He argues that hierarchy and inter-group competitiveness – direct results of organizational structures – lead to structured distortions in information. Similarly, we know that organizational operational efficiencies achieved through processes and routines honed by years of experience and use, may create obstacles to innovation and experimentation. *Exploitation*, argues March (1991), is organizationally in tension with *exploration*. That is to say, when organizations are committed to achieving and exploiting operating efficiencies, they find it hard to spend time considering and exploring new possibilities – new things to do and new ways of doing them. They are, in the distinction developed by Argyris (1999), focused on *single loop* learning (identifying and solving problems) at the expense of *double loop* learning (surfacing and exploring underlying assumptions and new possibilities). So a paradox emerges: when organizations are accomplished at operating efficiencies, this may reduce other capabilities. Hence, core capabilities, as has been noted, become core rigidities.

In the rest of this chapter we explore, through two case studies based on our recent research, some of the complex and paradoxical ways in which strategies and structures interrelate.

Two case studies: EngCon and contract cleaning services

The two cases which we describe below reveal different complexities. In one case (EngCon) the business strategy developed by the senior team is dependent for its success, the team believe, on the ability of the organization to attract, recruit, retain, develop and deploy talented, creative individuals. This in turn, they maintain, requires a very particular type of organization – structures, culture and processes – all of which are the object of explicit attention and management by the senior team and which are designed and selected to ensure that talented staff are encouraged, directed, deployed and rewarded so they stay and their talents contribute to the high quality work which attracts clients. So, one interesting feature of this case is that it illustrates how senior managers define the relationship between a business model and a model of business – in this case a strategy based on high quality products and services dependent on talented individuals attracted, retained and deployed by explicitly agreed and designed organizational systems and structures. For EngCon's executives the source of competitive advantage – talent – is entirely dependent on the business's structures, culture and processes.

However, there is a second point of interest in this case because a complication emerges: the very success and growth of the firm, which are caused by the firm's success at managing talent – arguably through the structures and processes designed explicitly for this purpose – also create tensions for the sustainability of these structures. Thus, there is a tension between the business model and the model of business: talent makes for success but success may undermine the ability of the firm to continue to manage talent effectively.

The second case (comprising a number of leading contract cleaning and allied building services companies) depicts firms in a very different business from that of EngCon and reveals different complexities. However, like EngCon, the businesses in the second case illustrate tensions between the business model to which some managers in the industry aspire and the current model of business employed in many businesses in the sector. In this case, the ability of these senior teams to develop, and, crucially to implement, a new business model is thwarted by their prevalent model of business: they cannot escape the limits of their current capability. The business model to which they aspire is one that the top teams in the sector recognized as the only way to escape the constraints of the low margin, price driven, low cost business in which they engaged. However, their ability to move their businesses towards this desired business model is thwarted by the existing structures processes, management styles and competences (and mindsets) which are geared up for success in a low-cost low margin business and not for the more value-added business model. In the sector in which these firms operate and compete the dynamics of competition are firmly and unequivocally based on price – or so most managers think. But there are some managers in this sector who not only recognize the benefits of moving up the value chain, of moving away from price-based competition towards different sorts of benefits for clients (and for suppliers) but who also believe it could be possible. The case describes the aspirations of some managers within this price-dominated industry where, as one manager put it, there is currently a 'race to the bottom', to move to a new set of propositions to clients and a new, quality-based and even innovation based business model. In essence, this aspiration involved a move from supplying a set of unskilled operations for clients (office cleaning) to (a) an increasing range of associated services (for example, maintenance, office administrative services, concierge, and others) and to (b) responsibility not only for carrying out operations but also for planning and coordinating these operations.

The cleaning and support services businesses case is revealing not only for insights into how even within a low-skill, non knowledge-based sector, where competition is dominated by price and a price war exists, where barriers to entry are few and low, certainly for small to medium-sized clients, managers are aware of the advantages of moving up the value chain and offering higher quality and a wider range of services (with all the associated implications for staff skills, employment conditions, etc.), and are prepared to try to establish the organizational bases for such ambitions. However, the case also reveals more than this: the obstructions to these aspirations may arise not from the clients but from the commitment of managers in the sector to historic routines and assumptions. Not for the first time, it seems that radical organizational change even when recognized and desired, has to start not with clients, not even with organizations, but with the knowledge and assumptions of key managers.

Case 1: The engineering consultancy company

EngCon was founded in 1984 and now numbers over 300 staff. It provides all the engineering services required for the design of buildings and bridges. Structural, civil and building services engineering teams are supplemented by specialists in civil engineering, building physics and infrastructure.

It now has engineers in six UK regional offices and a new Dubai office of 25 staff. The firm is committed to becoming a multi-disciplinary practice. As its structural engineering roots have grown, it has also branched out into infrastructure, geotechnics, bridges and a multitude of other areas of engineering. Following the downturn in commercial building it has established strong credentials in new areas such as schools and healthcare. EngCon directors expect 30% UK and 100% overseas growth per annum up to 2012. Design software and computing power play an important and central role.

EngCon designed an IT system geared to job administration which has helped free up team leaders' time that was dedicated formerly to paperwork and cost-tracking. The firm's business plan involves recruiting 200 new staff. EngCon has a staff turnover of only 6% which is half the industry average.

EngCon needs to take no lessons from consultants and politicians about the importance of expertise and talent in their propositions to clients and as the basis of their strategy and their success in the knowledge economy. This is a point they had taken wholly to heart. Expertise and knowledge – and the talent which is required to use these in innovative customer-focused ways – were seen as fundamental to the competitive edge, the business strategy and therefore to the organizational structures on which these were seen to rely.

EngCon senior managers recognized the crucial role of knowledge as a mainstay of their success but they did not see knowledge as sufficient: it had to be combined with other qualities that were noted frequently and valued enormously: talent, innovation, enterprise and responsiveness. Professional knowledge experience and expertise, used innovatively and creatively, were the mainstay of EngCon's business proposition, the heart of its strategy, the secret of its success. The ability to develop and deploy these professional resources effectively and creatively was a result of individual talent harnessed, developed and deployed by the organization.

These qualities were defined at strategic, organizational and individual levels. Designing an organization that was capable of attracting, retaining, motivating and using expertise and 'talent' – the most important and elusive of all the core attributes – was crucial. The role of organization (structures, systems, processes and crucially culture) was (a) not to damage or demoralize; and (b) to allow full expression and deployment of talent and knowledge.

The concepts of knowledge, talent, innovation and enterprise were regarded by senior management as central to EngCon's culture, strategy and business approach. They had constructed a model of business (the key determinant of organizational structures and systems) and its business model (seen as critical to the dramatic success and growth of the company) around these ideas.

The Managing Director explained the reason for the firm's success:

> Our ability and desire is to look at every engineering problem with a fresh outlook, to see if there is any better way of providing a solution. Our youth – I think we are a young firm, our average age is quite young – so there's a freshness about us. But I think the biggest thing that categorizes us to the outside world is our enthusiasm for what we do, and I think we are fresher, more enthusiastic, than other firms. The people who join us … are surprised by the energy levels that come across.

The firm's success lay in its talented people and in its organization (especially its culture and systems which encouraged enterprise and talent) – and in the way the organization supported talent. Its model of business was seen as fundamental to the success of the business model. The CEO and other directors drew a clear and strong connection between the features of the organization which attracted and encouraged enterprise, innovation and talent, and the organization's success.

EngCon is interesting because of the ways in which these qualities were not only defined as individual qualities, but were also developed, deployed and rewarded explicitly by organizational arrangements.

The ultimate source of these qualities is at the individual level – the people who are recruited and the way they are then 'managed'. When asked what made EngCon distinctive, another director answered:

> We have a great passion for finding, holding on to, promoting and nurturing talent … We set out to get them. We designed this business around the emerging generation of young people …We realized that talented people could grow very quickly when placed in the right environment. Recruitment is key but so is retention and both are the result of deliberate policies and practices, the latter requiring explicit and deliberate choices of organizational structures and business strategies. Senior managers including the founder MD see themselves as enterprising and they try deliberately to recruit others who share this quality: we recruit people around us or we promote people who are like-minded, and they in turn surround themselves with like-minded people.

Expert, talented and enterprising individuals had to be found and nurtured. Despite the recent rapid growth of the company, senior management was clear that if enterprise was to be preserved and cherished, the organization must retain its small size features even though it was becoming larger. So, keeping the features of smallness was an explicit strategy for organizational design. The MD remarked that EngCon: '... retains small firm adaptability, creativity, buzz – but on an increasingly large scale'.

Another director commented:

We are still a relatively small business and we were probably one of the first consultants to really work closely with contractors – looking at how we were going to build it and how we're going to procure it and putting a whole package together. So we were very much 'hands on', giving the overall picture of how something was done. So it's not the traditional engineering consultant's approach of 'That's our design and that's what you [building contractors] are going to go and do'. So we challenged, we did a lot of work leading to the challenge to procurement routes and how we're going to build it, we helped clients move from standard methods. It's the culture and the 'hands on' approach to doing standard things.

This 'hands on' approach was expected of everyone, regardless of seniority.

At the organizational level a small number of key principles, which all focused on the importance of encouraging and developing (and, critically, not suppressing) talent, innovation and enterprise, determined organizational design even when the organization was growing. One principle was the 'rule of 25' – that no one would work in a group of more than 25 people, or manage a group bigger than this. Twenty-five was seen as the number which would permit informal working relationships, informal contact, access, communication and familiarity and would reduce the need for formal systems. The MD commented: 'The idea is that you maintain the structure of the firm, which is sort of 25ish teams of people, each led by a director – the context of unit management ... there are things we have discovered work, and also when they've been changed, we've discovered how they don't work. So, what we want is quite a flat structure, where you don't have too many people gathering those groups of 25 together, and then holding them as their own ... The danger is that those people compete. If that happens, fiefdom develops'. The small teams were seen as responsible – with the other organizational principles – for creating some strategically critical features of EngCon, giving the firm '... the sort of small, light on our feet approach'.

Another principle was that the organization should permit the necessary and timely development and promotion of the talented, enterprising and ambitious people who had been recruited and whose retention was critical to the business model and client value and satisfaction. This had implications for business strategy – it placed an emphasis on growth in order to create roles and spaces for talented people; and for structures – which must permit the development and encouragement of talent. The MD commented: 'We're aware that everybody in the business has a career ahead of them and it's only going to help if we grow the business to meet their demands, their desires. And we have lost people when we have not grown fast enough. We strive to evolve a position for them which means that they can play a major role in the business …We're taking on 20 brilliant graduates this year, and they are really top class; we've got to at least tell them to stick with us, and in five years' time we have moved a lot of other people on, in order for them to have a role. It's very hard *not* to grow in the circumstances'.

EngCon's senior managers were also strongly hostile to excessive systems and administrative procedures which they regarded as antithetical to the development and deployment of talent. Knowledge management, for example, was achieved largely through informal systems – the involvement of the directors in the teams, and the critiques that occurred whereby projects were publicly presented and analysed. 'So our culture is made up of that sort of philosophy [which] hates red tape, dislikes bureaucracy because it feels constrained by it. So, to a large extent, the reason we don't trap data, is we don't like … the rigorous administrative procedure that comes with trapping and using data … We're engineers; we enjoy engineering; we're good at engineering. We're not and we don't want to be data collectors and administrators'.

This antipathy to formal systems was supported by a conviction that organizational systems and cultures should not suppress or limit individual enterprise and initiative: '… the organization is structured so that it has no problems with people exploring these opportunities. There are no real constraints on people who want to explore a new sector, or opportunity'. However, this emphasis on individuals (and the organization as a whole) 'being reactive, customer-focused, adaptive, flexible as opposed to systematized', was supported by a clearly recognized need for 'visibility'. Visibility entailed the directors' ability to check right down to the detail of a project – 'checking to the core'. The checks were carried out by directors on a personal basis.

'Visibility' was central to the firm's capacity to encourage initiatives from the staff (which in turn was central to the firm's success with clients) without suppressing it by smothering talent and expertise with formal systems. The regular 'critiques', the involvement of the directors and the role of the MD in quality checks, all supported this. So too did the process known as the 'Job Management System' (JMS). The role of this system was to ensure that the costs associated with a project were kept in line with the fee chargeable. It was designed to ensure that engineering innovations did not run out of control. The JMS 'focuses on the fee so that everybody is aware of the spend so there's a culture in the business of getting a fee, setting your workload to it, you can adjust the workload you need to do it by affecting your profit factor but by having that [JMS] system you can look at the overall workload of the company. It means everybody in the company is open to knowing what fees are there. So there's a culture certainly through the business from very early days of knowing what you're doing'. Hence, informality was underpinned by a systematic process built on fee income.

Quality was also managed through a variety of mechanisms. The directors could overlook any project; a pairing system existed whereby the teams of 25 staff were run by two associate directors ('so there is support and challenge'); the 'external review' system consisted of directors reviewing work from other teams; and each director set a review regime for his or her project. On complex projects these reviews could apply at a number of project stages.

Lessons from EngCon

The role of management in deploying and defining the qualities *they* deem as critical to the successful achievement – through appropriate organizational structures, cultures and systems encouraging, motivating and developing the capacities of knowledgeable and talented staff – of necessary business strategies for operating successfully in a globalized knowledge economy has been insufficiently studied. Over-determined analyses of organizations underestimate the key role of senior managers and underestimate the nature and significance of their theories of organization and strategy which play an important role in decisions on strategy and structure.

The case of EngCon contributes usefully to our knowledge of the ways in which managers, competing in a knowledge-based sector where expertise, talent and knowledge (and the ways these are used and applied) are defined as critical to firms' competitive advantage and performance. It reveals how the senior managers developed the business model around knowledge and talent, and then explicitly and thoughtfully develop organizational structures and processes designed specifically to ensure the appropriate context for developing and deploying talented staff.

The case reveals to us how managers theorize strategy and organization and the links between the two within the environmental context so often emphasized by Cassandra-like politicians and consultants. The case shows us how knowledge, expertise and enterprise are defined and used by managers as a major element of their business model and their model of business. Both revolve around knowledge and its innovative and enterprising application, the model of business being explicitly and comprehensively designed.

The case of EngCon suggests some ways in which high level discourses of knowledge and talent management are incorporated into senior management thinking – theorizing – about strategies and structures. The case reveals the critical and determinant role of management knowledge and decision making about organizational structures and systems that attract and ensure the appropriate deployment and development of employee and organizational knowledge and expertise. The directors of EngCon maintained that there are clear linkages between the organization, business strategy and the required qualities and attributes of individual employees. Strategic success arises from the attributes and talents of employees. Employees are therefore recruited specifically in terms of these criteria. However, for these talents and qualities to be deployed successfully, certain clearly designed and discussed organizational arrangements are necessary which retain the informality and looseness of control within a large (and growing) organization, and which combine autonomy and enterprise within a system of visibility and quality control. Deploying the talents of ambitious enterprising staff, however, will fail unless there are arrangements in place which allow the timely promotion and development of talented ambitious employees. The emphasis on growth as an organizational strategy is driven significantly by the need to ensure development/promotion opportunities for talented staff.

Two things are – from our point of view – of interest in this case. One is that the value placed on innovation, flexibility and enterprise in EngCon was associated with specific forms of organization, culture and processes.

However, these organizational factors not only allowed and encouraged and deployed talent, but also controlled employees. Control was largely a matter of visibility of both work outputs and cost outputs through professional critique, senior management and peer monitoring and the cost control system. So, in effect EngCon had developed a form of organization that was simultaneously loose/tight. The project review regimes; the 'critique' system by a group of directors; the JMS system, the twinning of associate directors for team leadership, the emphasis on professional standards and quality ('challenge' was as much applied internally as externally); the explicit role of the MD in quality assurance; and most of all the dominant and pervasive cultural emphasis on high professional standards and on challenge, open critique and on innovation – all these exerted clear and strong pressure on employees, as did the explicit emphasis on career management and progression. The able and successful progressed; the others did not.

EngCon is interesting in two ways. First, although explicitly anti-bureaucratic, the EngCon organization was anti-bureaucratic in unusual ways. Although employing the conventional devices of decentralization (small autonomous work teams) and flat management structures, EngCon also incorporated a strong focus on normative control allied with a series of explicit review/critique structures. However, the main point of interest lies in the attempt by directors to create a form of *ambidextrous organization* with respect to two dimensions: large/small, and professional/managerial. EngCon combined elements of conventional organizations (a work management system, group work, etc.) with features of small, informal organization, and features of professional organizations (explicit professional review processes and structures).

Directors were determined to create an organization which encouraged and utilized knowledge and talent by achieving the benefits of small size within an organization that was no longer small – and also tried to combine the encouragement of innovation and responsiveness with minimal systems for ensuing financial constraints and quality visibility. This provides a clear example of a corporate attempt to exploit and thrive on paradox.

One of the central values was 'how they treat people'. Deviation from the EngCon norms on this issue was a serious breach of the culture. The MD commented on one regional office which was defined as 'a problem': 'There is a measure of whether they appreciate our values in that respect. And that's terribly relevant and we're out to correct that'. Of staff in the new Dubai office, the MD remarked: 'None of them [a diverse, international group of engineers] has ever worked with us in London so some of the game is going to be to pull some of them back, to indoctrinate those people'.

While EngCon staff were expected to be, to a considerable degree, autonomous and independent – to take responsibility for the quality of their work, to be challenging, independent, resourceful, reliable, talented, competent, innovative and enterprising – they were also expected to accept and be bound by a clear and powerful shared organizational culture ('being us'). So there is an extent to which this could be seen in terms of self-regulation in that it unequivocally places a considerable burden on the individual to self-manage.

However, this self-regulation is not disguised or implicit: it is overt, obvious and discussed. The nature and role of the culture were analysed openly. The expectations of recruits and staff were similarly overt and discussed. Also, if some aspects of the EngCon control system could be seen as an overt set of requirements and standards which impacted on individuals and which they were expected to internalize, accept and meet, other aspects were clearly externally derived and applied – for example, the JMS system and the review systems. The systems for review were emphasized strongly but they could not be seen either as 'action at a distance' or as attempts to define the subjectivity of the employee.

In some interesting and unusual ways EngCon could be seen as seeking to achieve an ambidextrous form of organization which avoids the problems of over tight or over loose forms of organization, creating an organization that is both controlling and liberating; however, our research also suggests that there may be some new tensions arising from the inter-relationships between some components of its attempts to retain talented staff. The retention of talent, as senior managers admitted, was significantly influenced by an explicit commitment to the development and promotion of talent. This meant that promotion opportunities had to exist. The only way to achieve this was through growth of the business. Growth also occurred as a result of increasing workflow. However, senior managers were beginning to realize that while growth was necessary it was also dangerous: the main risk being a reduction in the nature and extent of shared values that were a key source of normative control of the business. This was, as we have seen, especially likely when growth occurred through acquisition or via franchise arrangements. Growth was desirable, even necessary; but growth could undermine the very principles that made it possible. It seems that solutions to some core paradoxes may in time only generate new ones.

We now turn to a very different context and a very different case. This concerns firms in an industry at the low skill end of the spectrum. We illustrate the dynamics here by a study of office cleaning companies and associated business services contractors.

Case 2: Commercial and industrial cleaning and support services contractors

This case is not a single business but a cluster of the large international and national firms and their industry association which represents the major contractors in the industrial and office cleaning and support services industry. We were approached by the leading half dozen firms who were exploring the idea of a new business model for the premium end of the industry. These members, while interested enough to investigate the idea of a new quality kite mark standard and premium end 'club', were far from sure that it is possible or even desirable for the cleaning industry to move away from price-driven competition to other more value-adding bases of competition.

However, the fact that the research reported here took place at all indicates that some senior managers within the industry thought that the idea was worth serious investigation. Over a two-year period we worked with six of the top contracting firms to help them think through and investigate this proposition. However, it was clear that the companies were some way from achieving this move from price-driven competition and had not managed to adapt their organizations to support such a shift. This relationship between a desired future strategy and business model and the current and historic organizational model (with its core components – a largely unskilled workforce, certain historic management styles and models) turns out to be an important source of dilemma and paradox.

The case tells us not how firms are managing to compete within a knowledge-based sector (as with EngCon) but rather how firms in a sector that is not (yet) based on value-adding competition *seek to make the transition* towards being able to make these propositions to clients and how they struggle to make the necessary adaptations to develop and support and deliver such strategies.

The company directors who steered the association were under no illusions about their industry, its dynamics and its reputation. While some of the leading contractors have made significant strides in recent years in raising the quality and competitiveness of their service offer (and their clients were aware of, and appreciated but also increasingly demanded such developments) the industry as a whole suffers from a poor public image – an image which reflects significant parts of the industry – but as we found, with some very notable exceptions.

The industry, despite certain changes, is characterized by low status, low pay, low margins and low quality. The value-added is relatively low (though some of the more enterprising firms are finding their own ways to escape from this price-based, low margins model). There are very low entry barriers into the industry and an approach to contracting and tendering which impels a 'race to the bottom' with firms under cutting each other on price to gain the business and clients using this to reduce costs. The model leads to a low demand for skills.

However, some firms in the industry, as noted, have identified a potential market opportunity in escaping from this part of the market into a more value-adding territory. The nature of this conceptualization is shown in Figure 3.2.

The drive to move up the value chain away from the price-based provision of cleaning services towards a wider range of services and a more plan-

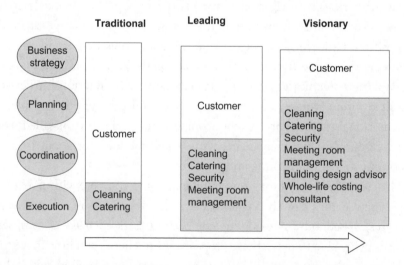

Figure 3.2 Actual and potential shifts in the business model in contract cleaning and associated services.

ning management and even strategic contribution is driven in part by the directors' aspirations. It was driven also by other factors, not least by their awareness of demands of the larger, more sophisticated, clients.

The following were some major sources of pressure for change:

- Consolidation in the industry.
- The move to larger contracts – sometimes global, often international.
- Clients' demands for (or being open to) providers moving up the value chain towards not simply supplying services but deciding strategies and implementing them.
- More professional management within the industry especially within the larger contractors.
- New technology especially ICT, new machines and new cleaning products.
- Increasing demands from clients for integrated service provision.
- Trade union, political and pubic pressure for change (e.g. campaigns against low pay and poor conditions in the industry targeted at high profile clients).

Firms within the industry were and are changing, often with competitive benefit, for such moves differentiated the firms which took them, and as we will see, clients were themselves pushing for change. The main business developments as indicated in Figure 3.2 above were:

- expansion in the range of services;
- 'bundling' of services into packages which were sold as integrated contracts;
- mergers and acquisitions, consolidation;
- increased professionalism of management;
- contractors investing substantially in training;
- contractors innovating with full-time rather than part time operatives;
- daytime cleaning rather than night time or twilight hours;
- interacting with and supporting clients staff and customers.

In some ways, carrying out cleaning during the day is more difficult since office staff are in the way. However, contractors who chose to do daytime cleaning did it deliberately to encourage the development of relationships between their staff and office staff and to make their workers *visible*. This was one of a number of ways in which the role, contribution and even identity and humanity of the cleaner could be improved and personalized. The more enlightened managers recognized that if the contribution (and value) of the cleaner was to be changed one simple but important step was making them visible and enabling them to build relationships and arrangements with the end-users – office workers and in retail environments the customers (shoppers). So, managers sought to enlarge the interface between contractor and client from contractor manager to client facilities manager to individual cleaner and office worker. In itself this could be seen as relatively trivial but it indicates a fundamentally different – and more sophisticated – understanding of the supplier-client relationship and an awareness of the need to widen and broaden and strengthen this key relationship: client management.

Increasingly, clients are expecting or hoping that contractors will move in exactly the way described in Figure 3.2: moving from simply supplying services by carrying out circumscribed, repeat operations to taking responsibility for planning and coordinating these services and for offering a wider range of services delivered in new ways and with new features. They want contractors to be innovative in terms of the services offered, the management of these services, the role and contribution of management. One client, a facilities manager in an international pharmaceutical firm, mentioned how, over time, the cleaning contractor had trained its staff not simply to clean the laboratories but also gradually to take over some routine preparation work within the laboratories, thus liberating the technical staff for more demanding work.

Another manager noted how the contractor had designed an effective ICT system whereby client managers received frequent and updated reports from the cleaning staff about the progress of the work and any issues which had arisen that needed attention. The introduction and benefits of day-time working have already been noted. Another client mentioned that the cleaning staff, although employed and managed by the contractor, wore the uniforms of the client firm and stressed that this had positive benefits for the role and contribution of the cleaning staff. However, most of all, they wanted to move away from the historic relationship with contractors whereby contractors, having won the cleaning contract largely on price, had an interest in employing cheap unskilled labour and in managing the contract tightly to ensure margins: thus setting up an adversarial or low trust relationship with the client. Many clients wished to move away from this model (or at least they claimed to want to do so).

With respect to changing client needs and expectations, a senior facilities manager responsible for one of the massive office blocks in Canary Wharf, commented:

> We will be looking at how our contractor takes *proactive* responsibility to handle the growing pressures. I will not be pleased if they simply try to hide behind me. I want to see them leading. What new ideas do they have? What are they doing for their staff? I want them to come to me and tell me what is going on, about market intelligence. I don't want them simply to say 'please can you give more money to pay my cleaners'.

The facilities managers recognized that contractors would have to change – radically – to be able to recognize and meet the new client expectations. However, many clients also noted that contractors would probably find making (or even recognizing the need for and designing) these changes difficult. Old, established routines and practices, skills and assumptions could obstruct both the recognition of the need for change and the ability to change.

Increasingly, clients in this industry wanted more and different things from their contractors. In particular, they wanted value for money – not simply lowest cost, but efficient and effective working. They wanted to share in the benefits of innovation and learning – not just at the time of the periodic contract tendering times.

The changes aspired to were both of type of service and level of contribution: horizontal diversification and vertical diversification. Horizontal changes – where the range of services offered is increased – were of a number of types. One type was where the suppliers of cleaning services could change the way they provide their traditional operation – office cleaning – for example, as noted, supplying this in new ways (day-working) or with new equipment and products or with new management supports (information systems). Another type of horizontal change was where the range of services was expanded and the contractor took responsibility for other facilities management activities: for example, reception or porter services or chauffeuring. Or, the change might be not in the number of activities within a broadly accepted range of facilities management activities, but might involve a move into office administration services (photo-copying, printing, etc.) or

low-skill support for production activities as in the case of the pharmaceutical company where staff from the cleaning contractor were trained to carry
out the routine, lower skill-end laboratory activities.

Vertical diversification of cleaning contractor activities involved not an
expanded range of operations, but the transition from supplying services to
taking responsibility for planning, coordinating the range of services and, in
advanced cases, developing and applying strategies for the most effective
design and employment of these activities, thus liberating client management from these responsibilities and changing the nature of the client–
contractor interface from one of wary and suspicious surveillance, to one of
clearly delegated and agreed responsibilities and outcomes within a partnership relationship. The aspiration was that cleaning and maintenance function specialists would be consulted at the building design stage so that the
whole-life costing for the building and its maintenance and cleaning could
be taken into account at the outset.

The clients (or some of them) want a change from the historic nature of
the client–contractor relationship. They want much more from their contractor. And the contractors too (or some of them at least) seem to have
developed radically new sorts of relationships with their contractors; they
have recognized this opportunity and have risen to it.

The 'high road' or high-value vision of the contribution, proposition,
strategies and structures of the alternative new type of cleaning contractor
has been indicated by the discussion above. It means a shift from the low-
price, minimal service, low skill, adversarial contractor–client relationship
to a series of interlocked propositions including not only a wider range of
services and management activities but also a different sort of relationship
between contractor and client. However, achieving this new model, although
widely desired by some contractors, required radically new ways of thinking
and managing: new competences, new attitudes towards staff, more full-time
staff, better trained and more motivated staff, capable team leadership and
management able to work with client's management and better career structures within the contractors.

Nevertheless, it became very evident over the course of our work that
many contractors, although recognizing the picture described above were
unwilling or unable to make the transition. In terms of Figure 3.3 below,
they were unable or unwilling to move from the historic 'low road' model
to the 'high road' model.

Low Road	High Road
Low status	Higher status
Low pay	Higher pay
Low cost emphasis	Business value emphasis
Low commitment	Higher commitment
High turnover	Lower turnover of staff
In the dark hours/out of sight	Daytime cleaning
Primitive technology	Advanced technology
Responsive	Proactive solutions; Advice on building design
Cowboy image	Professional image
'Just cleaning'	Integrated services (e.g. hotel-type suite of services)
Marginal part of customers business	Integral part

Figure 3.3 Contrast between the high road and low road business models.

High performing companies in this sector, as any other, are able to iden-tify changes in the sector and to rise to the new demands these offer and to change the bases and rules of competition – they do it themselves and this constitutes a sustainable basis of competitive differentiation. However, we found that market research and analysis was by no means sufficient. The paradox was that these owner-managers and professional directors aspired to the new business model, but in some other regards they were simultane-ously suspicious of it and found comfort in cleaving to the old, familiar, model.

Identifying and understanding and meeting and exceeding clients' needs are essential to business success. Some firms in this sector are good at this: finding new products or services (with higher margins) or delivering existing products in new and better ways. However, many companies – perhaps most – were less good at making this change. They found it hard to move from their historic ways of competing. We began to realize that the 'obstacles' they encountered came partly from their own established ways of thinking and partly from established ways of doing and the skills and structures and routines they had devised and consolidated. They found it hard to really believe that price was not still the bedrock of competition, hard to believe that a new less price-conscious, less adversarial management model was required (for their staff and for client relationships). They began to insist that price was still the dominant criterion even though clients stressed to us that increasingly their concern was not price in an absolute sense but value for money where more innovative value-adding contractors could not only be more than a source of cost, but could also assist the client organization to achieve their goals.

Understanding – or anticipating – customers' needs and delivering on these propositions would require listening to and understanding customers' wants, developing smart strategies and creating an organization to deliver these. We found that many of these companies were fundamentally ill-prepared to deliver on these; they were conservative, introverted and slow to change.

It was clear – to the contractors themselves very often – what was required:

- Better understanding of clients' changing needs.
- Better strategic analysis and thinking.
- A more proactive and innovative approach not only to clients but to their own organizations.
- Greater willingness – and ability – to change.

However, although these elements were widely discussed within the Managing Directors' group, many contractors remained ultimately unwilling or unable to move in the necessary directions even when they agreed at an intellectual level that such change was advantageous and necessary.

They realized that 'high performing' companies 'force' change, and they realized also that this requires a heightened understanding of clients' needs (supplemented by an enhanced ability to meet these needs). But they remained imprisoned by their historic mental models and assumptions, constrained not only by their unwillingness or inability to think in new ways about what their relationship with and propositions to clients and indeed to staff, but also limited by historic and organizational arrangements (management styles and professionalism, staff capacities, organizational systems and cultures – which seriously limited the capacity of the organization and its staff to deliver anything other than low-cost, low-skill, provision of conventional, and limited services.

Discussion

These two cases reveal ways in which existing organizational strategies and business models impact on the ways in which directors react to and try to develop strategies to meet, environmental challenges and opportunities.

EngCon shows how managers in a firm offering a professional technical consultancy designed organizational structures and processes which they believe will support a value-based strategy and set of business propositions and which will enable their firm to attract recruit, develop, motivate, retain and deploy the talents and creativity of talented staff.

This case offers insight into the ways in which the senior managers sought to escape from a classic paradox: the tension between the need to control and to motivate, to inspire and encourage creativity and innovation through a series of explicit organizational principles, and the need to ensure surveillance and control – but through mechanisms that would not be experienced as obstructive or obvious or unnecessarily burdensome or unreasonable. EngCon's executives have developed a form of organization which not only liberated staff, but also ensured control through self-motivation and encouragement (developing talent and ambition) and through a variety of control mechanisms working at personal, peer and small group and organizational levels, all supported by normative control and thorough financial control.

They were, in subtle and intelligent ways, seeking to overcome and collapse some of the established polarities which govern thinking about organizational design – large/small; structured/organic; professional/managerial; innovative/operational – by developing hybrid organizational forms. Most interesting of all, are the ways in which these senior managers define the essential features of value-adding organizations – that they attract, retain and use talented people who combine knowledge with other critically important qualities about the way knowledge is used. However, it also reflects the dilemma between the consequences of success (growth) and the necessary supports of growth – the organizational arrangements necessary to maintain the deployment and motivation of enterprising, innovative and talented staff.

The second case presents a very different picture in a very different industry. Here the issue is less *how* to develop value-adding strategies and capabilities (although these are important questions) and more the difficulties that arose for these firms in escaping from the historic and existing mind-sets, systems, structures and competences developed over many years which had served the original business model well but which have had to be unlearned and modified if the businesses were to support a radically new business model. For the senior managers the issue rather was whether this new business model was feasible. This case describes an industry that is changing. Although it is unlikely that it will ever achieve a similar degree of complexity as the engineering consultancy industry or ever require the degree of expertise which that industry requires, nevertheless many clients in the cleaning sector stressed that they wanted more and different services from their contractors. In many cases they not only wanted the contractors to carry out new services in new ways; they also wanted them to take over the planning and management of facilities operations as a whole, to move from just 'doing' to thinking about, and making decisions about, a wide range of associated services, sometimes on a national, international or even global scale depending on the clients' needs.

Being able to meet these changing and more demanding expectations requires not only greater and different expertise from suppliers to support the new business propositions, it will also require new structures (for example national, international or even global client account management); new expertise (for example, strategic thinking and decision making); and new skills to develop and execute the new business propositions. This will require new sorts of attitude: the highly oppositional, low trust win/lose attitude which was associated with the price-based business model – and the management practices and attitudes and employment practices associated with it – will have to be replaced by practices, management styles, account-management structures and skills required by the new business model. A difficult shift – for many firms it seems simply far too difficult.

This is where the problems (for some firms at least) arise and are revealed – in being able to recognize and adapt to meet the emerging changes in the dynamics of competition away from simple (and often aggressive) price-based competition around the provision of basic cleaning services to clients who are often viewed in adversarial terms, to a value-adding, differentiated and greatly enlarged range of services to clients viewed in terms of partnership and shared benefits. Here, the supplier is expected 'get off the beaches' and establish positions and responsibilities within client management.

The cleaning contracts case shows that under these circumstances some firms manage to make the radical adjustments required; others do not. The crucial variable, in both cases, is managerial perceptions and interpretations.

The first case highlights the key role of EngCon directors' definitions of their competitive situation and the nature and role of the theories of management which they bring to the design of appropriate talent-managing organizational structures and systems. The second case shows that the factors which distinguish between those cleaning companies which recognized and rose to the changing requirements of clients, and those that did not, were managerial knowledge and assumptions and the willingness and ability of managers to move beyond and overcome the established and historic expectations, mindsets and practices. These were deeply embedded not only in management thinking but also in organizational routines, relationships and practices.

Both cases reveal that the key factor which determines how, how well, and indeed if, firms rise to the new demands their situation is ultimately their model of business. Organizational arrangements which could be sources of strength in some circumstances can be sources of restraint in others. Operating efficiencies once achieved can, because they become organizationally embedded, serve to act as sources of restraint when a significant shift of strategy requires radically new structures and processes. These are the essential dilemmas and paradoxes of business models.

4

Dilemmas and paradoxes of organizational form and structuring

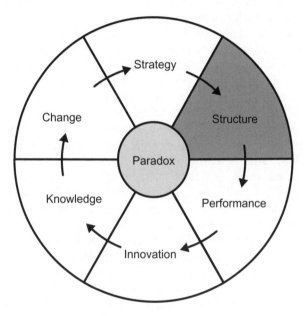

Figure 4.1 The six paradoxes: structure.

In this chapter we turn to consider the second of the six dilemmas and paradoxes – the design of organizational forms and structures. Getting organizational forms and structures 'right' can be very difficult. As the extract below from an interview with a senior BBC executive reveals, the impression is gained of a constant attempt to try one solution and then another. These changes are often reactions to the previous set of changes.

> I've worked for the BBC since 1970 and I can tell you that the BBC restructures itself on average every four or five years.

Such changes are not uncommon in all sorts of organizations. However, what lies behind them? Let us observe another senior BBC executive's struggle to explain *the thinking behind the structuring*. Note, in particular, the diversity of principles that the manager seeks to reconcile and also the attempt to explain the historical unfolding:

> When it started as an organization, the BBC was engineering led. The content came after the method of distribution. Then, the content dominated for many years. When television came on the scene, the organization became about the way in which you packaged that content. The presentation and so on and the commissioning. In a sense we're back to content again now but the infrastructure that you need to do something as complex as delivering twenty-one, I think, main national services, not counting the thirty-six local radio stations. And the complexity of the digital world which is now upon us means that there – you have a bigger, flatter structure looking after presentation and transmission and so on. And a bulk of people making programmes, not all of them in the BBC anymore. Here we are funded by the licence fee for most but not all. And it comes in to the centre of the BBC which keeps some of it to run itself. And it then disperses it chiefly to something called BBC Broadcast, and another bit to BBC News which also commissions as well as produces. And if I've forgotten anything I'll come back to it later. So the money flows down. Within broadcast you've got subsets, education, the regions as we boldly call them, which is quite a lot. It's the three, it's four big regional centres, it's Scotland, Wales, Northern Ireland and England. Because each of those has got specifically regional broadcasting as well as making programmes for national distribution. It's got television and it's got radio are the main subsets of broadcast. So, the money's flowing down and they all then commission. And they commission from internal BBC production. There is also production within the regions because it's not a nice clean division. And then there is production outside the BBC from independent production houses. The News is in fact still vertically integrated so they have their own production. I'm not surprised anybody is confused about this. So, the money flows down there and prices given for programmes and then the production people buy their resources which may be studios or people. But they also buy traditional engineering resources and also buy talent, they're spending money on talent and that's a kind of crude way of saying, performers. But it also means writers, it may mean musicians, so your performer may be an actor, it may be – he/she may be an actor, a musician. It may just be a contributor. Somebody like yourself who's interviewed and gets payment for it. So the money flows all the way down like that. It actually gets more complicated I am afraid because there is also The World Service, BBC Worldwide which is the commercial wing, BBC Prime and BBC World, various joint ventures and so on … not to mention our huge on-line activities …

Here, we can observe a senior manager's struggle to literally 'make sense' of a complex set of diverse and competing principles of organizing. The manager begins with the engineering origins, then describes the rise of content as a new organizing principle, before moving on to a 'modern' way of thinking about the organization based on the logic of arranging the form around the way the 'money flows'. In addition, there is a dominant narrative of the commissioning versus the provider of services split. Running alongside that is a geographical organization structure. In addition to that, there is a product principle (for example, news versus entertainment). Then, there is a further organizing principle – types of staff (most notably talent versus support staff and administrators). From time to time, while each of these principles seems to remain in play in some form, the salience of a particular principle raises to the fore as a presumed dominating logic.

Anyone attempting the design or redesign of organizational structures and forms is soon made aware that this domain of management work is especially prone to dilemmas and paradox. Anyone who has ever worked in an organization is probably familiar with the periodic oscillation between more centralization and then a counter move to decentralization. There are similar shifts between greater control and alternative shift to devolved autonomy. In this chapter we seek to explore the underlying dilemmas which lead to such familiar patterns of 'reorganization'.

Let us begin with an example from the public sector.

Case example – social services

Social services departments in the UK, which cover services such as child protection and adult social care were fundamentally redesigned and reformed in 1971 by the Seebohm committee. However, following the lapses in child protection revealed by the death of a small child, Victoria Climbie, new, dedicated children's departments were created under a Children's Act in 2004 in order to ensure 'focus' and joined-up thinking in relation to the needs of vulnerable children. This clarity seemed an appropriate response to a very sensitive political climate. However, by 2008 a significant number of councils had started to combine children's departments and adult social services under a combined directorate. It is argued that this allows better focus on the needs of the 'whole family'. Hence, some senior local authority executives have been made 'joint strategic directors' of both children's services and adult social care. Is this mere opportunistic cost saving, a redis-covery of the value of the wider view and a reaction to 'compartmentaliza-tion', or a betrayal of the previous commitment of strong child-focused strategy? (Improvement & Development Agency 2008)

This case reveals a common tendency – to deal with dilemmas by fluctuat-ing between one pole of the solution and then the other, depending upon the immediate pressure being experienced. The anxiety provoked by the Baby P Case in the London borough of Haringey, soon after the IDA report was published, led to serious questions about this possible loss of clear focus. However, there are also other drivers impacting on organizational design.

In recent years, many organizations have been seeking greater flexibility and agility, and as a result, they are relying more on market and market-like forms of coordination – this has been especially notable in the UK National Health Service which we have been researching and where 'providers' (e.g. hospitals offering services) have been separated from commissioners/purchaser organizations. The meanings and the tensions created by these reforms are still being worked through.

The ways in which work contributions are brought together and are coor-dinated have thus become much looser and more varied. Even the term 'organization' begins to seem too restrictive a concept to capture the variety of forms which the multiplicity of modes of coordinated work now takes. Externally, networks, supply chain management, various forms of contracting and outsourcing all tend to loosen the construct of a singular employing organization. Internally, we see a growing reliance on market-oriented projects, network structures and process management approaches. Increasingly, coop-eration runs alongside competition both within and between organizations.

Yet, while the 'end of bureaucracy' has been heralded many times, there appears to be evidence that successful organizations are operating with dual forms – i.e. introducing new flexible and agile features while also maintain-ing the stabilizing and controlling advantages of more traditional forms. As has been noted (Graetz and Smith 2007) 'the paradox is that if organizations discard the key planning, co-ordinating and direction-setting mechanisms of traditional forms of organizing, they also remove the stabilizing dimen-sions of organizational form that are essential to periods of uncertainty and change' (2007: 1). Hence, leaders and managers have to learn to manage the tensions arising from the duality of these forms and principles. And there is evidence to support this assertion. Dunford et al. (2007) and Palmer and

Dunford (2002) found that 'new organizational practices' based around flexibility tended not to displace traditional formal and centralized structures including tight financial controls but to co-exist with them. In other words, the different approaches were found to be compatible.

In some organizations there are indeed still notable attempts to introduce more procedure (bureaucracy). For example, Rothschild Banking has traditionally been franchise-like and managers had considerable autonomy to run their distinct territories. As Andreas Raffel, Executive Vice Chairman of NM Rothschild & Sons and formerly CEO of Rothschild GmbH in Frankfurt, told us:

> We could run our businesses with considerable entrepreneurial freedom. However, we have grown to such a size that that there has to be a limit to what you can do with that form of organization; we feel a need to put more structure in. But there is a dilemma here. On the one hand people are attracted to us because they like the entrepreneurial spirit, the independence, the freedom and the culture and not everything is defined. But, on the other hand, now that we have grown to a global size, there is a need to be more stringent and hold people and businesses more to account. We need to put more structure in without overdoing the admin and the bureaucracy and without creating the wrong culture. It's a problem.

This admix of the principles of hierarchy, market and trust (Adler 2001) leads not only to some interesting and novel forms, but also throws up some novel management challenges and dilemmas. Even putting the wider context aside, there are at the heart of any attempt to 'organize' a fundamental set of perennial dilemmas. The key ones are shown in Figure 4.2.

We will be examining many of these core dilemmas in the course of this chapter. However, in the first instance we need to note that shifts in organizational forms carry many important implications for other aspects of management. These include, for example, implications for strategy, for customer service, for career opportunities, for job design and job satisfaction, for learning and development opportunities, work content and skill levels. Moreover, in some senses these new forms themselves constitute alternative management approaches – for example, organizational boundaries may be redrawn based on an assessment of which skills are considered 'core'. The causal link between organizational structures and management strategies thus run in both directions. The purpose of the chapter is not to try to locate the prime mover here. Rather, the aim is to explore the mutual ramifications

Component of Choice	Examples of choice
Hierarchy: levels	Tall versus flat
Hierarchy: authority	Centralized versus decentralized
Specialization	Based on which principle – function, product, process or region?
Roles	Clear specific job definitions or fuzzy
Schedules and protocols	Mandatory or discretionary
Integration	Vertical or horizontal
Control	Which strategy: personal, target-based, bureaucratic or commitment based?
Planning/Acting	Planning or improvising
Processes	Conformance or variation
Boundary-crossing	Intensity of network Contract versus trust Short-term or long term links

Figure 4.2 Key basic dilemmas of organizing.
Source: Adapted from John Child (2005: 10).

and the patterns of fit and misfit between these aspects of organizing and to review how managers cope with these tensions.

To a large extent, the aspirations and principles underlying many recent structural changes seem to reflect those which also underpin the ideas of Human Resource Management (HRM). There are even the same 'hard' and 'soft' logics at play. From an organizational restructuring point of view the 'hard' aspects are to be found in cases of downsizing and outsourcing. The 'soft' side of the rationale is to be found in cases of empowerment, learning and team working. The hard and soft approaches proceed apace: that capitalism marches on two legs – market discipline and mutual commitment – and that these two legs sometimes work together and sometimes undermine each other.

As noted earlier, the term 'ambidextrous organizations' can be used to capture this duality. These forms build on and utilize both tight and loose coupling simultaneously. This means they manage process-efficient exploitation units alongside more loosely-managed exploration units. We noted that in order to achieve this, management need to be 'consistently inconsistent' as they strive to be both long-term and short-term focused. In other words, the ambidextrous organization amounts to 'a mental balancing act' (O'Reilly and Tushman 2004: 74).

The analysis of these issues in this chapter is organized as follows. We begin with a brief review of the interplay between the organizing principles of bureaucracy and market; we then present a figure which maps the variety of forms which have emerged or are emergent; each of these is examined in order to tease out the implications for managing dilemmas and paradoxes.

From bureaucracy to market

The large organizations which grew after the end of the Second World War typically took a form described by Edwards (1979) as 'bureaucratic control'. The key attributes of bureaucracy in the descriptive, social science, sense (as distinct from the pejorative, colloquial sense) were a clear division of work with stipulated boundaries to responsibilities; officials given authority to carry out their assigned functions; referral by role occupants to formal rules and procedures which ensure predictability and routinization of decisions; a well-defined hierarchy of authority; and appointment to posts arranged not through patronage or bribery but on the basis of technical competence.

This bureaucratic form was based on internal labour markets and winning employee commitment through the prospect of long-term career advancement, job security, welfare packages and seniority pay systems. The elaborate job ladders were underpinned by company-provided training and development. Where they existed, trade unions also supported these internal labour markets. Such arrangements formed the matrix within which emerged the principles of modern human resource management. The material elements were in place to encourage a psychological contract based on commitment; extensive investment in training and development made sense; and the system ought to have encouraged careful recruitment and selection, systematic appraisal and elaborate performance management systems.

However, there were limitations. The model in its totality gave rise to impersonality – this was one of its intended characteristics. Impersonality had the advantage of overcoming nepotism, favouritism and arbitrary decision making; and the principles seemed well suited to the administrative needs of the new democratic states and the emerging large industrial enterprises. On the other hand, however, the emphasis on control prompted rigidity of behaviour and defensive routines. The division of task and responsibility elevated departmental goals above whole system goals – that is, led to sub-optimizing behaviour. Rules and procedures often became ends in themselves. These 'unanticipated consequences' and 'dysfunctions' of bureaucracy gave rise to a voluminous literature that helped buttress bureaucracy's bad press (Gouldner 1954; Merton 1957; March and Simon 1958; Selznick 1966).

A senior manager at Oxfam observed:

> In the international division, if you're a field officer overseas and you have a bright idea about how to work, you have enormous freedom to get on and do it ... over time as we become more aware of things like measuring impact, and as we introduce more planning, clearer analysis and so on, these freedoms may become curtailed.

If bureaucracy's internal structure was too rigid, its external structure – the form it gave to inter-organizational relationships – seemed no more reliable. In their relations with peer organizations, big bureaucratic 'core' firms appeared to be all too comfortable in their oligopolistic 'easy life'. On the other hand, the big core firms held their smaller suppliers at arm's length, forcing them into brutal price competition with each other, and keeping them in a subordinate, 'peripheral' sector.

In sum, the bureaucratic form tended to degenerate. Complacency and the link with customers became tenuous; as competitive conditions changed, these systems found it hard to adapt; bureaucracy was used to command and control; initiative was stifled; and supplier relations became markedly antagonistic. As a result, much of the innovation in organizational form over the past few decades has been a response to the perceived limitations of bureaucracy and to the very real limitations of its degenerate forms.

The uncertain place of bureaucracy in an 'age of enterprise' has attracted considerable academic scrutiny (see, for example, the Special Issue of *Organization* January 2004). Some reform initiatives suggest a desire to restore the integrity of the bureaucratic form. In many of these 'restorative' cases, the goal has been to strip away unnecessarily complex structures and to streamline key processes; General Electric's famous 'Work-out' process reflects this faith in the power of streamlined bureaucracy. The then CEO, Jack Welch, said the purpose was to abolish bureaucracy; but a more sober assessment is that GE was simply streamlining it – and with great benefits to the organization's efficiency and profitability. This effort to restore bureaucracy has often been accompanied by greater attention to the fabric of informal relations needed to allow it to function effectively. New forms of 'soft bureaucracy' can be detected (Reed 1999; Courpasson 2000).

Other reform initiatives, often in combination with these restorative ones, sought to partially or wholly replace the process-based controls characteristic of bureaucracy with market-like output-based control. This has led many organizations to decentralize – to reduced sub-unit size, and devolve responsibility. Starting in the 1950s, many large corporations moved to a divisionalized form, based on strategic business units. In recent decades, this move has continued, with many organizations breaking up larger divisions into a larger number of smaller ones that are more rigorously market-focused. Down in the business units, this reorientation towards the market prompts trends towards project and process management approaches.

In their external structure too, we see a proliferation of reforms aimed at creating simultaneously greater market discipline and mutual commitment. On the one hand, firms are outsourcing non-core activities and encouraging more rigorous supply chain management. Conversely, organizations are increasingly forming alliances and joint ventures, partnerships and networks. Information and communication technologies carry the capacity to bridge – in some sense, abolish – organizational boundaries and allow work to be done in new ways on a distributed basis. A related reform has been the shift from hierarchy to network or modular forms in order to increase flexibility (Schilling and Steensma 2001). The past identity of an organization, resting as it did on a physical place and associated perhaps with distinct products, is becoming less important and even less valid.

In this buzzing landscape of changing organizational forms, ideas and practices have been shaped powerfully by an ideological shift which urged the primacy of the market. There was a parallel attempt internally to promote the idea of 'enterprise'. This logic led to extensive deregulation and the consequent pressure on large organizations which had previously enjoyed oligopolistic conditions. It also manifested itself in the pressure to shift from internal transactions and process controls in favour of actual or near-market controls.

Faced with rapidly changing environments and encouraged by this market ideology, many employers engaged in radical downsizing and in the process also retreated from long-term commitments to employees which the internal labour market model allowed and facilitated. Littler and Innes (2004) have analysed patterns of downsizing across the world. In the United States it is estimated that over one million middle managers lost their jobs as organizations flattened organizational structures.

However, this push towards the market has provoked a backlash, and not only among its victims. A growing chorus of consultants and managers argue that even if market forms support flexibility, they do not create the collaborative commitment needed for innovation. As a result of these moves towards a market logic, Hamel and Prahalad noted, 'In many companies, one cannot speak meaningfully of a "corporate strategy" because the corporate strategy is little more than the aggregation of the independent strategies of standalone business units. Where the corporate role has been largely devolved, corporate officers have no particular responsibilities other than investor relations, acquisitions and disposals, and resource allocation across independent business units' (Hamel and Prahalad 1992: 288). In adopting a 'hard' market model, the synergies and the potential advantages of the big company are lost: the potential to use core competencies across units is undermined, and the creative combinations that generate innovative products become less likely.

Figure 4.3 locates the diverse initiatives on a conceptual map. While some authors see a simple spectrum between markets and hierarchies, we follow Adler (2001) and others in arguing that both market and bureaucratic organizing principles can be more or less salient in structuring real institutions, and that some institutional forms reflect powerful influences of both. Our argument is that recent decades have seen a 'swelling' of the middle zone between the top left (arm's length pure market relations) and the bottom right (pure bureaucracy), and the emergence of forms that combine strong influences of both market and hierarchy.

The journey through the chapter reflects the climb from the bottom right of the figure to the top left. Having considered aspects of bureaucracy above, we begin the review at the next stage with project management.

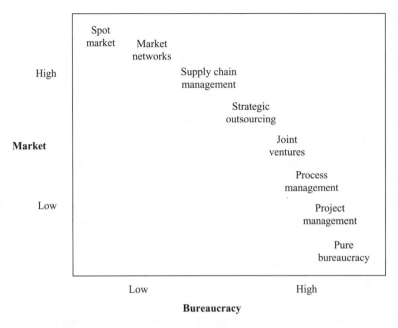

Figure 4.3 Mapping the forms of work coordination.

Project management

Project management has been perfected over centuries by civil engineers as a way of mobilizing people and skill sets towards a market goal. However, over recent decades, project management has penetrated an increasingly broad spectrum of industries and firms. As the business environment becomes more turbulent, and as customer demands become more idiosyncratic, many businesses find they need to respond with less standardized, more customized solutions. Even where customer needs are relatively standardized, competitive pressure pushes firms to find ways to optimize the resolution of the competing considerations of the contributing functions (marketing, engineering, manufacturing, etc.)

Project management implies significant changes to the traditional bureaucratic form. New roles are needed. Project leaders assume more authority and influence. The resulting 'matrix' forms of organization have become almost ubiquitous in a growing number of industries. Structural forums for reconciling the competing demands of concurrent project emerge. In their most radical form, these project-based organizations do away with functions altogether, and the organization adopts a 'network' form, discussed below. Matrix forms, of course, are not restricted to project-based structures. Arrangements such as those we found at Citibank where 'product heads' at director level are responsible for territories covering many countries also act as functional specialist leaders in a 'staff' role (e.g. for marketing) for a different territory, can be found in various forms in many companies. They represent a distinct way to manage the choice dilemma between function versus product.

The logic of project management has also been scaled up to a more aggregated level with the 'front-back' structure. Here multi-divisional firms redefine the charter of their units so that a first set serves distinct customer or market segments, and a second set serves as internal resources for this first set. Galbraith describes the way Nokia and other big corporations have reconfigured themselves in this manner (Galbraith 2002).

Project management requires new skills. Individual contributors need to learn some of the skills used by other project participants, leading to the idea of 'T-shaped' skill sets. Rotational assignments become more valuable in this environment. Team members also need new interpersonal, team working skills, since more of their work now requires face-to-face discussion of how best to resolve the competing functional requirements. Project managers need both 'managerial' skills of coordination, budgeting and planning, and 'leadership' skills that equip them to lead heterogeneous teams towards goals that are often ambiguous. Functional managers too learn to operate in a more complex political landscape, where their power is counter-balanced by that of project leaders.

Evaluation and rewards shift in project oriented organizations. Organizations find that they need to reward teams and not just individuals. Galbraith (2002) identifies some further implications for the front-back model. Most importantly, where the traditional multi-divisional firm typically rewards people based on the performance of their own division, now rewards need to recognize their contributions to the performance of the organization as a whole.

Evaluations and rewards are typically set not only by the functional manager, nor only by project leader, but by the two jointly. Moreover, these people often find they need input on employees' performance from other team members and other people outside the team that the focal team member may have worked with. As a result, a growing number of project-oriented organizations are using '360 degree' evaluation methods.

The inherent capability of Information and Communication Technologies (ICT) to allow 'virtual teams' to operate across the globe raises new questions for HR. Typically, these include whether to encourage face-to-face interaction or not, if so how much, and to what extent they should be empowered. A study by Kirkman and Rosen (2004) of 35 virtual sales and service teams revealed that team empowerment was associated positively with both process improvement and customer satisfaction. The degree of face-to-face interaction, however, played a mediating rather than a direct role in that its effects depended upon the amount of empowerment. Other studies too have found that social cohesion and network range affect the efficacy of knowledge transfer within a network (Reagons and McEvily 2003). People management choices are thus closely associated with organizational choices.

An arguably more sophisticated variant of project teams are 'communities of practice' (Wenger 1998). These communities are self-forming and last only as long as the members wish them to do so. They can be powerful agencies for generating and sharing knowledge. However, they have a paradoxical relationship with management. Arguably, they cannot be 'managed' in the traditional sense but their proponents do suggest that they can be encouraged rather as a gardener encourages plants and that supportive infrastructures and non-traditional evaluation methods are necessary.

Process management

While project management represents a temporary structure laid over the bureaucratic functional structure, the market can influence even more strongly the internal organization of the firm with the introduction of process management. The starting point of process management is the discovery that operational improvements and innovations are often located across, rather than within, existing activities. In its more modest forms, workers are encouraged to collaborate in occasional 'process improvement projects' to seek out improvements in the way their work is divided up and coordinated. In its more radical forms – as 'business process reengineering' – the power of new technologies is marshalled to automate activities, allowing whole families of activities to be combined and reducing correspondingly labour costs and administrative, coordination costs (Storey 2002). It can apply to services such as healthcare just as much as manufacturing (McNulty and Ferlie 2002). The objectives are drastic cost reductions and major improvements in quality, flexibility and service levels.

Proponents of process management claim that it has far reaching implications for organizational structures and human resource management. Thus, according to the founders of the business process reengineering (BPR) movement, 'everything that has been learned in the twentieth century about enterprises applies only to task-oriented organizations, everything must be rethought' (Hammer and Champy 1992). In this statement the originators of the business process reengineering concept make clear their radical intent. The central idea of reengineering was that companies should reorient themselves around their core processes – the start to finish sequence of activities which create customer value – no longer arranged according to the vertical authority structure of bureaucracy but horizontally, towards their market targets. The key elements of this more radical BPR programme are:

- a 'fresh start', 'blank sheet' review;
- a process rather than functional view of the whole organization;
- cross functional solutions;
- step change;
- the exploitation of information technology;
- attention to work activities on and off the shop floor;
- adoption of a customer's view of the organization/producing value for customers;
- processes must have owners.

(Hammer 1996) in *Beyond Reengineering* explains how the 'process-centred organization' differs from traditional functional structures. In a process organization, workers engaged in operating a machine will see their role is not just running the machine but contributing to the 'order fulfilment process'. Hence, if production flow backs up, these operatives will be expected to first investigate and then seek to resolve the problem. Such behaviour will simply be part of the new job. According to BPR proponents, the term 'worker' should be replaced by the term 'process performer'.

Further new roles are required beyond the 'process performer'. There is a need for 'process leaders', 'process owners' and 'process managers' whose jobs are to engage in process design and redesign, coaching and advocacy. This last means it is the process owner's job to obtain the necessary financial and other resources to meet the process need; and to occupy a seat on the 'process council' (which is a forum of process owners and heads of remaining support services to discuss the business as a whole). Such a body is seen as necessary to avoid functional silos being replaced by 'process tunnels' or process protectorates.

This kind of process focus implies jobs that are considerably enlarged: jobs which require understanding, insight, autonomy, responsibility and decision making. Supervision is not supposed to be required. Hammer (1996) talks bluntly about 'the end of the organization chart'. There are no departments or departmental managers and very little hierarchy. This, in retrospect, seems like hype, since the creation of a whole hierarchy of process performers/leaders/owners/managers/councils signals that the old bureaucracy is being updated to reflect the new pattern of interdependencies. Moreover, the old functions persist, although they are now an overlay on the process-oriented structure, as 'centres of excellence'. These are to be thought of as in-house versions of professional associations. They are supposed to enable skill formation and continual development, and are intended to provide channels of communication which enable the sharing of knowledge and expertise.

The origins of BPR are traced to the late 1980s when a few companies such as Ford, Taco Bell and Texas Instruments began programmes of business improvements which differed in kind from the usual run of the mill variety. They engaged in radical changes and redesigned their processes. The take-up of reengineering world-wide has been very extensive. In Britain, for example, it has been reported that 70% of large organizations have embarked on what their own managers say was a BPR programme. In America, Ingersoll Rand, Shell, Levi Strauss, Ford, GTE, Chrysler 'are all concentrating on their processes' (Hammer 1996: 8). In 2009 one still finds major organizations seeking to adopt a process-based review of their organization and operation.

Initially, this process approach was adopted in a highly coercive, top-down manner: it was an effort to streamline bureaucracy without the participation of the people doing the bureaucracy's work. BPR programmes thereby often dramatically undermined whatever trust may have obtained. Subsequently, Hammer himself argued for a version of process redesign closer to the vision propounded by the humanistic wing of lean production and proponents of 'continuous process improvement' – where workers themselves learn the art and science of process (re)design and work together with managers and engineers to improve processes.

The implications, according to Hammer, are far-reaching: 'For a world of process-centred organizations everything must be rethought: the kinds of work that people do, the jobs they hold, the skills they need, the ways in which their performance is measured and rewarded, the careers they follow, the roles managers play, the principles of strategy that enterprises follow' (1996: xiii).

In the changing of mind-sets and behaviours which are required under such a radically different organizational form, one such change is 'job enlargement'. Evaluation and rewards need to change too, to reflect these broader responsibilities. New process measurements are important in order to track performance and plan improvements.

Shifting from a traditional mode of operating to a process-based one is no easy task. Employees fear that a process reengineering initiative means job losses and extensive change. They are usually correct on both counts. Even years after the introduction of such a change employees may harbour resentment and blame the consultancy firm that was used. The implications for future commitment-winning measures can be problematical. More recent BPR programmes therefore often take a more participative approach and attempt to allay job loss concerns by assuring employees that process innovation will not lead to firings although perhaps to attrition.

In the more radical form of BPR, process management has often brought to the fore in a rather stark way some of the fundamental contradictions of the capitalist enterprise and in the process, challenged the hegemony of the unitary view of the firm. In a telling section, Hammer criticizes those corporate heads who so readily nowadays mouth the mantra of the primacy of 'shareholder value'. This is not what business enterprises are about, he maintains: they should instead serve to create 'customer value'. The tension here is between the alienating effects of subordinating the enterprise to the pursuit of exchange value and the motivating effects of orienting the organization to creation of use value. BPR programmes often appeared as brutal, job-destroying exercises aimed only at enhanced profit.

Joint ventures and alliances

Partnerships take place for a number of reasons: most notably, to exploit new opportunities and also in order to access resources and capabilities which the organization does not currently have. Citibank uses 'co-branding' on its credit cards in different territories in order to reach new customers. In the US it co-brands with airlines and the customer is offered air miles; in India and other emergent economies the co-branding is often with mobile phone companies and customers are offered free minutes of mobile phone use. In the UK, BT alone has more than 70 joint ventures and overseas distribution arrangements. Some pharmaceutical companies form as many as 20 to 30 new alliances per annum. The iPod was not successful until Apple developed the alliances necessary to manage and sell digitized music using iTunes.

Companies often use partnerships in order to innovate. Those which succeed in this have to handle a multiplicity of variables. According to the results of a worldwide study on collaborative innovation by MacCormack and Forbath (2008) such firms 'figure out how collaboration can improve the top line as well as the bottom line, and they organize themselves to work effectively with partners. What isn't widely appreciated is how much time and effort these companies put into getting better at collaborating' (MacCormack and Forbath 2008).

Through joint ventures, organizations are able to achieve a number of objectives. Large companies using their marketing expertise and systems can bring new products developed by smaller companies to market somewhat faster than a small company acting alone. For example, this is common in the area of genetic research enterprises. Additionally, large companies may seek a joint venture in order to gain a foothold in new product areas and to acquire new expertise rapidly. This has been the case with large agrochemical companies which have allied with small and medium sized biotechnology companies. A third reason for joint ventures is to enable the partners to reduce their cost base by pooling resources. Companies have often cut their staffing levels and reduced their distribution costs. A fourth factor is that certain developing countries such as India and China may disallow inward investment which is not tied to some form of joint venture with a domestic concern. Salomon Brothers, the American investment bank (a subsidiary of Citigroup), and

Dresdner Bank of Germany have both entered into joint ventures with Chinese financial companies as a result. Likewise, Royal Dutch/Shell invested in a power generation plant in India in a joint venture with the Essar Group, an Indian industrial company.

Despite these attractions and the frequency of occurrence, the failure rate is high. The challenge involves blending corporate cultures, compensation schemes and overcoming staffing problems. According to the results of the study by MacCormack and Forbath (2008), the successful firms 'alter their recruitment, training, evaluation, and reward systems to focus on "soft" skills such as communication so that managers can better learn to motivate and coordinate team members who are outside the firm and, sometimes, in vastly different cultures. Many of these companies also help to train partners – for example, by inviting them to internal development programs so that future teams learn together what it takes to collaborate'.

Strategic outsourcing

'Outsourcing' refers to the situation when a company subcontracts to another supplier work that it was previously performing in-house. In recent times it has been one of the more popular ways to cut costs and to refocus on core competencies. One graphic sign of the trend was that by the mid 1990s the labour agency Manpower Inc. had displaced General Motors as the largest employer in the United States. While some sporadic signs of insourcing can be found the general trend has been towards continued outsourcing. For example, in the US, the growth of off-shore IT outsourcing in the two-year period 2003–5 was estimated at 55% (http://www.intergroup.com).

The BBC has been outsourcing around 25% of its programme production. An Executive Director explained to us one of its functions:

> The independent production companies from which we source programmes tend to be very small organizations. And there are lots of them. The reason we introduced 'Producer Choice' which is our version of the purchaser–provider internal marketplace idea was so that we had good comparators on price between independent productions and internally. It means we could use it to drive costs down internally, which is indeed what it has done.

It also had knock on effects which were not anticipated: it meant that other support 'activities and services that either producers did not want to purchase or activities which could be more cheaply purchased outside – design and makeup facilities are a good example – were cut back'.

The reasons for the growth of outsourcing are many. In a complex, fast-moving market it is a speedy way to gain access to specialist services. Alternatively, it can be a means to reduce costs by sourcing from low-cost producers many of whom are likely to be non-unionized. In this regard, advances in information and communication technologies have played a part in that companies headquartered in high wage cosmopolitan areas can outsource routine billing, etc. to remote stations almost anywhere in the world.

Problems of scrap can be drastically reduced or even eliminated as defective components can simply be rejected. Outsourcing also enables flexibility in that supply can be more readily turned on or off – at least in theory. In some instances it is merely a device to respond to pressures of 'headcount control' – i.e. a means, on paper at least, to show that the critical measure of direct employee numbers is being kept under control. However, according to the more cutting-edge theories of 'winning' companies, the outsourcing phenomenon is, above all, a manifestation of enterprises clearing out peripheral, distracting activities, in order to focus on core functions and core competencies.

In practice, there are many different types of outsourcing activity and usage. Some of the instances are piecemeal and opportunistic with little strategic character. Office cleaning is an example in most circumstances. The commissioning client has low vulnerability in relation to this kind of service and likewise the contribution to competitive advantage is not likely to be high. Here arm's length market contracting is the norm.

However, for other services the outsourcing decision might permit strategic advantage. Nike thus considers it a strategic advantage to outsource all of its manufacturing; similarly Apple Computers outsources 70% of its components, while GM has outsourced its car body painting activities. In these cases, outsourcing often necessitates much closer ties between supplier and customer: here arm's length market relations are replaced by a complex mix of market and bureaucratic mechanisms.

In addition to the commonly outsourced services such as catering, security, IT services and the like, various HR functions can themselves be outsourced. To date, the most popular candidates have been training, retirement planning, outplacement services, relocation, counselling and various forms of consultancy. American Express, for example, has outsourced its retirement plan and benefits system. In February 2005, BT signed a renewed contract with Accenture for the provision of HR transactional work including recruitment, payroll, employee benefits, health and safety and some HR advisory services. This new long-term (10-year) deal covers 87000 BT employees in the UK and 180000 pensioners plus another 10000 BT employees in 37 countries. BT's Group HR Director said that the agreement would enable BT's own remaining in-house HR staff to concentrate on the strategic aspects of the HR role (see also Adler 2003).

A variant on outsourcing is an arrangement whereby companies enter into cooperative arrangements to invest in and share common services – such as a local training facility. In a more formal way this is exemplified by the Shared Service Centre established for the BBC by a joint venture company formed by PricewaterhouseCoopers and EDS, the US systems group. A 10-year contract has been signed under which staff will eventually work for the joint venture company – but on BBC premises. The shared service centre has allowed the finance function the opportunity to offer career development to two quite different groups of staff. High quality finance staff 'are not going to spend a lifetime pushing debits and credits. We want to build skills in the value-added areas', claimed the Finance Director. In time, other companies may use the SSC as it effectively becomes an outsourcing centre. For the present time it is located inside the BBC. Shared service arrangements have also been launched by General Electric, Seagram, Bristol Myers Squib and Whirlpool. Essentially, an SSC does all those tasks that do not need to be kept close to the heart of a business. Placing an order with a supplier is a decision that must be taken at the centre – but the payment of the bill and recording of the transaction can be done at the SSC. Meanwhile, the staff working on processing transactions find themselves in a larger, single organization with greater career opportunities. There has also been a need to put in place management structures to ensure the main customer/contractor is able to keep a measure of strategic control.

Organizational hierarchies are somewhat simplified, since there are fewer functions to be coordinated. On the other hand, relationship management and the negotiation of contracts with the providers become critical. There are issues of confidentiality, risk sharing, continual improvement and so on. Even where there are clear opt-out clauses for non compliance, the management of the actual occurrences may prove difficult.

While not all contracted staff are in the vulnerable, low pay category, there has been some widening of inequalities as the remaining few permanent staff enjoy higher earnings, fringe benefits and better access to skill acquisition. This presents a further challenge to the maintenance of an organization which is low on formal control structures but is supposed to score high on shared values.

Supply chain management

Traditionally, supplier relations were managed by a specialized purchasing function. Personnel here identified potential suppliers and wrote contracts with those who could produce to the organizational specifications at the lowest price. Over recent decades, a growing number of firms has seen a potential competitive advantage in developing a more strategic approach to the management of this function. The process management logic can extend beyond the organizational boundaries to encompass the entire 'supply chain' – not only direct suppliers, but also those suppliers' suppliers further 'upstream'. Supply chain management has been stimulated by the globalization of supply options which creates new opportunities for a variety of suppliers including those offering low cost options but often accompanied by a greater risk of disruption. These concerns are exacerbated (in some industries) by social activists who campaign for corporations to take responsibility for the employment practices and environmental policies of their suppliers.

In some cases, supply chain management consists of enforcing a strict market discipline on suppliers, demanding sizable price reductions with every successive contract on pain of losing the contract to competing suppliers. In other cases, however, customer firms work to establish a denser fabric of relations with their suppliers. This typically takes the form of what Stinchcombe (1986) calls 'hierarchical contracts', where the purchase agreement stipulates not only the standard enforcement clauses, but also an extensive specification of how the two firms will coordinate their activities – effectively introducing important elements of bureaucracy into inter-firm market relations, especially where continually cost reductions, quality improvement and timeliness are critical. This kind of supply chain management is also often characterized by higher levels of trust and collaboration – especially where innovation is expected.

Supply chain management means that middle managers and first-level supervisors often find themselves dealing directly with external suppliers. This is a role that previously was reserved for top executives and for specialized staff in the purchasing department. Middle managers now need to learn the art of 'influence without authority', which is a skill which managers have typically been expected to acquire only at more senior levels. HR is pressured to respond with new criteria for selection, promotion, training and rewards.

Organizational members need to adjust their mind sets so that the well being of the whole value chain is kept in mind and enhanced. For example, GE Appliances collaborates with key suppliers. Together they can plan for, and respond more quickly to, changes in the production schedules. Production, inventory, sales, specification and scheduling data can be coordinated. A monthly data package is shared with 25 main suppliers. An organization may be considered well linked into its value chain if it scores high on a set of measures of joint development in marketing plans, product development planning, production and inventory planning, distribution planning and information systems planning. And for the management of resources and capabilities the indicators would be shared resources as opposed to separate resources in the areas of technical expertise, financial expertise, management skills, information systems and training and development.

Networks and virtual organizations

Network forms have attracted immense attention in recent years, as signalled by the Special Issue devoted to the theme in both the *Academy of Management Journal* (December 2004) and the *Academy of Management Executive* (November 2003). An organization such as Benetton is characterized by its organized network of market relations based on complex forms of contracting. It operates a retail system based entirely on franchising. On the other hand, its sourcing for garments is based on a putting-out system which has a long history. Nowadays, information and communication technology allows the total complex system to operate with a rapid feedback system enabling it to operate with the absolute minimum of stock. In this system it is the wider network rather than the organization which is the interesting unit of analysis – indeed arguably Benetton, as such, is not an 'organization' at all in the conventional sense (Clegg 1990). Organizations such as Coca Cola and Visa, despite their strong world-wide presence, are likewise not traditional organizations. It is very hard to pin down the 'ownership' of these forms; some of them have no fixed assets.

A network organization has been defined as an economic entity that operates through a cluster of compact business units, driven by the market, with few levels of decision making and a willingness to outsource whatever can be better done elsewhere (Snow and Miles 1992). It can be expected that new management functions will be needed – for example, brokers, architects, lead-operators and caretakers.

However, we can also find network forms of organization within the ownership boundary of the firm, such as have been documented in several large consulting firms. Here teams are continually formed and reformed, regardless of administrative or geographic location, as a function of the clients' needs. Functional or divisional structures recede into the background, as mere support for this constantly evolving pattern of interactions. There can be wide variation in the strength of network ties from weak to strong over time depending upon founding conditions and network processes (Elfring 2007).

This free-flow across internal or external organizational boundaries can reach a stage when the organization per se becomes indefinable and unrecognizable – what Davidow and Malone (1992) have described as the 'virtual organization'. They ask: 'What will the virtual corporation look like? There is no single answer. To the outside observer it will appear almost edgeless, with permeable and continuously changing interfaces between company, supplier and customers. From inside the firm the view will be no less amorphous, with traditional offices, departments and operating divisions constantly reforming according to need. Job responsibilities will constantly shift, as will lines of authority – even the very definition of employee will change as some customers and suppliers begin to spend more time in the company than will some of the firm's own workers' (1992: 5–6).

The underlying logic of network organizations as presented by their advocates and practitioners is that 'know-how' and resource capability are now critical factors and these are increasingly difficult to locate within the boundaries of a single organization. Know-how and capability are increasingly distributed across a network of different business and contractors.

However, if this is so, the management challenge to identify, retain, develop and appropriate such scarce resources is immense.

Part of the know-how resides in the identification of the parties and the capability to bring them together. In the 'the boundaryless organization' there are huge uncertainties about who, if anyone, is managing these processes. External boundaries are barriers between firms and the outside world including customers and suppliers but also government agencies, special interest groups and the community at large. In traditional organizations there are clear demarcation lines separating 'insiders' from 'outsiders'. Role expectations were relatively clear. Management dealt with the former group and had mechanisms and techniques to help them do this. However, these traditional methods are of doubtful validity in the network situation.

Under the network arrangement, there are contracts of a more commercial nature. Equally, there are connecting lines based on repeat business, trust and reputation. Mind sets and attitudes have to change considerably. Traditional methods of negotiation, competition, win-lose, information withholding, power plays and the like may cause difficulties.

Increasingly, boundary maintenance behaviour is seen as having dysfunctional consequences. When the boundaries are dissolved or drastically reduced, customers and suppliers may be treated as joint partners. Employees, as such, may be hard to identify. A range of parties may be expected to help the firm solve problems and to innovate. Effective network organizations need to make permeable the external boundaries that divide them from their customers and suppliers. The key concept here is that of the value chain. This is the set of linkages which creates services and products of value to the end user. In the traditional view each company is supposed to maximize its own success with disregard for that of others. The overriding idea is that of competition. Under the new value chain concept the idea is to loosen external boundaries so as to create a win-win situation across the whole value chain.

Under the network concept, cooperative relations between organizations are given high priority. As the cost of innovation increases, as complexity increases and everything changes so much faster, many companies have come to the conclusion that they simply cannot work alone (Storey and Salaman 2005). Business partners, customers and suppliers are urged to work together to co-produce value. This entails reconfiguring roles and relationships. The use of cooperative arrangements of a network kind has long been well developed in Japan. The *keitsu* consists of cross-locking companies often straddling very different sectors. They have shares in each others equity but there is no governing holding company.

The successful network companies cooperate in both strategic and operational business planning. Network organizations require managers and staff to change their assumptions and behaviours. Instead of developing plans and strategies independently, planning needs to be coordinated and even shared with other participants in the network. Information therefore must not be hoarded and protected but shared to allow joint problem solving. Moreover, measurement and auditing systems need to be coordinated.

Information therefore must not be hoarded and protected but shared to allow joint problem solving. Moreover, measurement and auditing systems need to be coordinated. How, and why, does a company become a core organization in a networks value chain? The main identifying feature of a core organization is that it 'manages the network' – a role that is not, however, legally recognized. The actual process of managing such a network is a difficult one and it requires skills for which, as yet, little or no formal training is usually offered.

According to proponents of networks, they offer answers to many of the dilemmas of organizing. They allow the involvement of as many employees as possible so that they become familiar with customer and supplier needs. This can be done through inviting customers and suppliers to meetings where outlines of plans, goals and problems can be explained; it can likewise be sought by sending employees on customer and supplier field trips to encounter the detailed operations of day-to-day work. An additional stage can involve experiments with collaboration through, for example, organizing cross-value chain task forces and sharing technical services. And a more ambitious step involves companies integrating their information systems while reconfiguring roles and responsibilities in the light of the collaboration achieved across the network.

Conclusions

Organizing and organizations are replete with dilemmas and are inherently paradoxical. Organizations are based on some notion of structured planning and yet, in reality, situated practice often requires adaptation and improvisation (Bourdieu 1977; 1990). Likewise, organizations are often characterized by specialization (of roles and departments, for example) and yet the more specialization occurs the more there is an apparent need for integration to pull the different strands together. Similarly, there are dilemmas and paradoxes concerning the poles of autonomy/empowerment on the one hand and control on the other. These are just some of the dilemmas and paradoxes.

A number of consultants and management scholars have sought to identify ways in which to exploit paradox in these instances. For example, Pascale explores the advantage of working at 'the edge of chaos' (Pascale 1991; 1999). Classic bureaucracies harbour a *dual potential*. They can emphasize the rigid rules, multiple hierarchical levels and impede horizontal communication along with a command and control approach to worker management. Or, they may emphasize the psychological contract of security for long-term commitment and loyalty along with an infrastructure of training and development and corporate identity. In so far as the classic form has not been entirely abandoned, these dualities remain.

However, as we have seen in this chapter, there have also been very many and very significant departures from this classic form. The alternatives have been numerous. Descriptions and prescriptions of these have proliferated. And, to a large extent, the alternatives are still unfolding. No one has a firm fix on the emergent form. Various key attributes have been championed: prominent front runners have been the process-oriented company, the network, joint ventures and strategic alliances, the boundary less organization and the virtual organization. We have argued in this chapter that there are some significant overlaps in these conceptualizations. For example, Ashkenas *et al.*'s (1995) concept of 'boundarylessness' both within and between enterprises shares very many features with Davidow and Malone's (1992) 'virtual organization'. Likewise, Nonaka and Takeuchi's (1995) description and proselytizing of the features of 'the knowledge creating company' shares a great deal in common with Senge (2007) on 'the learning organization', Quinn (1992) on 'the intelligent enterprise' and even Hamel and Prahalad (1992) on the vital strategic importance of building core competencies. Further discussion of the variety of meanings hidden in similar language can also be found in Palmer, Benveniste *et al.* (2007).

Thus, similarities and overlaps abound. Each management consultant and would-be guru is seeking to crystallize a complex set of developments into a central idea which can be made appealing, be packaged and sold. The variations around certain underlying themes should not therefore be too surprising. This is not to say, however, that the whole set can simply be dismissed as manipulated 'fads'. The numerous accounts of the nature of 'the new organization' are capturing, albeit it in a selective and partial way, critical features of important trends in organizational formation and reformation.

5

Dilemmas and paradoxes of performance management

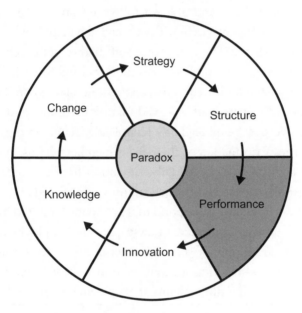

Figure 5.1 The six paradoxes – performance.

This chapter turns to the third of the 'Six Paradoxes' that we identified in the introductory chapter.

A medical consultant and a lawyer were in conversation over a beer in their golf club. The consultant was retelling how his car was off the road due to an accident. The lawyer advised how the substitute car clause in an insurance policy worked. The consultant not only acquired a high class loan car, he and the lawyer devised and subsequently launched an entirely new model of business based on persuading motorists involved in collisions to agree to accept a loan car arranged through this agency and this agency promised to ensure they had a high-range quality car delivered within a matter of hours. The rest of the insurance claim continued to be processed in the normal way. There was, on the surface at least, no charge incurred by the motorist (they signed a contract which meant the motorist carried the risk if the cost of the loaned car could not be reclaimed after all; this occurrence was quite rare). The new business required access to very timely information from garages and it required call-centre staff willing and able to follow up and 'covert the leads'. Garage staff was incentivized with a small payment for volunteering customer information. The call centre staff had to act quickly – within hours of receiving the tip-off – to contact the motorist and persuade them, using a standard script, to assign their claim handling to the agency. The call-centre staff was paid mainly by results and was monitored intensively by 'team leaders'. Team leader remuneration depended largely on the performance of their team members. Thus, team leaders monitored performance sheets daily. Deviation from set targets resulted in meetings with the leader at which training was offered and new targets and deadlines set. Failure to respond to this 'support' resulted in dismissal. Constant job advertising in local newspapers and employment agencies attracted a steady supply of substitute recruits. The recruitment, selection, induction and training sessions were in routine operation. So too was the routine for handling claims at Employment Tribunals.

When people come together or are brought together to form an organization, various questions concerning effort and contribution tend to arise. Ensuring that people do the 'right things', and do the 'right things well', are inevitably fundamental issues. Even when individuals and teams meet these two requirements there is usually an additional need – namely to ensure that there is coordination between the various inputs of right things done well. And when these three hurdles are passed there is yet another – to ensure that performance meets organizational strategic objectives. For these four reasons at the very least, some form of performance management is usually thought to be required. However, this intent is beset with dilemmas about which of the many performance management and control devices to utilize. And this dilemma is compounded by the paradox that such devices and interventions can result in unintended consequences and can provoke behaviour contrary to that intended.

Attempts to influence the performance of individuals, teams and of course the whole organization can be made in numerous ways. These may be direct or subtle, autocratic or participative. The methods are numerous and yet the endeavour is ceaseless. Hire and fire, payment by result inducements, culture building, peer influence and so on. When formalized, the various attempts to influence performance may be termed a 'performance management system'.

While the emphasis on performance management is not new, the forms it takes change, to some extent, over time. Recent years have witnessed senior executives emphasizing the importance of 'adding value' to shareholders and customers. A corollary has been a drive to manage and measure corporate performance. Thus there has been increased emphasis on value-based performance metrics, such as EVA (economic value added) and other similar measures that take the place of earnings per share, return on-equity and return-on-investment. The latter group reflects reported earnings while the former reflects the extent to which earnings exceed the cost of capital. These and many other related shifts have signalled a huge increase in attention to performance management.

There have been two sets of consequences for organizations. First, there is greater emphasis on value-added techniques at the executive levels. These, in turn, drive behaviours downward. Second, there is pressure to measure performance based on these objectives throughout an organization. However, attempts to deliver on such a mission can be highly problematical and paradoxical.

Let us take an example of a core dilemma of performance management from the world of marketing and market research services. The Chief Executive of one of WPP's many businesses states his personal style of performance management and contrasts it with the wider framework of corporate financial control:

I would prefer to manage in a permissive way, to set the framework and let people get on with it. But, when you work within a massive, multi-brand organization like WPP which has lots of companies sitting beneath it focused on lots of different things such as a marketing communications business, a market research company, creative agencies, a media phone company etc., in order to manage that range of businesses we have to manage with financial controls. These tend to be pretty rigid. So, whereas in my business, I would prefer to work through empowerment within a framework, that's in contrast and in tension with how we manage centrally which is as a financially managed organization. We are ratio-based (for example, revenue per full time staff equivalent, operating profit margin etc.) it's just too complicated otherwise. You have to have some control from the top and some predictability, on the other hand, the nature of our work depends on creativity and autonomy. There is definitely a tension there.

(David Day, Chief Executive Europe, for one of the WPP businesses).

Of the various 'factors of production' (land, materials, labour, capital, technology) the human factor is the most open-ended and uncertain. Steel or oil can be bought in known quantities and grades. However, the 'purchase' of labour power is always subject to a degree of open-endedness. Effort and initiative can be withheld in numerous ways; people can be 'busy' but essentially unproductive. In order to seek to manage performance various control devices have been deployed over many years. Direct control using an 'overseer' is one of the more basic methods. However, it can lead to resentment and conflict. It is also costly. Hence various 'indirect' methods have been used. One indirect method is payment for performance – and low or no pay for low or no performance. This allows for self-drive but designing and maintaining such payment systems can also be costly. If people are paid purely by the hour – or any other unit of time – the employer may fear that insufficient effort will be offered. If, on the other hand, payment is by the piece the employer may now fear that quality will be compromised as the employee seeks to maximize pay by turning out large quantities irrespective of quality. To overcome this tendency, regimes of inspection were introduced. But again, inspectors are essentially unproductive labour and as we will see later in the chapter, inspection regimes had their own unforeseen and unintended consequences. Moreover, the very idea of 'performance management' is in many settings a strange one. This is illustrated by the observation below made to us by a very senior executive at the BBC:

Until recently we would never have used the word 'performance' or for that matter 'strategy' or have the concept of a work place 'objective'. I mean the history of the place is that there were, and there still are, a group of people who made programmes who were seen as creative and colourful and slightly freaky and strange. And then there were a group of administrators who struggled to manage them and imposed systems and procedures and bureaucracy and civil service type arrangements on them. The latter group, the administrative group would not have regarded themselves as business executives until recently. And as a result had none of the language of the business world. We just simply didn't use that kind of vocabulary. It would have been more the language of the civil service of fifteen years ago.

This insight into the use of language also reflects insight into the importance of attitudes and the framing of the very nature and presumed requirements of management work.

This chapter will examine the nature and implications of performance management and of management control more generally. In particular, we will see that certain forms of control can be counter productive and they produce their own dilemmas and paradoxes. The chapter will also investigate the various main types of control and their varying consequences. Performance management and control is a social process and is a more complex and interesting phenomenon than is implied by simple mechanistic models.

The meaning and implications of performance management

Performance management can be thought of as the various processes used by managers in order to try to ensure that human inputs contribute to organizational effectiveness.

The range of techniques and processes can be extensive but in essence there are a number of core elements. Typically, these include some combination of goal and/or target setting; some kind of monitoring of behaviour and of output; selecting indicators in order to measure either inputs or outputs or both; offering guidance, coaching and training to help raise productive effort; designing reward systems to encourage conformity with desired behaviour; designing and implementing disciplinary systems to help discourage undesirable behaviour; and finally the design of 'exiting' strategies to aid the removal of unreformed members.

When each of these elements is aligned within a consciously designed architecture, we can speak in terms of a 'performance management system'.

Organizations may have 'tight' or 'loose' performance management regimes. There is no necessary correspondence between these and high performance. Ad hoc, arbitrary attempts to control may be viewed as unfair and may be counter productive. Tight regimes may discourage spontaneous effort. Loose regimes may allow space for malingering if there are no alternative support mechanisms or, on the other hand, could allow space for the growth of trust and creativity. Thus, each of these processes is beset with dilemmas and the domain as a whole is replete with paradoxes. This chapter will examine the main instances.

Thus, the whole process of management control contains many paradoxes. Tighter controls have been seen to result in greater resistance and, as was once famously remarked, management can, under certain circumstances, most effectively 'regain control by sharing it' (Fox 1966). In some instances attempts to impose controls in one relatively minor area of activity can result in disastrous consequences for the whole of the enterprise. While in other circumstances, as we will see, more effective controls actually appear to be associated with higher levels of satisfaction for some employees.

It is often observed that control is one of the key functions of management. Management controlling can be seen as a *process* – not merely as a set of tools and techniques. This process is social and it has interactive properties. This means that the imposition of a control in an organization will trigger behavioural responses. These, in turn, may prompt an adjustment to the control. Sometimes these responses are wholly positive and the intended service outcomes are achieved. However, in other circumstances the unintended consequences of controls can be very negative. Creativity, for example, may be easily stifled under the weight of imposed formal controls. Too little control can be dysfunctional – an organization can be literally 'out of control'. On the other hand, simply adding more control may not always be helpful – an organization can be over controlled. So, the first challenge is to create the optimum amount of control and the second challenge is to use the most appropriate forms of control for the prevailing circumstances.

There is a tendency to turn to 'key performance indicators' (KPIs) which are based on financial accounting measures, published metrics by trade groups, or best practices provided by consulting firms and software firms. A performance indicator on its own carries little meaning, but as a carefully selected measure derived from a strategic plan and designed to yield specific bottom-line outcomes (contrasted with input or process outputs), it can have real significance. At the heart of these systems is the balanced scorecard, a framework that translates strategy into long-term, measurable performance objectives and balances financial and non-financial metrics. The 'balanced scorecard' has been adapted to allow monitoring and management of multiple scorecard levels that identify value-based performance objectives at the strategic, tactical, operational and individual levels.

Another tool is Activity-Based Management (ABM) which encompasses activity-based costing, activity-based budgeting, and business-process activity analysis. While ABM has been used primarily for cost reductions, profitability analysis, target costing and continuous improvement programmes – all of which support value-driven strategies – it is argued that it is even more powerful when used for value-based financial planning and resources budgeting as part of a balanced scorecard initiative. It can be tied to the balanced scorecard methodology so enabling a number of non-financial performance measures to be incorporated into ABM metrics. Various enabling technologies such as data warehousing, analytical simulation processing, graphical and interactive displays facilitate this.

The above represent at least some of the technologies of performance monitoring and control. However, they are only part of the story. In the next section we place them in the context of human behaviour.

The paradox of control

From the days of the early classical administration theorists such as Fayol (1916) onwards, it has been conventional to note that control is one of the basic 'functions of management' alongside planning, organizing, commanding and staffing. Many contemporary management textbooks adopt the same stance. Controlling, in this technical sense, refers to the process through which managers *ensure conformity* with plans and targets. For example, control has been defined as 'a process of monitoring performance and taking action to ensure intended or desired results' (Baird *et al.* 1990: 454). However, other commentators, as well as many managers, commonly adopt a much wider definition. Thus, it is sometimes suggested that management control encompasses 'commanding' as well as 'controlling' in the narrower sense. For example Tannenbaum (1962: 2) defined it as 'any process in which a person or group of persons determines, that is, intentionally affects, what another person or group will do'. Here, Tannenbaum is equating control with influencing or shaping behaviour.

However, while elaborate plans can be formulated and missions and goals set-out, the achievement of these can easily go awry. Control is the mechanism, or set of mechanisms, designed to ensure conformity with a plan and to enable corrective action should this be necessary. One commentator has expressed it thus: 'Control, like a ship's rudder, keeps the organization moving in the proper direction' (Barney 1992: 379). Without adequate controls much wasteful activity can take place even if people are working very hard. For example, in one manufacturing facility known to the authors, defective parts and assemblies were being produced in such quantity that a large proportion of the workforce were employed simply to take corrective action on these components. In that factory, quality controls were extremely poor. Likewise, in a fast-food chain, unhygienic conditions were often found and this could also be attributed to an inadequate set of quality controls. Similarly, in some parts of the public sector (such as in health and social services) suitable controls will need to be installed and maintained if services to the public are to be equitably distributed and to an acceptable standard.

There is usually a need for horizontal control as well as vertical control. Managers have 'tended to pay considerable attention to the achievement of control in the hierarchical sense of ensuring that instructions are carried out and this may be at the expense of giving attention to the lateral dimension of integration across organizations'. That is, heads of department have high expectation that they can show they have 'authority' over their employees as a demonstration of competence but they have tended to place less emphasis on coordination with managers in other areas and departments (Child 1977: 118).

The performance control process

Most analysts of the control process in standard management textbooks depict the performance control process as comprising a number of *stages* – typically these are identified as:

- establishing standards;
- measuring performance;
- comparing performance against standards;
- taking corrective action.

The conventional model for this process is the thermostat which controls a heating boiler. In this simple technical example each of the four stages noted above are occurring. Drawing heavily on this type of technical process, many classic management writers and system designers have suggested that the process of management control is a reflection of this. But, in reality, management control in organizations is much more complex than this traditional model suggests and numerous dilemmas and paradoxes are inherent.

For example, at stage one – Establish Standards of Performance – it is said 'Without objectives and plans, control is not possible because performance has to be measured against some established criteria' (Koontz and Weirich 1988: 490). If objectives are vague, and poorly defined, no system will be able to measure whether they have been attained or not. An example of a standard of performance target could be to reduce the reject rate of components from 20% to 2%. However, the problem is that the choice of standards is likely to lead to unintended consequences. Focusing on one or a few selected targets tends to lead to a relative neglect of others.

Then at stage two – Measure the Actual Performance – managers may develop quantitative measures of operational performance that can be reviewed daily, weekly or monthly. These may relate to quality, quantity, timeliness or customer service – or all of these as a basket of measures. There is an issue, however, concerning the extent to which it is possible to manage through the numbers. Many managers, perhaps most, do not rely on quantitative measures. As some hospital doctors advise: manage the patient not the test results. For managers of organizations there are questions about *what* precisely to measure and *how* to measure. Possible sources of information include personal observation, computer counts, written and oral reports – each has strengths and weaknesses (Robbins 1988). What to measure is especially critical – the selection of criteria can, and (if the measures are at all taken seriously) almost certainly will, influence behaviour. The consequences of this heightened attention to certain measures can be dysfunctional.

Stage three – 'Compare Performance to Standards' – appears deceptively straightforward when viewed simply from a technical viewpoint. Managers may use data reflecting performance alongside targeted performance on a whole range of measures. However, in practice, management control is *not* like a thermostat in a heating system. If actual performance measures do show a shortfall compared with targets, all manner of subjective judgements tend to come into play. Most managers will have some sense of priority among the measures and so will focus, quite sensibly, on the important and mission-critical measures while paying little if any regard to the less important measures. However, what is judged to be critical can change over time and is also likely to vary between different managers.

Stage four – 'Take Corrective Action' – simply comparing and noting is one thing, what *corrective action* to then take, following the interpretative phase, is quite another. Does a clinician's performance record depart from national norms? Is the clinician likely to be supported by his or her medical college? Does an operative need training? Has the standard been set too high? Have circumstances changed? Are other priorities diverting attention from this particular measure? What will happen to morale and motivation if criticism is delivered – let alone if disciplinary action is taken? Moreover, what action, if any, needs to be taken when a group consistently meets, or exceeds, the target? Is this simply ignored while attention is focused on the shortfalls or is the group given positive reinforcement through rewards and praise? What if the group exceeding key targets is also the one failing to meet other targets? And what if a manager who is failing to meet a target (let us say, for example, in arranging sufficient training for staff) is an otherwise excellent performer on a whole range of operational and financial targets? And what if this same manager simply refuses to take action on the training front? This kind of scenario raises all sorts of dilemmas and complications, including, for example, who will take 'corrective action' and what leverage they will be able to bring to bear.

The social complexity of the process

For each of the steps examined, the technical (and in a sense *abstract*) conceptualization of the control process is an incomplete and imperfect depiction of management control. The reality of management control is much more complex and socially embedded. That is, the way in which this form of control is perceived and understood is highly conditional upon social expectations, social relationships and social meanings.

For example, the technical abstract model begins with the idea of 'setting standards'. But, in an organizational setting, this would leave a number of important issues unaddressed, such as: who should set the standards; with, or without, whose agreement; and what kind of standards should be set. Answers to each of these will vary in practice between workplaces. To use the well-known saying, 'the devil is in the detail' and these details may influence whether the controls are accepted, understood or ignored. Nor is that all, the setting of standards may have little impact unless there is also some understanding about who is responsible for ensuring that the standards are met. For instance, will this be the responsibility of a group of people or one individual? Moreover, will it be acceptable to meet the standard without trying to exceed it? Who will take corrective action and what will this entail? Many studies of piece rate-payment systems have revealed that work groups will tend to set and enforce norms which are designed to protect the rate – i.e. paradoxically, incentive pay systems can serve to hold down output.

Types of control

So far, we have considered: the meaning of the term 'management control'; the rationale for such control; and some of the processes involved in management control. Now we need to take another step. It is necessary to gain a deeper insight into the *variety of types and means of control*. These are rather wide and varied and the essential point here is that managers have *choices* to make about the nature, extent and mix of controls.

Managers are faced with a whole array of options. Each has its own attendant difficulties and paradoxes. A classification of the main types of options is shown in Figure 5.2:

Direct supervision

Direct supervision is one of the more traditional methods of management control. Early in the industrial age, factory supervisors ('foremen', 'charge-hands' and 'superintendents') exercised control through personal observation and instruction. It has sometimes been thought that the 'maturation' of management would see this method displaced by more formal and impersonal rules. But, paradoxically, the method has been given endorsement in the 'Management By Walking About' (MBWA) recommendations of gurus such as Tom Peters. This latter mode, admittedly, is given a more social and

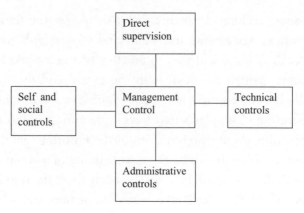

Figure 5.2 Types of controls.

friendly gloss but the element of direct supervision is still evident. An added complication for the modern manager, however, is that this mode of direct supervisory-style management is potentially susceptible to allegations of 'bullying'. For this reason, many managers prefer more impersonal control devices. Practice also varies between different industry sectors. Direct supervision is still a favoured method in a number of sectors. In certain settings such as health and social work there is virtually a built-in formal requirement for professional supervision.

Managers face the dilemma that on the one hand supervision may be required in order to allow coordination of effort and unified effort towards a common goal, yet on the other, is the limited knowledge which any single manager is able to build and maintain. Even if a manager happens to accumulate sufficient knowledge to match that of a number of subordinates that alone would not be enough. As the free market economist Friedrich Hayek noted (1948: 80):

> Today it is almost heresy to suggest that scientific knowledge is not the sum of all knowledge. But a little reflection will show that there is beyond question a body of very important but unorganized knowledge which cannot possibly be called scientific in the sense of general rules: the knowledge of particular circumstances of time and place. It is with respect to this that practically every individual has some advantage over all others because he possesses unique information of which beneficial use might be made, but of which use can be made only if the decisions depending on it are left to him or are made with his active cooperation.

To overcome the limited knowledge problem, control and performance management are frequently divided up into divisions and departments. Sears stores in the US in the 1930s and 1940s were divided into regional divisions. This may have allowed for more direct control within the divisions but, conversely, it risked another paradox – the loss of central overall control to a series of 'baronies' (Katz 1978: 17):

> In the spirit of decentralization, each vice-president in charge of one of the five sovereign territories developed his own administrative procedures. Each had authority to design and drop his own new stores. They could take out bank loans at will. They protected the right of local store managers to price the goods and select the things they wanted to carry from the warehouses. They could structure a staff around themselves in whatever way they liked … the territory kings preferred to dole out raises and bonuses even to the most junior executives. The territories had gained so much control over company communications that corporate directives from Chicago were rewritten when they weren't thrown away.

Technical controls

One way to exercise control is to embed it in the technology of work. The best example of this is the assembly line. The technology of the assembly line allows the pace of work to be controlled by the speed of the moving line and the fragmentation of the assembly into numerous separate elements installs a further controlling feature. In effect, what has to be done, when, by whom, in what sequence, at what pace and, to a slightly lesser extent, how, are all predetermined and built in to the technology of production. Similar techniques have been transposed into the modern service economy. For example, many security guards have their patrol routes and timings controlled through the use of hand held scanning devices which they have to use to scan bar codes at predetermined points on their designated routes. This technology is designed to encourage compliance with the planned procedure. Similarly, call centre staff have their activities monitored technologically through computer logging of their work and through recordings of their calls. Indeed, call centre research points to the multiplicity of control approaches in these settings – technological monitoring plus team-based pressure (that is both vertical and horizontal modes of control). A paradox in call centres is the heavy emphasis on teams in the context of what is a very individualistic work system (Kinnie *et al.* 2000; Korczynski 2001).

Even under such circumstances, studies have shown that workers find ways of resisting the controls. In call centres, forms of resistance have been tracked by Knights and McCabe (1998). In manufacturing, methods include, for example, 'working up the line' (that is altering the predetermined pace by working faster for a while and completing a number of units so as to take a break), missing some units if the line is considered to be moving too fast, compromising on quality, absenteeism and even sabotage of the line itself. It has also been noted that assembly lines and other technologically based ways of supervising and controlling were instrumental in provoking collective conflict and that these conditions helped to promote unionization. Even without such overt forms of resistance, the limits of assembly line control have revealed themselves in high labour turnover and difficulties in the recruitment of quality labour. In response, various alternatives have been tried including, for example, the rearrangement of machine technologies and groups into manufacturing 'cells'. These allow more flexible working and greater group autonomy concerning task sequencing, pace, method, task allocation and so on. In call centres, routinized tasks and tight controls usually result in high levels of labour turnover and absenteeism. Managerial attempts to counter this include loosely organized 'teams' with, for example, Red Team competing against Blue Team for monthly prizes. Such supplementary activities seem to acknowledge the limits of technological controls.

Administrative controls

Administrative controls are another form of impersonal control. Here control is achieved through formal rules, budgets, job categories, promotion procedures, discipline procedures and definitions of job responsibilities. Administrative or bureaucratic controls routinized the management control function. Company 'policies' replaced supervisory whim. Most of our organizations today retain some elements of bureaucratic controls though perhaps in a scaled-down form compared with the highpoint of its use. For example, the Polaroid camera company in the mid-1970s had approximately 300 job titles for its manual employees alone. And for each job, seven pay steps were possible. Thus, for hourly paid workers (let alone the salaried) there were

2100 different slots (300 times 7) for its 6397 hourly workers. In addition, there were seniority bonuses, job families, pay grades and so on (Edwards 1979). Companies such as GEC and Ford typically had fifteen to twenty levels between shop floor and Chief Executive and each level had its multiple grades. Formal rules, allied with finely-graded hierarchy, enabled a type of control based on the impersonal characteristics of bureaucracy. The multiple job grades also allowed plenty of scope for control based on hopes of promotion through a complex series of steps.

It has become fashionable in more recent times to roll back many of these types of administrative controls – thus hierarchies have been reduced through 'delayering' and job categories have been collapsed. Evidently, new forms of control are being tried – as noted in Chapter 4 on Organizational Forms. A subcategory of administrative controls is the use of *budgetary controls*. There are two classic studies of the use of budgets as a mode of worker control. One is *The Game of Budget Control* (Hofstede 1968) and the other is *The Impact of Budgets on People* (Argyris 1952). Central to the analysis in the first is the conflict between organizational control and individual autonomy. By budgetary control, Hofstede meant budgets as financial plans – i.e. planning translated into monetary terms along with operations budgets included 'standards' – i.e. quantities, hours, percentages and quality levels. He argues that 'early budgeting theory started from a mechanistic, materialistic view of human behaviour' (1968: 40). However, by the 1930s the Human Relations movement had identified the 'unanticipated consequences' and these ideas and the prescription for 'participation in budget setting' became increasingly common.

Likewise, Argyris pointed to the tension that can be created by the use of budgets. Although on the surface they appear to offer a neutral means of control, in practice they are usually perceived by all concerned as open to manipulation and hence their use requires subtle managerial skills. Moreover, Argyris warns that participation in budget setting is no panacea. He cites cases of 'pseudo-participation'. A good example of this is the case of one controller who spoke about how participative budget setting was undertaken in practice (1958: 28):

> We bring them (the supervisors) together and tell them that we want their frank opinion, but most of them just sit there and nod their heads. We know they are not coming out with how they feel ... Then we request the line supervisor to sign the new budget. Then he can't tell us he did not accept it.

Argyris suggests that while this type of ploy has no real long-term beneficial outcome the dynamic does illustrate the inherent dilemmas and paradoxes in these forms of performance management attempts.

Quality and Just-in-Time manufacturing

Traditional forms of control owe a great deal to the legacy of Frederick Taylor. They were based on mistrust and the division of labour. The quality movement in the West which has flourished from the 1980s in response (initially) to Japanese superiority in manufactured consumer goods seemed to challenge many of the long-held and deeply-held tenets of performance management. Instead of individualizing work there was a celebration of quality circles and other forms of team working. In place of more and more quality inspection there was a move to eradicate inspectors completely in place of worker self-inspection. Instead of seeking to ensure uninterrupted work flows through building numerous buffer stocks along the way, the radical alternative of removing these stocks completely and relying instead on perfecting smooth flow through Just-in-Time manufacturing was extolled. The contrast between traditional performance management and Just-in-Time methods is summarized in Table 5.1.

As this table reveals, the central profound idea is that in place of the assumed 'trade-off' between quality and quantity this duality is resolved through a form of paradoxical thinking. In this new mode of thought an uncompromising focus on quality and Just-in-Time 'pulls' along other desired attributes. Thus, the apparently irrational idea that the removal of buffer stocks would expose the production system to a massively increased risk of interruptions was countered by the transformative notion that the removal of such a 'crutch' would concentrate minds. Hence, production planners and schedulers had to do a better job. Suppliers were carefully selected, vetted, trained and then held to strict account. Any interruptions that did occur were used as significant learning opportunities to uncover their root causes and to correct for these so they did not occur again. The buffer stock system would have masked such problems.

In these and other ways, the quality movement and Just-in-Time and business process engineering used the power of paradoxical thinking to reframe the problem and thus to challenge long-held assumptions about dualities.

Table 5.1 Traditional versus JIT quality approaches.

Key ideas	Traditional	Just-in-Time
Ways to achieve quality	Inspect for quality	Build quality in
Objectives	Cost and quality need to be balanced; trade-offs expected	Quality is dominant goal
Material and incoming parts inspection	Statistical acceptance inspection	None, once vendor is established
Acceptance levels of defects	Parts per hundred	None
In-process inspection	Separate checks by inspectors	Employees inspect own work
Final test	Statistical sampling	All units inspected

Source: Based on Eisenhardt and Westcott (1988: 178).

Incentive payments as a form of performance management

Incentive payments are designed to harness individual interests and efforts in pursuit of organizational goals. They seem the logical answer to the problem of reconciling the individual's temptation to withhold effort and the organization's desire for productive effort. Yet relatively few organizations actually firmly link effort and pay (Lawler 1987: 70):

> Employees engage in numerous behaviors in order to have rates set in such a way that they can maximize their financial gains relative to the amount of work that they have to do. They engage in such behaviors as working at slow rates in order to mislead the time study expert when he or she comes to study their job. They hide new work methods or new procedures from the time study person so that the job will not be restudied. In addition, informal norms develop within the organization about how productive people should be with the result that workers themselves set the limits on production.

Managers face short-term incentives to choose inefficient incentive regimes for subordinates. Employees have little reason to trust employers with information that would allow alternative decisions.

Self controls and social controls

It is suggested by some observers that there is a shift in the nature of man-agement control. Changes to the global economy have made the controls that were characteristic of the industrial age somewhat inappropriate. In the post-industrial – or as some term it, the 'post-modern' economy – a premium is placed not on mere obedience and conformity but on commitment, responsiveness and flexibility. The precise meaning of 'post modernism' in organizational theory is rather contentious. In essence, it signals a shift from one set of interlocking ways of organizing and controlling to another. For example, a rigid, conformist and mechanistic organizational mode developed under the umbrella of the 'Fordist' model. However, with new forms of competition and new market characteristics there seemed to be a need to move towards more flexible modes of production and even towards the design of an enterprise culture overall and 'enterprise cultures' in work organizations. Some commentators, when referring to this shift, use the terminology of 'Fordism versus Post-Fordism' – the latter denoting more flexible structures, multi-skilling, individualization, and so on. For our pur-poses, we can regard these two terms as broadly equivalent to the distinction between classical forms of managing/organizing/controlling and the post-modern forms.

A stylized contrast between the industrial/modern and the post-modern, in so far as their characteristic modes of control are concerned, is shown in Table 5.2. This table only attempts to show an *indicative* contrast. The research and the literature (for example, Piore and Sabel 1984; Harvey 1989; Clegg 1990) go much further in elaborating the differences. Crucially, asso-ciated with this point is that the shift in organizational controls is only a small part of a more wholesale transformation extending across the design of organizational forms, the nature of market conditions and economic competition, technology, politics and culture.

For our purposes here, a notable feature of 'post-modern' controls is the concerted attempt to communicate organizational values and norms. Pro-grammes such as Total Quality Management (TQM), organizational culture change and Business Excellence are viewed by some observers as geared towards social and psychological control. Top management values and objectives may be embedded in training and development programmes with

Table 5.2 The shift to 'post-modern' controls.

Classical/modern organizational controls	Post-modern organizational controls
Mass production of standardized products, assembly lines	Flexible production systems; multi-batch production for niche markets
Hierarchical organization structures, bureaucratic, vertically-integrated	Flat, flexible structures, decentralized
Administrative controls (rules, timetables)	Normative controls (through cultures, values, manipulation of meanings and attitudes)
Institutional controls (collective bargaining)	Identity control (e.g. through programmes such as service excellence; TQM)
Insecurity experienced as collective sense of social and economic injustice	Insecurity based on individual self-doubt; weakness or absence of alternative allegiances

the aim of achieving the *internalization* of these by all employees. Such post-modern controls may not be confined to formal culture change programmes. Similar ends may be sought through careful and sophisticated methods of recruitment and selection, by means of elaborated induction programmes and through the use of appraisal, promotion and rewards.

Depending on your point of view, it may be possible to draw a distinction between these forms of control and 'self-control'. Self control is arguably exercised willingly and knowingly by mature adults making informed choices whereas control through corporate values and social control through peer-pressure and work groups is externally driven.

Whilst the economy in the early 1960s may have been more mixed in terms of competitive and environmental conditions, it might plausibly be argued that the turbulent and unstable conditions described by Burns and Stalker (1968) as characterizing just some *parts* of the economy, have now spread much more widely as to impact on most, if not all, constituent organizations to some degree. By implication, one might expect that, currently,

Table 5.3 Mechanistic versus organic control systems.

Mechanistic control system	Organic control system
Fragmentation of tasks	Contribution of specialist knowledge to common task
Supervisory and vertical control to ensure relevance of tasks	Continual adjustment of tasks through interaction with others
Precise task definition	Flexible and wide role responsibilities
Obligation attaching to functional position	Commitment to the concern as a whole
Vertical structure of control, authority and communication	Horizontal and network communication
Instructions and decisions issued by supervisors	Information and advice rather than instructions and decisions

Source: abbreviated and adapted from Burns and Stalker (1968):119–22.

most organizations are likely to benefit from, or even require, a shift towards the right-hand column of Table 5.3.

It has been suggested that self controlling systems might, especially, be expected to operate in voluntary sector organizations where members may be intrinsically motivated to achieve high performance standards (Johnson and Gill 1993). In so far as this may prove to be the case (and it is clearly not so for every person who happens to be employed in the voluntary sector), it is indicative of the importance of the nature of the psychological contract in governing the way in which controls of various types are perceived and received.

Control and resistance

There is a crucial distinction to be drawn between an abstract model of control (let us say a control plan on paper) and the implementation of such a plan in organizational settings. Having a control plan is by no means the same as exercising effective control. Control involves the regulation of human performance and behaviour.

The vicious circle of control

In the attempt to control an organization managerially, a number of different things can go wrong. A number of factors can intervene with the result that a system of formal controls, feedback loops and sanctions that looks technically proficient on paper, may turn out to be ineffectual – and even counterproductive. For example, managers may get drawn into a vicious circle whereby tighter and tighter controls result in greater degrees of resistance and an eventual loss of control. The paradox here is that more controls can result in less actual control. This cycle is depicted in Figure 5.3.

In this vicious circle, the manager's (or it could be a management team) analysis is that the situation requires the imposition of more and more controls as expectations are not met. Employees perceive the introduction of controls as a clear declaration of mistrust and blame. In such circumstances, morale is likely to suffer and discretionary effort and goodwill may be withheld. As a result, productivity and quality standards may decline further. In direct response to this deteriorating situation, the manager may decide that even tighter controls are required – in part to counter the recalcitrance that has been engendered. These tighter controls are, in turn, perceived by the workforce as unfair and oppressive and, as a result, higher degrees of resistance may be provoked. The vicious circle thus takes a further turn.

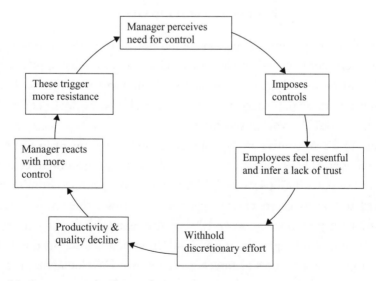

Figure 5.3 A vicious circle of control.

Even in situations where the vicious circle of control is avoided, the imposition of management controls may still affect behaviour in an adverse and unplanned way. It has been noted frequently that simply engaging in measurement is likely to affect behaviour. Even more likely is that behavioural consequences will result from the installation of new control systems. Some of these consequences may be unanticipated and highly adverse.

For example, during the latter half of the 1990s, the BBC was subjected to major reforms and new systems were introduced in order to gain better control over budgets. Recent research reports have suggested that the overall outcome of these measures was highly damaging to the productive and creative core of the organization. Programme makers and producers reported demoralization and the loss of a sense of mission and excitement. Programme quality is said to have suffered greatly. Some of these reports may possibly be exaggerated and there will undoubtedly be some who will not agree that these have been the consequences. Nonetheless, the case serves to make a more general point – namely, that even where direct resistance is not provoked, and where the vicious circle of control is avoided, the price of winning control over a process (say budgets or delivery times) may, under some circumstances, trigger an undermining of an organization that can strike at its creative core. The action taken to cure may risk killing the patient.

Positive responses to controls

However, the preceding subsection should not be interpreted to mean that management controls will invariably produce adverse effects, or even that people will necessarily react adversely to them. On the contrary, there are research reports which suggest a positive correlation between certain controls and recorded levels of satisfaction.

Thus, in a comparative study of managers and management in Britain and Japan (Storey et al. 1997), extensive control systems were found to be in place in all of the organizations studied. More than three-quarters of the managers sampled had been given clearly specified objectives; there was systematic evaluation of performance; only 10% of the managers felt that they were evaluated either infrequently or not at all. Interview transcripts pointed to a sense of growing pressures as targets were refined. Developments in control systems were subtle and multiple. The nature of control was undergoing change. However, when analysing the statistics which correlated satisfaction levels with the existence of types and amounts of control, the researchers found that close monitoring was, overall, accompanied by *increased* satisfaction in both Britain and Japan. This is yet another finding on management control which might be considered a paradox.

Reconciling control and autonomy

Performance management dilemmas centre on dual theories of how to influence bahaviour. Organizational economics suggests a focus on incentives based on economic rationality – essentially on price. This implies the use of economic incentives, setting targets, monitoring employees and enforcing contracts. Conversely, a perspective rooted in organizational behaviour emphasizes the importance of leadership and inspiration and the power of non financially-based motivational factors. For example, Chester Barnard urges managers to inspire subordinate 'sacrifice' by the 'breadth of the morality' they bring to bear (Barnard 1937).

Competitive market forces will enforce the appropriate disciplines and managers do not need to lead or inspire. However, the Organizational Behaviour literature, on the contrary, sees the manager's primary job as to lead, to innovate and take risks and go beyond a narrow definition of effort implied by market contract. A third stance brings into play political factors: 'While competitive market forces may tend to reward the more efficient leaders, other leaders may be able to insulate themselves from the disciplining force of the market by political stratagems that result in governmentally enforced entry barriers or restrictions on capital markets' (Miller 1992: 2). Thus, the manager may be pulled between economic, organizational leadership and/or political action.

Performance management systems

When the various elements of performance management such as goal setting, monitoring, feedback and so on are brought together in a coherent way they can be considered to form a performance management 'system'. As a process, performance management is not a single event or a series of discrete events, but rather an integrated series of interactions. As a system, the components relate to each other in a continuous cycle that is affected by external factors (e.g. demands and opportunities) and internal factors (e.g. self-expectations and monitoring). At the individual level, there are the employee's or manager's goals and performance in relation to the strategies of the organization and department. At the group level, there are the department's or work team's goals and performance affected by organizational expectations and the demands from other work groups. Departmental goals affect individual employees' goals and performance, which in turn affect those of the department, other departments and the entire organization.

The performance management cycle, depicted in Figure 5.4, reveals an interlocking suite of processes and procedures designed to enhance individual and group performance in order to shape it to meet organizational objectives. It is continuous, it occurs over time and it is repetitive and cyclical. Goals are revised as expectations change, competition shifts, feedback is received and interpreted and training is experienced. The design process includes ensuring that the methods are reliable (meaning, for example, that behaviours are perceived similarly by multiple raters who have similar roles) and valid (meaning, for example, that performance ratings accurately reflect important performance outcomes).

The first stage is ideally the clarification and then communication of organizational objectives and the strategy to achieve those objectives.

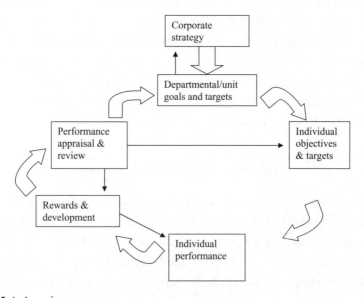

Figure 5.4 A performance management system.

Departments and units should ideally draw on these overall organizational objectives to design their own goals which will help support the overall organizational objectives. Likewise, individual objectives should reflect and align with their departmental objectives. The next step in the performance management cycle is that individual performance should be reviewed systematically in the light of these pre-agreed objectives and measures. Rewards and development and possibly revision of individual objectives may follow the review.

The model suggests a rational approach to management. As we noted above, this mechanistic assumption derives from cybernetic models outside the management sphere. In reality organizational behaviour and indeed learning is much more complex and derives from competing rationalities and motivations. Different parts of organizations often have rivalries and these are not acknowledged in the formal performance management model.

The wider context

Performance management techniques within particular organizations tend to reflect their situated contexts in terms of time and prevailing assumptions and norms about work systems. For example, a significant shift occurred in the early twentieth century when the Ford motor company sought to break away from the prevailing casual labour market system (Miller 1992: 11):

> One of the purposes of Ford's decision to impose a $ 5 day was to make sure that the labor market in his industry would be transformed from one that was competitive, fluid and voluntaristic to one in which a decision to work for Ford Motor Company meant a long-term commitment to a system of *political economy*.

In the NHS we find an illustration of the same dilemmas – market, hierarchy and collaboration all combined in a complex web which managers seek to negotiate and resolve. When internal controls in an NHS are deemed to have 'failed' the external hierarchy may parachute in an 'agent' to sort out the situation. Thus, turnaround directors and teams are increasingly imposed on NHS trusts whose performance management has been judged to have been defective. These externals sometimes bring novel frameworks to bear. One very senior Turnaround Director who was imposed on a very powerful hospital trust which was in deficit observed to us:

From where I'm sitting, this hospital trust is a big, professional services business; it's not a hospital. It's a big professional services business within the health service, and I deal with big professional services businesses and I know how to deal with them, and I've got a lot of experience of doing so.

I was imposed on the Trust. The first thing you have to realize is that the Trust did not think they needed anybody. They had had a big involvement with KPMG, initially on an assessment of the problem, and then working on massive projects setting up a stabilization team, financial recovery plans and all that. But it became clear that more was needed.

Using new performance management methods he managed to reduce the deficit by many millions of pounds in a 12-month period.

Hence, the NHS is currently seeking to performance manage with an interesting combination of quasi-market forces (Foundation Trusts Hospitals have to compete for business through offering appropriate services), through networks (constituent parts of the NHS are often dependent on other parts) and through formal control (through centrally imposed targets and, on occasion, as in the turnaround case cited above, through direct intervention).

The justification of the free market was articulated by Adam Smith in 1776 (Smith 1976: 194):

As every individual therefore endeavours as much as he can both to employ his capital in support of domestic industry, and so to direct that industry so that its produce may be of the greatest value; every individual necessarily labours to render the annual revenue of society as great as he can. He generally indeed neither intends to promote the public interest, nor knows how much he is promoting it … he intends only his own gain, and he is in this as in many other cases, led by invisible hand to promote an end which was not part of his intention … by pursuing his own interest he frequently promotes that of society more effectually than when he really intends to promote it.

However, on the other hand, this rationale assumes the efficient operation of the market and in practice there may be the problem of market failure. Failure stems from three sources: information asymmetry, monopoly power and externalities. For example, as Miller points out, the McDonalds franchise system may tempt some managers to 'freeload' by reducing expenditure on cleaning, etc. and thus they seek to trade on the general reputation of the universal brand sustained by the efforts of others.

The purpose of hierarchy even in a firm with incentive payments is to 'apportion rewards observing the input behavior of inputs as means of detecting or estimating their marginal productivity and giving assignments or instructions in what to do and how to do it' (Alchian and Demsetz 1972: 782). The supervisors earn their keep by the costs saved and the extra revenue gained through the increased effort he or she encourages.

Conclusions

Many of the dualities and dilemmas about performance management covered in this chapter have their roots in underlying and deep-seated assumptions about how business organizations and other types of organizations work. Traditional thinking from Adam Smith onwards focuses on the engineering of incentive and disincentive systems that will induce efficiency and profitability by appealing to worker self-interest. This meant rewarding – or as appropriate disciplining – workers based on an essentially economics-based notion of behaviour. However, an alternative set of assumptions based in psychology, sociology and political science stresses instead the importance of managerial leadership and cooperation among employees.

Gary Miller (1992) suggests that these alternative frames reflect a schism that has developed in organization theory between the traditional organization-economics based mode and an organizational behaviour approach harbouring alternative assumptions. Miller seeks to bridge the gap between these literatures. In this chapter, we have sought to build on his work with a different purpose in mind: and that is to reveal how the various alternative ways designed to 'performance manage' each contain their paradoxical qualities and further to show how, by using these paradoxes rather than seeking to avoid them, better outcomes can be achieved.

6

Dilemmas and paradoxes of innovation

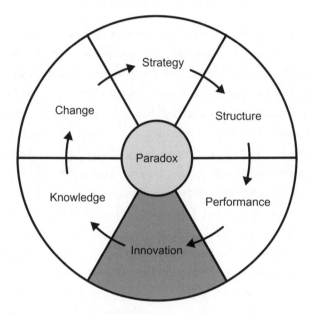

Figure 6.1 The six paradoxes – innovation.

This chapter attends to the fourth of the Six Paradoxes.

Simply put, when the best firms succeeded, they did so because they listened responsively to their customers and invested aggressively in the technology, products, and manufacturing capabilities that satisfied their customers' next-generation needs. But, paradoxically, when the best firms subsequently failed, it was for the same reasons – they listened responsively to their customers and invested aggressively in the technology, products, and manufacturing capabilities that satisfied their customers' next-generation needs. This is one of the innovator's dilemmas: Blindly following the maxim that good managers should keep close to their customers can sometimes be a fatal mistake.

(Christensen 1997)

In my business, its imperative that I have the talent in place for when I need it, so, that may mean I have to recruit ahead of the curve – and frankly that's a pretty tough thing to do in a business which is managed via ratios which are scrutinized quarterly by analysts and which then affects the stock price.

(David Day, Chief Executive Europe, Lightspeed, a WPP Business)

Introduction

One of the classic books on the management of innovation in fact focuses on one of its inherent dilemmas. Christensen's (1997) *The Innovator's Dilemma* describes in fine detail the fundamental dilemma facing market-leading firms. It is not simply that a leader may become complacent or that core capabilities may become core rigidities; the phenomenon that intrigued Christensen was even more perplexing. He found that when leading firms with established products did follow the marketers' advice to focus on customers they were often badly misled by loyal customers. Consistently, when asked about their preferences for future developments, established customers would report that they wanted cheaper and upgraded versions of existing products or existing products with minor improvements. Meanwhile, new entrants would be undercutting the lead product with novel products that established customers would initially deny they sought.

The essential innovator's dilemma then, concerns when to abandon a successful market-leading product. Accordingly, the list of major firms which collapsed in the face of disruptive technologies turns out to be a very long one indeed. They include Digital, Apple, Sears and IBM. The common element in the decisions that led to eventual failure of these firms is that they were taken when the firms in question were at the top of their game and were considered the leading companies in the world. The paradox is that these firms were not badly run. They were in fact in conventional terms very well managed. They did listen to their customers. Indeed, it was 'precisely *because* these firms listened to their customers, invested aggressively in new technologies that would provide their customers with more and better products of the sort they wanted, and because they studied market trends and systematically allocated investment capital to innovations that promised best returns, they lost their position of leadership' (Christensen 1997: xii).

However, this is not the only innovator's dilemma. Another is the problem of cannibalizing the market for a dominant product or service by offering substitutes and alternatives. And yet another is the tendency for successful large business units to want to defend their lead position and thus crowd out new interloping ideas. But, as Prahalad and Krishnan (2008) point out, the dynamic of innovation increasingly entails an intermingling of episodic breakthroughs with the continuous change that is impelled by new levels of connectivity (markets, technology, convergence of industry boundaries and consumer engagement – such as the cocreation of value illustrated by iGoogle) (Prahalad and Krishnan 2008).

These are the kinds of issues explored in this chapter.

Innovation issues

In accord with our focus on dilemmas and managers' use of theory, we begin the chapter with a review of those studies of innovation concerned with the management – or encouragement – of innovation within organizations. This embraces aspects of business strategy and new product development, entrepreneurship, the use of alliances and networks. It also covers the role of cognitive aspects of organizations – mindsets and recipes – which encourage or discourage innovation.

The difference between achieving improvements to an existing product or process and achieving a radical departure from historic products and practices is one of the most fundamental distinctions in the innovation literature (Moch and Morse 1977; Freeman and Soete 1997). However, this distinction needs further refinement. Henderson and Clark (1990), for example, argue that apparently modest alterations to existing products may produce dramatic competitive benefits. These arise, they argue, because the apparently incremental innovation reconfigures an established system or arrangement to link together existing elements in new ways. They call this 'architectural innovation'. Incremental innovation may involve relatively minor changes to the existing design though it may cumulatively have very major economic consequences. Radical innovation, on the other hand, is based on new principles and so can open up completely new markets. Which type of innovation to strive for is itself thus a dilemma.

Radical innovation can create special difficulties for established firms by challenging the extant advantages bestowed by their existing products and technologies. Conversely, it may allow major opportunities for new entrants. Radical innovation can also, by the same token, be difficult for established firms to achieve. While incremental innovation reinforces the nature and dominance of existing organizational arrangements and competences, radical innovation potentially challenges these – 'it forces them (organizations) to ask a new set of questions, to draw on new technical and commercial skills, and to employ new problem solving approaches' (Henderson and Clark 1990).

A number of analysts explain this in terms of the conflict between operational competence (including incremental innovation and improvement) and the capacity for radical innovation which not only involves ways of thinking and seeing and imagining which are outside of the established channels of thinking, but also competences and processes which are radical departures from existing organizational arrangements. This paradox has been noted by many writers, and we found that it exercised many managers. As Tushman and O'Reilly (1996: 10) note in relation to the reasons for long term failure in the semi-conductor industry, a major cause was cultural:

> Companies failed *because of their inability to play two games at once*: to be effective defenders of what quickly became old technologies and effective attackers with new technologies. Senior managers in these firms fell victims to their past success. (emphasis added)

One way of conceptualizing the relationship between competing in the present and in the future is by an understanding of the notion of 'path dependency'. Developments are usually not random. Innovation avenues are forged and, at the firm level, history may heavily shape the contours of the future that is, 'a firm's previous investments and its repertoire of routines constrain its future behaviour' (Teece *et al.* 2002: 192).

Business strategy and the management of innovation

Many researchers and commentators have examined the ways in which innovation is intertwined with business strategy, or have advocated the importance of innovation as a business strategy. Central to this strategic sense of innovation is the development of innovative products, as the previous discussions have emphasized. For some companies new product development is the single most important factor driving success or failure. Effective new product development usually requires the combined efforts of multiple specialized capabilities. However, integrating these specialities can be difficult.

Barriers and enablers

What factors facilitate innovation and what factors act as barriers? These are two interconnected and vital questions. One common explored variable is organizational size, another is the maturity of the organization. In addition, entrepreneurship and innovation are often closely linked and both have been associated with size. Mintzberg and Waters (1982) have identified one link between size and entrepreneurship and innovation. In the entrepreneurial phase of development organizational strategies are carried out by a 'single informed brain'. This, they argue is why the entrepreneurial mode is at the 'centre of the most glorious corporate successes'.

The point about the barriers to innovation within large and established firms has been argued in numerous studies (for example, Tushman and Anderson 1986; Henderson and Clark 1990; Leonard-Barton 1992). A central thesis of such writers is exemplified by Markides's proposition that 'Compared to new entrants or niche players, established companies find it hard to innovate because of structural and cultural inertia, internal politics, complacency, fear of cannibalising existing products, far of destroying existing competences, satisfaction with the status quo, and a general lack of incentive to abandon a certain present (which is profitable) for an uncertain future' (2002: 246).

In consequence, it is often urged that large firms need to emulate many of the characteristics of small entrepreneurial firms (Kanter 1983), to combine the characteristics of large and small, mature and new, organic and mechanistic firms – Tushman and O'Reilly's 'ambidexterity' as noted earlier. However, achieving this combination is difficult. Prescriptions in the literature vary and are often rather obscure and lacking in practical details.

Schumpeter (1934; 1942) pointed out that in some respects large size could have benefits for innovation, suggesting that, in the modern age, significant innovations would be the preserve of the large corporations with their centralized R&D labs and greater financial resources. Others argue that large and small firms interact in a symbiotic way. Modern examples of symbiosis can be found in pharmaceuticals and biotechnology, and in telecommunications and semiconductors. Significantly Lefebvre, Mason et al. (1997)

report results from a study which reveals that it is the *perceptions of the chief executives*, rather than any objective variables, which best explain technology policy and innovation strategy.

Pavitt (1991) identified what he termed the 'key characteristics of innovative firms'. These he suggests are:

- That accumulated competence is crucial.
- Because of specialization some organizational mechanisms must be in place to orchestrate working across disciplines.
- The improvement of competences requires continuous learning.
- Systems for allocating resources have to take into account benefits gained from *learning from doing* and not be purely focused on conventional outcomes.

Looked at another way, these 'characteristics' are the central tasks and challenges for the strategic management of innovation.

The literature also points to another factor, namely, the firm's relationship with others – that is, the issue of networks. A major reason for the appeal of networks or relationships with other organizations is that this allows large, mature, organizations which may suffer from the list of obstructive characteristics offered by Markides and others the opportunity to overcome these intrinsic constraints by combining with smaller, newer, niche entrepreneurial firms and to use these smaller younger more entrepreneurial firms to carry the burden of innovation.

Alliances and inter-organizational networks seem to offer a way to handle the paradox of 'neither market nor hierarchy'. While networks are used for a variety of purposes, their role in fostering innovation has been especially noted. Networks reduce the risk inevitably associated with innovation by distributing it, and overcome inevitable competence and other limitations of any one organization by the addition of other complimentary competences.

The underlying theme is the need for cooperation rather than, or *as additional to*, competition in today's market conditions. Collaborative networks are sometimes regarded as a new hybrid organizational form – neither the traditional individual firm, on the one hand, nor the formal alliance, on the other. Collaborative networks offer a source of requisite variety and flexible access to shared resources and diverse capabilities. The role of *inter-*

organizational networks in shaping the diffusion process rather than simply the usual supplier–user relationship or network can also be important. This is also a central pillar of Prahalad and Krishnan's (2008) book: there is a global 'trend', they suggest, propelled by two interrelated forces: first that value is based increasingly on the individual consumer's experience and second that because no firm on its own can satisfy this demand, firms must access resources from a variety of sources – a variety of large and small enterprises from a global pool. Hence, they contend, the challenge is to be able to access resources not to own resources (2008: 11).

However, resolving the practical issues involved in working through inter-firm strategic alliances will require specific, and possible scarce or unavailable management capabilities and competences.

Exploration versus exploitation

As we have noted, many who have commented on the organizational determinants of innovation have identified a major paradox, that the organizational qualities necessary for successful and effective operations are dysfunctional for innovation. In other words, exploitation is at odds with exploration. There are many aspects to this paradox.

Despite the importance of product innovation, 'research shows that established firms have difficulty developing and marketing commercially viable new products'(Dougherty 1992: 77). This prompts the further observation, 'solutions to this puzzle require consideration of the question: "Can large, old firms in fact change their fundamental principles of management or must they 'die' to make way for new forms?"' (Dougherty 1992: 90). Institutions construct taken for granted routines and, as a result, they become rooted in conformity. In consequence, other, potentially disruptive actions are regarded as illegitimate. Barriers to innovation in established organizations are in this sense normal because product innovation often involves illegitimate activity. Under such circumstances, innovators have to 'creatively reframe' their activities in order to legitimate their work.

There are elements integral to mature successful firms which can *obstruct* innovation. Leonard-Barton (1992), for example, noted that being competent at activities required for current operations may block the ability to develop new competences: 'core capabilities' can also become 'core rigidities'. This presents managers with a dilemma: how to take advantage of core capabilities without being hampered by the associated flip side, namely the paradox that core capabilities simultaneously enhance and inhibit new product development. This is similar to what Argyris (1985) has termed 'trained incapacity'.

From one perspective it could be suggested that innovation is the antithesis of both organization and management. Innovation tends to be idiosyncratic, unpredictable, high risk and not easily amenable to planning. Despite this, one central line of enquiry has been the search for the ways in which organizations can *build the capability* to innovate.

The role of established cognitive structures and recipes

Recently, an intriguing literature has developed concerned with the analysis of processes of strategy formulation by senior teams, which addresses the various ways in which organizational, historical and group factors can influence the way strategy makers think, what they think about, how they define and solve key strategic issues and which issues they see as strategic. This literature is very relevant to the understanding of the capability of organizations to innovate. Innovation is an intellectual, cognitive process. If aspects of organization encourage or discourage innovation they do this by influencing how managers and leaders think and what they think about. The study of ways in which aspects of organizational structure, systems, history and culture can influence innovative thinking is therefore crucial.

The importance of managers' perceptions and (literally) 'sense-making' with regard to innovation has been noted by a number of researchers. Valentin *et al.*, for example, argues the significance of history and complacency born from past certainties and successes. They note, on the basis of a case study of strategic failure, that: '... past successes and ideological rigidities can foster dysfunctional inertia and mindsets. The study centred on a strategy rooted largely in speculative and predominantly false analogies and conjectures that became so vivid and available during the planning phase that their verity was eventually taken for granted without the benefit of serious objective enquiry' (Valentin 2002: 58).

There is a close association between the issue of managerial perspectives on, and understandings of, innovation and that segment of the strategy literature which deals with the problem of 'strategic persistence' in mature firms (Lant and Milliken 1992). Persistence with a known strategy has been recognized as a function of managerial interpretations (Milliken and Lant 1991).

Managers' subjectivity also helps explain their resistance to potential innovations. The 'perceptual lens' of the top management team, how senior managers define their business environment, which environment they see as relevant to their organization's success and which aspects of it they regard as relevant, are important factors in influencing their reactions. And these perceptions are socially and historically structured.

This possibility, that historic (and successful practices) limit future possibilities through the embedding and institutionalization of established and historic search activities, data gathering processes and analysis, is further strengthened when senior managers have a personal commitment to, or investment in, the status quo. This is a tendency we found among managers we have studied. As Lant *et al.* (2002: 157) suggest, 'managers who are the architects of past strategies may be reluctant to acknowledge the validity of information that signals the failure of their strategies'.

In the classic article about organizational learning and communities of practice, Brown and Duguid (1992) reveal the interrelationships between the three vital processes of work, learning and innovation. As they point out, these three are often thought of as in conflict with each other but, in an attempt to bring about a 'conceptual shift', these authors reveal the interplay and interdependence between them. By focusing on *practice* they show how learning is the bridge between working and innovating. Moreover, they reveal how 'evolving communities-of-practice are significant sites of innovating'.

Most organizations depend, in practice, upon significant amounts of informal activity. But, ironically, the incipient intent to routinize (and thus de-skill) work may drive what Brown and Duguid term 'non-canonical practice' (i.e. as distinct from the canonical practice which is found in official manuals and organizational procedures) further underground. In consequence, this kind of knowledge and practice becomes even less visible to the organization as a whole. As a result, subsequent reorganizations and/or official changes to practice are likely to 'disrupt what they do not notice'. Thus, the gap between espoused and actual practice may then become simply too large for the informal organization to bridge. Dysfunctionality is likely to result from this vicious circle of control and reaction. To avoid that fate and to engender healthy interplay between working, learning and innovating, organizations need to reconceive themselves as a 'community of communities'.

But, problem solving and innovation usually require new combinations of information and knowledge – and these can be costly to transfer to a new location and costly to use in a new location. This characteristic of 'stickiness' affects the location (or locus) of problem solving (von Hippel 1994; von Hippel, Churchill et al. 1998). This realization is reflected also in the work on 'absorptive capacity' by Cohen and Levinthal (1990).

Having sketched the wider field of inquiry relating to innovation, in the second part of this chapter we now describe our findings from a series of case studies that we have conducted into the management of innovation. A number of the dilemmas and paradoxes already noted from the wider literature are exposed and illustrated. But, in addition, we are now able to reveal a more fundamental duality – or dilemma concerning the choice between two very different overall models of organizational design and management.

Our findings about managers' use of theory and the choice between two divergent models

The main general finding from our various studies of innovation is that senior managers in effect, normally employ their own 'theory of innovation' to their organizations. By doing so they generate two distinct ways in which managers of organizations (individually and collectively) define, value and seek to manage innovation. One of these tends to construct a negative pattern, the other a positive pattern. Clarifying the nature of these two polarized models of how organizations approach innovation will help senior managers and indeed policy makers to understand rather more clearly why organizational innovation performance so often fails to meet expectations.

Hence, our intention is to describe and to analyse managers' theories and to show how paradoxical thinking could help. Our analysis will occur on two levels. First, we will offer descriptions of the theories managers used when understanding and explaining their organizations' approaches to innovation. This will show that managers differentiated two polarized organizational approaches. Second, we will move beyond managers' explicit theories to an analysis of underlying themes which, while apparent to us in what managers said, may not have been stated or acknowledged explicitly by the managers themselves.

The implicit level of meaning contained a 'moral' dimension. It revealed a deeper psychological attitude towards innovation. Managers did not explicitly and self consciously state them or admit to holding them. They did not openly say: 'In our organization we regard innovation as a potential threat, as something dangerous, only marginally illegitimate, and self indulgent'. Nonetheless, in effect, views of this kind were apparent in many separate comments managers made about the way innovation had to be controlled. They were apparent too in the stories they told about the dangers and problems of innovation, in the way they stressed the importance of controlling the excesses of innovation and in the organizational arrangements they made for managing innovation.

Our analysis centres on managers' theories of innovation and, as noted earlier, we see these theories as having two core elements which constitute the main focus of our discussion:

- How do managers comprehend, define and value innovation (i.e. what do they think it really means and implies, and what priority do they give it)?
- How do managers explain and understand the ways in which their organizations encourage or discourage innovation – which aspects of organization do they regard as important? What causal connections, propositions or theories do they work to?

We have also attempted to identify underlying patterns and themes which may not have been obvious to our respondents or explicit in their comments. Our analysis of interview transcripts revealed two types of insight:

- The first relates to the *explicit explanations* which managers were able to offer of the problem or successes of innovation within their organizations.
- The second derives from *our interpretations* of what was unsaid or only partially said, or hinted at, or assumed – the meanings and interpretations we derived and developed from managers' comments.

Below, we summarize respondents' views in terms of these two levels of manifestation. In operational terms the underlying factors are certainly as important as the more obvious factors – possibly more so in that they support and legitimize these explicit factors, and make them sensible in terms of the underlying logic.

Managers displayed a high degree of consensus on both the elements of a theory of innovation – the dimensions they employed in analyzing their organizations' attitudes towards and management of innovation – and on the qualities of these dimensions that would produce or obstruct innovation. These dimensions – the components of the theories – are shown in Table 6.1.

Although we have frequently referred to managers' *theories* of innovation – expecting to find considerable variation in how managers explained innovation performance – in fact we have found that, in the main, managers shared one (duality based) theory to explain what factors encouraged and discouraged innovation. They used this theory to identify two polarized organizational approaches to innovation. In their view, their organizations adopted one of two possible positions in terms of the key variables, one broadly supportive, one obstructive. The table therefore uses the theories – or the elements of the managers' theories, to describe and differentiate two polarized organizational approaches to innovation, one positive one negative.

In the negative approach, the organization (in the shape of its executive top team) adopted a limited and conventional definition of innovation, and was relatively limited in the value it placed on innovation. This was fundamentally different from how innovation was defined by more successful innovators. Managers saw this as a causal relationship: organizations tended to design their ways of encouraging or controlling innovation in terms that were consistent with their view of its value.

Not surprisingly, the two types of organization differed markedly in the ways in which they were structured, and these differences were seen by all respondents as highly significant for innovation – one approach limiting it, the other encouraging it. However, these differences were not seen as accidental: on the contrary they were recognized and welcomed. In organizations that were seen as poor innovators, senior managers justified the repressive impact of their organization's structures and systems as necessary to control the risky excesses of uncontrolled innovation. Poor innovators stressed the necessary function of existing structures and systems, stressing their historic and current role in operational successes; in good innovators

Table 6.1 Managers' *explicit theories* of innovation.

Core elements of managers' theory of innovation	'Poor' innovating organizations	'Good' innovating organizations
Definition of innovation	Conventional, limited	Radical, all-encompassing
Value placed on innovation	Guarded, qualified, marginal, limited not strategically central	Very high, seen as strategically critical
Structures	Constraining, rigid, long established and strong divisions, centralized, hierarchical, stable	Changeable, flat, fluid, decentralized
Attitude towards structures	Defensive, justifying	Questioning, critical, destructive
Innovation management system	Elaborate, structural formalized, many-layered, thorough, cautious, reduce risk, focus on control	Informal, if present all, to encourage innovation attempts, culturally transmitted
Specialist/Generalist	Innovation a specialist activity and function	Innovation expected of everyone
Role of leadership	To protect against risks of innovation, to defend status quo, to pursue historic strengths, and market applications, to ensure that innovation is controlled and contained. Present-oriented	To ensure innovation occurs ubiquitously and continuously across all aspects of the organization. Future-oriented
Culture	Deference, compliance, fatalism, cautious	Autonomy, enterprise, assertive, positive
Operational versus innovation emphasis	Operational	Innovation

senior managers actually defined their key priorities in terms of mounting critiques and attacks on existing structures. This finding suggests that critical to an organization's stance on and approach to innovation (how it defines, values and seeks to manage innovation) is its attitude towards radical

change. This suggests that it is worthwhile and necessary to explore managerial perceptions of *the need for change*, managerial perceptions of *the opportunity to change* and the perceptions about *the way to change*. Perceptions,
beliefs and assumptions are thus vital aspects to be understood. It was this
realization of the need to pay attention to issues of perception and cognition
which led us to emphasize two major themes in our research: the first concerns what has been termed the 'illegitimacy' of innovation in established
firms (Dougherty 1994); and the second the strategic issue of an organization's capability and preparedness to innovate and to change.

Poor innovators had elaborate, formalized and structured innovation
management systems. The purpose of these was to reduce the riskiness of
innovation; good innovators placed greater reliance on encouraging innovation (while making sure it remained 'visible') through a culture which
encouraged experimentation and innovation. In poor innovators' organizations, innovation was seen as a specialist activity or function and was often
seen as necessarily separated from operational activity (although often controlled by the product businesses).

Underlying these explicit elements of managers' views of how their organizations encourage or discourage innovation we discerned a number of less
obvious but crucially important themes. These are listed below in Table 6.2.
Once again, the central column shows how these issues are defined and
addressed in poor innovators; the right-hand column shows how they were
managed in good innovators.

Ostensibly, the key determinants of an organization's innovation record
are those structural, cultural and systems features which encourage or
obstruct innovation. However, underlying these mechanisms is a more
primary determinant – the way the organization views, defines and values
innovation. This constitutes one of our key propositions.

Managers' interpretations of the nature and priority of innovation

What did innovation mean to the managers, and how did they value it?
Definitions of innovation (and the value placed on these definitions) are
crucial elements in managers' analyses of their organizations' innovation
performance and potential. These analyses display strong interrelationships

Table 6.2 Managers' *implicit theories* of innovation.

Core elements of managers' implicit theory of innovation	'Poor' innovating organizations	'Good' innovating organizations
Underlying attitude towards innovation	Dangerous, potentially improper, irresponsible, childish, conservative	Positive, celebratory, encouraging, radical
Consensus/differentiated definitions	Differentiated	Consensual
Recognition of role of balance, 'ambidexterity'	Conviction that one set of values should dominate	Search for balance, recognition that any 'solution' will fail
Innovating innovation	Traditional view and approach	Open, radical approach
Debate and discussion	Discouraged, not necessary	Encouraged seen as central
Priority of organization or Innovation	Organization, stability	Innovation, change

between the way innovation was defined and the way managers said their organizations managed innovation. Managers insisted that the way their organization – i.e. senior managers – defined innovation and the significance they attached to innovation were central to the way the organization was geared up (or not) to achieve innovation.

In some cases, managers defined innovation in relatively traditional terms – as incremental improvement or radical transformation of product or process. And these differences had significant organizational implications. However, in other organizations, managers defined anything and everything as a potential object of innovation and accorded it enormous priority. And while some managers defined innovation as an exotic extra ingredient, as something that could with benefit (but often also with risk) be added to the organization, in others innovation was defined as coterminous with the organization itself: not a desirable optional extra to be added when possible to everyday, 'real business', but absolutely integral to and essential to it.

What managers said reflected important differences in the way innovation was understood, defined and valued. Some definitions of innovation were very circumscribed and conventional; others were wide-ranging and unconventional. Limited definitions focused on products – and sometimes processes – while the more comprehensive and radical definitions encompassed any and every aspect of organizational structure process and functioning.

Hence, some of the managers believed that the first and proper object of innovation was the process of innovation itself. They judged that those traditional definitions which were limited to certain forms and certain objects (products, processes) and to certain people and certain times and places (e.g. R&D labs or special innovation units) were in fact obstacles to the genuinely innovative organization.

In organizations where managers rated their organizations as 'poor innovators', managers and other key organizational members tended to argue that the fundamental root problem was that senior management were only interested (if they were interested at all) in conventional, unambitious, limited and incremental forms of innovation.

It may be a consequence of the fact that, in these organizations, managers' hold a view of and place a value on innovation which leads them either to define it in limited ways (which when achieved strike the observer who holds more ambitious and radical views of innovation as evidence of a gap between intention and achievement), or to seek to achieve it in limited ways which then limits its incidence. However, this too, while it may appear as evidence of an apparent discrepancy to the outsider, may in fact be a logical consequence of how innovation is defined and achieved.

Thus, there were differences between the organizations in how innovation was defined and valued and these differences are important in themselves. They were also important because of the implications they carried for how these organizations set about achieving the sort of innovation they valued.

Different interpretations and their consequences

There are other ways in which interpretations of and values placed on innovation are important. The organizations we studied differed in a number of respects. One difference, which our respondents suggested was significant in itself, was the degree to which the managerial cadre within an organization agreed or differed in their definitions of innovation and the value they placed on it. Within some of the organizations there were marked variations in the ways in which innovation was defined and valued. However, in general, in successful and less successful organizations – as assessed by the managers – there were patterns. In successful innovating organizations we found that senior technical staff, executives and managers in general agreed essentially on the factors that encouraged and discouraged innovation. But, in the less successful innovating organizations, while some managers and staff agreed on what obstructed and facilitated innovation within their organization, their senior managers articulated a markedly different analysis.

In fact, this lack of agreement in the less successful innovators on how to encourage innovation was seen by the technical specialists and middle to senior managers as a major source of frustration and dissatisfaction, and a fundamental source of the failure to innovate. Within these organizations, for example, the perceived failure to innovate was ascribed to the deliberate policies of senior management who designed and encouraged organizational structures and systems in order to reduce the risks they associated with innovation or to reduce the incidence of types of innovation they found less desirable.

Among the organizations seen as poor innovators, conflict, confusion and ambiguity over organizational direction and purpose were seen frequently as major obstacles to the realization of innovation. Clarity and consensus about the direction and strategy of the organization were seen by those in success-ful innovating organizations as one of the most important factors in encour-aging innovation.

The moral and affective dimensions

How senior managers regarded innovation centred around the way the very nature and implications of innovation were defined. Innovation is inherently messy: it is hard to control (arguably impossible to control). Innovators often behave differently from other types of staff; places where innovation is encouraged are often (in accordance with theories of innova-tion which stress the necessary role of creative individuals) distinctive – more 'creative'. Innovators are often treated differently – with greater licence. Innovation is risky and expensive. We found that managers differed sharply in their views of these aspects of innovation. For some, innovation was defined as dangerous, almost inherently irresponsible, childish, unsettling, threatening to the organization and its established controls and disciplines, desirable possibly (as long as it was controlled) but not essential.

In other organizations all these aspects of innovation – its creativeness, its quirkiness, its capacity to break through barriers and constraints, its inherent riskiness, etc. were seen far more positively – as highly valuable, as strategically essential, creative, exciting, exhilarating, the source of advantage and competitive success.

These differences underpinned radically different organizational approaches to the management of innovation. Those organizations where senior management saw innovation as a threat, a danger that must be controlled, were more likely, our respondents insisted, to seek to manage and discipline innovation. When innovation was seen as a desirable and exhilarating source of competitive advantage the stress was likely to be less on controlling innovation and more on encouraging it. In both types of organization, managers recognized what the innovation literature also emphasizes – that the achievement of radical forms of innovation requires definitionally a willingness and commitment at senior levels of the organization to question and critique the existing organizational order. However, senior managers differed in their reaction to this. Some welcomed it and stressed how the search for innovation meant that they had to continually reinvent their organization in order to ensure that vested interests and ways of thinking didn't become established. 'It's a self critical culture. Hence it's always changing. We like to shake up every three to five years to seek out complacency and shake them out. We seek a balance between order and chaos' (Board Director, Nortel).

In organizations that were seen by managers to be obstructive towards innovation, it tended to be defined by the senior managers as something potentially dangerous, as something that must be controlled and tightly regulated. In one poor innovating company, senior managers described innovation as 'an indulgence'. In this atmosphere, those managers who encouraged innovation spoke of it as if it were an illicit activity that had to be protected and hidden – and given 'air-cover'.

The illegitimacy of innovation?

Innovation is in some cases 'illegitimate' almost by definition. Departing from the norm is close to rule breaking. Consistent with this view, some of our respondents expressed very firmly the point that within their organization innovators required senior sponsorship and protection. Innovation was clearly viewed as a contested terrain. It was understood to be the source of tension and even conflict about a range of important issues: for example, about the allocation of resources (including the deployment of some of the best staff), about the most appropriate product and service offerings and about, in consequence, the operating procedures and infrastructure of the organization which would be needed to support the new activities.

However, in organizations where a radical and ambitious view of innovation prevailed (and was supported from the top) the underlying view of innovation was far more positive and a radically different organizational response was accorded to it. When innovation was seen as a risk it had to be controlled; when it was seen as a virtue and a benefit it was treated as something to be encouraged.

Analyses of the source of the problem

Established companies find it hard to innovate meaningfully. The reasons, as Markides (2002: 246-7) noted, include 'structural and cultural inertia, internal politics, complacency, fear of cannibalising existing products, fear of destroying existing competencies, satisfaction with the status quo, and a general lack of incentive to abandon a certain present (which is profitable) for an uncertain future ... A prerequisite for strategic innovation is a fundamental questioning of the way we do business today'. We found this kind of analysis being articulated by managers in our innovative companies. This research confirms that managers also believe, drawing on their own experience, that there is a dilemma between whether to emphasize and build on existing organizational strengths, or seek to downplay them by pursuing new, innovative paths.

Managers in some cases made a virtue out of the ways in which established structures limited innovation and argued that such control was necessary and desirable. In these cases, if innovation was to be tolerated and even encouraged, this was only so *within the parameters* of existing assumptions, structures and systems. But, in the cases where organizations were effective innovators it seemed that the solution to the paradox articulated by Markides and others was not to adapt innovation to the organization *but to adapt the organization to innovation*. Under these circumstances, managers interpreted

their role as combating and neutralizing the inevitable forces of conservatism that would obstruct innovation and which could emerge only too easily
within large organizations.

However, in those organizations where managers were unimpressed by
their organization's innovation performance, senior managers did, indeed,
seem to be trapped by their commitments to structural and cultural inertia
and all of the other characteristics noted by Markides. *But this is not of course
how they saw it.* To understand just how these sorts of managers did 'see it'
is of course one of the most important points arising from this study. This
is because it is precisely these sorts of managers (seemingly the majority)
who have resisted for so long the messages coming from governments, gurus
and academics. Just why have they been so resistant?

The answer appears to be because they hold deep, emotionally-based
attitudes which inure them to the intellectual arguments. These managers
regard themselves as guardians of the integrity and traditions of the organizations. They explained their stance on innovation as justified by the need to
curtail the 'risks' of innovation. It was, they said, underpinned by the need
to ensure that valuable resources were not 'squandered' on 'self-indulgent'
initiatives. Far from seeing this attitude as a negative, they converted it into
a claimed strength.

According to findings from our various projects, successful and unsuccessful innovating organizations differed markedly in two ways:

- In their *awareness* of the various ways in which existing and historic structures, competences, processes and mindsets could obstruct innovation.
- In the *reaction to this awareness*. They differed in their willingness to
  address and resolve these obstacles.

In organizations adept at innovating, managers saw their role in terms very
similar to those propounded by Teece *et al.*, that is, senior management's
key role is 'appropriately adapting, integrating, and reconfiguring internal
and external organizational skills, resources, and functional competences to
match the requirements of a changing environment' (Teece *et al.* 2002:
183). The managers in the successful innovating organizations we studied
saw their roles precisely in these terms. However, the less successful innovators saw their role very differently: not as constantly reshaping the organization but as 'defending it'.

Managers' thinking about the 'causes' or drivers of innovation were generally consistent across the organizations. They agreed on how innovation is encouraged and discouraged. The list of factors they articulated was broadly consistent across the organizations and sectors studied.

In the more successful innovators, participants argued that the organization was, on the whole, geared up to encourage the sort of innovation they viewed as critically important. A number of factors were identified:

- A clear and genuine strategic emphasis on innovation.
- A high value placed on innovation; clarity of strategic vision; senior managers' positive attitudes towards innovation and risk-taking.
- The quality of staff and how they were managed and rewarded.
- Supportive structures and processes, and crucially, cultural values which genuinely encouraged innovation.
- The availability (through various means, formal or informal) of sources of funding.

In the effective innovating organizations, managers at all levels recognized these factors as positive. In the less innovative organizations, managers, while sharing this view of what was necessary, tended to focus on the ways their organizations deviated from these standards. Conversely, in organizations seen as more successful as innovators, managers stressed a combination of elements, all mutually supporting each other.

Formal and informal systems

One interesting example of the ways successful and unsuccessful innovators were positioned with respect to these key variables is the way the organizations tried to 'manage' innovation. Organizations often have some sort of innovation management system. These procedures vary, from highly formalized to less formalized, from centralized to decentralized, business-based to autonomous. We found that organizations that defined innovation in unambitious terms as a potentially dangerous activity requiring discipline and regulation tended to lay particular stress on these kinds of formal processes.

Organizations which were perceived to be poor innovators had the most formalized innovation management systems. This is a counter intuitive finding. In these organizations informants were seriously critical of these systems, claiming that they applied inappropriate criteria and methodology to the encouragement of innovation being, for example, more concerned with eliminating risk than encouraging innovation. Innovation was seen in terms of its potential dangers not its potential benefits; and it was only acceptable if it was capable of being accepted by or was consistent with, structures and logics arising from the organization's operational regulation and disciplines.

Paradoxically, in the organizations which were seen as more effective innovating organizations, our managerial informants were far *less* likely to talk in terms of these formal innovation management system. Since innovation is at odds with organization, it is not surprising that formal attempts to organize, assess, review and control innovation end up limiting it.

Informal systems

In the effective innovating organizations, there were virtually no complaints of this sort. And the reason for this is revealing; they didn't complain about the formal system because there often was no obvious formal innovation system. Not only is there no formal system, although of course there is an informal one, but the managers also did not see the need for one, or advance any arguments in favour of one. Managers in the effective innovating organizations believe that within their organization people with good ideas exist and are encouraged. They also believe that the organization has creative people and that the nature of the organization and its clear purposes, allied to available funding and associated with a pervasive skill at networking, allows innovation to occur.

It also ensures that would-be innovators can believe that it is safe for innovations sometimes to fail. This is crucial. Innovation, virtually by definition, means at least some failure. A key test of an organization's approach to innovation is revealed in its attitude towards failure. If failure is not tolerated, innovation will not generally occur ('If you fire people for trying something they won't try it and you get the behaviour that you reward' – Manager, Nortel). In organizations that were rated as 'good innovators' by our respondents, they do not, on the whole, see the need for any institutionalized system to generate innovation; they think that innovative, intelligent people with good managers and a clear view of what they are trying to do is enough. Furthermore, on the whole they believe that this is the situation that currently exists. They don't want formal systems because they don't see the need for them. What is required is the *absence* of formal systems which could obstruct the creative energy of talented and focused individuals.

Managers in organizations which were defined as less successful innovators were quick to identify aspects of their organizations which in their view blocked innovation. One such feature – a common one – was the structuring of an organization into separate product businesses, with innovation being accountable to these businesses. Since the product businesses were managed by annual business plans with demanding levels of targeted performance they were unlikely to squander this year's profits on extravagant innovation projects, especially when these were uncertain of delivery, required long-term development, or were not tied to existing products and markets. The result was that little innovation was encouraged and what was encouraged was incremental improvement, not radical innovation.

Organizational cultures

Culture was seen to play a pivotal role in the encouragement or discouragement of innovation in organizations. Its most powerful positive role is when organizations make available shared and taken for granted ways of thinking that encourage and value innovation, that assume organizational members will innovate, that reward those who do and that castigate those who claim they are unable to find organizational support. They are most important negatively when the prevailing norms do not accord sufficient value to innovation, when compliance and conformity are emphasized, when innovation is seen as illicit, dangerous, threatening and when the organization is presented as an obstacle from which there is no escape.

Cultural values are particularly important when they are so pervasive that senior managers do not even realize that they share them. Or they do not recognize that their collective way of thinking is just one of a number of possible ways of thinking. Thus the authority and dominance of entrenched ways of thinking can become unquestioned. This is particularly likely if the way of thinking is based on a shared technical discipline background, or if, historically, it has been beneficial to the organization in the form of a recipe for success. In poor innovators, managers identified a number of such shared ways of thinking which limited innovation. One important charge was that an understandable emphasis on operational efficiency within the product businesses and the gradual accretion of institutionalized structures and systems resulted in a preference for the known over the unknown, the tested over the untested and the reliable over the uncertain. In short, 'the older, larger, and more successful organizations become, the more likely they are to have a large repertoire of structures and systems which discourage innovation while encouraging tinkering' (Van de Ven 1986: 596). Managers in the effective innovators seemed to fully recognize this; those in the ineffective innovating organizations seemingly did not.

Middle managers in the poor innovators identified a number of such shared assumptions and mindsets. Top managers were regarded as unwilling to challenge existing organizational arrangements – especially arrangements they had devised, or which had, historically, proved successful. Organization was seen as easily (but not inevitably) generating conservatism among senior managers.

Among the effective innovators, not only do professional or technically-based mind sets not determine attitudes towards risk and innovation, but the organizational culture also positively encourages innovation. It does this in three ways.

- First, the organization supplies a clear sense of the direction of the organization so that people are able to see how they could contribute to the achievement of shared purpose. One manager in a good innovator noted: '... I think the role of senior managers is to create a shared vision in the organization. I think that would really channel this innovation and encourage innovation in a productive way ... It gets everybody aligned.'
- Second, the positive cultures encourage debate and discussion about the ways in which the organization manages innovation. It makes the organization's innovation performance discussible, which ensures that any blockages (and there are bound to be blockages) can be identified, discussed, confronted and resolved. In poor innovators although the development of innovation was, according to managers, discouraged by features of the organization, managers were not prepared to identify and confront these obstacles in the organization – although they were prepared to complain about them to us and our researchers.

- Third, dialogue had to be associated with a degree of discontent: not just with a willingness to be critical of the organization (while being prepared to try to improve it) but with the recognition that it is acceptable to be critical as part of a search for improvement. One manager noted: 'I think that one of the ways that innovation thrives here is that there's a bit of an organizational culture of never being satisfied'.

We found a number of examples of cultural conservatism. It was very evident, for instance, in retail banking and in some engineering settings. An emphasis on engineering values is not surprising in a telecoms business with a real and important reputation for engineering excellence. The trouble was, the managers in one telecoms company observed, that this engineering mindset was less appropriate and indeed was a serious obstruction when it was applied to the management of innovation in general.

The dominance of an engineering mindset had other consequences. Managers argued that it resulted in an excessive concern for technological innovation at the expense of market-driven innovations. And it placed excessive emphasis on product innovation at the expense of channel or process innovations. It also meant that value was placed on attention to detail rather than on an intuitive, far-sighted, approach. However, the main complaint was in the attitude towards risk inherent in an engineering culture, which, with its understandable concern with risk elimination and the reliability of performance, was seen to breed an approach to risk which was seriously antithetical to the encouragement of innovation.

The cultures that were seen by managers to be most favourable to innovation were those which confronted the dilemma between exploitation and exploration. In successful innovators, managers expressed the conviction that individual creativity and innovativeness would and should emerge in their organization regardless of the existence of organizational obstacles or supports. In successful innovators, managers believed that individuals with good ideas would and should be able to find sponsorship and support – they would be able to triumph over any organizational barriers. In unsuccessful innovators, on the other hand, managers saw themselves as powerless in the face of organizational obstacles.

The two types of culture defined and constituted the individual innovator in startlingly different and distinct ways which reveal the respective core values. In the organizations which were least effective at innovating, the individual innovator tended to be seen as a solitary, heroic individual who through personal qualities of energy, genius and bravery had managed to overcome the organizational obstacles strewn in his or her path. The heroic innovator triumphed despite the organization. In the more successful innovating organizations the individual innovator was seen as a product of the organization: in these organizations everyone was expected to be able to gain support and sponsorship for innovative ideas, or be unworthy of the organization.

Also, in successful innovators the cultures stressed the value of the individual over the organization; in less successful organizations, individuals were not able to escape the dominance of the organization. The former stressed individual entrepreneurship within the organization; the second saw the individual as powerless in the face of the system. It is not possible for us, given our research design, to assess how true these beliefs were in any absolute sense, but certainly managers believed them to be true and acted as if they were true. Moreover, the belief patterns did seem to accord closely with more objective evidence about innovative performance of the organizations studied.

Mindsets and values

In unsuccessful innovators, actors' accounts suggested that innovation was limited by the dominance of historically-derived mindsets and values which permeated senior management thinking and culture. This was illustrated in one case by the observation 'People are comfortable with the way things were ... They find it hard to change, hard to see the need for change'. Some actors thus recognized the role of history in influencing an organization's capacity to innovate. History matters because 'firm's previous investments and its repertoire of routines constrain its future behaviour ... opportunities for learning will be "close in" to previous activities and thus will be transaction and production specific' (Teece et al. 2002: 192).

Organizations learn and this learning tends to influence future learning – it influences, for example, what environments are scanned, for what data, and how these data are processed. Established routines and processes establish guidelines and channels for learning. The more learning becomes focused and speedy the more efficient it is. However, this efficiency at single loop learning and at immediate fixing, as many commentators have noted, limits future learning. As Henderson and Clark have suggested, 'An organization's communication channels, both those that are implicit in its formal organization ... and those that are informal, develop around those interactions that are critical to its task' (1990: 236). However, this does not occur as an automatic, self-correcting function. The channels once developed can act as filters not only of what is seen as relevant and useful knowledge, but also of where this knowledge will arise and its value. The paradox here is clear: old learning thus limits new learning.

Approaches to innovation: a danger to be controlled or energy to be tapped?

Our research illuminates two important issues and the relationships between them. It shows that managers in organizations committed ostensibly to innovation as a strategic priority used an interlocking series of ideas to explain the level of incidence of innovation within their organizations. Regardless of the level of success of their organizations at innovation (as assessed by the respondents themselves), these managers showed a high degree of consensus about the key organizational factors which determined the level of innovation.

However, our research shows much more than this. When managers used their theory of innovation to understand differences in the production of innovation they differentiated two polarized organizational approaches, one positive, the other negative. They think they know why organizations succeed or fail at innovation and they offered detailed analyses of the ways in which different organizational responses to innovation encourage or obstruct it.

They differentiated two categories of organization. The first consists of organizations where, according to actors' accounts, the way innovation is predominantly defined and valued in the organization and the way the organization tries to manage innovation are deeply unhelpful to the achievement of the sort of innovation the organization actually needs. In the other sort of organization, where actors judged the organization was more successful, the informants argued that while they were not entirely sure how innovation could be achieved, they were sure that certain structures, process and values were unhelpful and others helpful, and that on the whole their organization was more disposed to be supportive than obstructive.

In the less successful innovating organizations, innovation was seen as dangerous, risky, almost illicit and somewhat self-indulgent. While recognizing – at least publicly – that innovation was important and strategically significant, senior executives by their actions sought to limit, control, corral and constrain it. If innovation was to be allowed or even encouraged, then it could only be permitted so long as it complied with the existing rules, discipline and procedures of the organization. Innovation must fit in with the organization, not the other way around.

Of course, in theory and according to espoused executive rhetoric, innovation in these poor innovators was encouraged; it was often an officially espoused corporate 'value'. However, in practice it was so constrained and regulated that it was permitted little chance of realization or impact. This approach is entirely consistent in its own terms. If innovation is risky it must be regulated. If the risk of innovation is that it takes on its own momentum with little recognition of the needs of the business then the way to control this risk is to make innovation in every way possible regulated and controlled by the business and not the other way around.

Loose/tight

Conventional thinking often asserts that the loose/tight distinction is closely related to levels of innovation and that in the context of innovation, the tight form of management is undesirable because it blocks innovation whereas the loose form of organization is desirable because it encourages innovation. Managers of course recognized this tension between innovation and organization and they argued that the form of organization most conducive to innovation was one that minimized the factors that were inherently anti-innovation (hierarchy, bureaucracy, regulation and centralization). However, in successful innovators this tension between loose/tight forms of organization was seen in a subtle and sophisticated manner. Control was seen as necessary. Too much looseness was seen as wasteful. The solution was not necessarily to replace one form of organization with another but to recognize the contribution of both types of organization and to switch between them as circumstances required. The key to resolving the tension between structure and innovation, managers reasoned, was not to insist on the superiority of one type of structure over the other but to live with a moving balance between the two.

The value of searching

Our research suggests that managers in innovating organizations think that the search for the pro-innovation structure may be important in itself. Their approach indicates that the way to deal with the loose/tight, innovation/ operational, present/future set of dilemmas and paradoxes is not to try to locate the right 'dividing line' or find the right 'balance'. They recognize that there is no one perfect answer yet managers must nonetheless continue to search for it. Their task is to discuss and critique, and when necessary, change the prevailing settlements on each of these; good innovators remain capable of exploring, discussing and confronting the way the organization establishes these sets of temporary balancing acts – and to hold up the underlying principles of decision for scrutiny and evaluation.

Indeed, in the proficient innovators, senior managers seemed to argue that being able and willing to engage in this debate – how to find the right balance or tension between exploitation forces and exploration forces – was more important than finding a formula for the precise balance. Finding the balance could easily lead to conservatism and complacency. However, any solution was bound to be wrong or unbalanced sooner or later. Therefore, the only safe and sure approach was to assume that any current solution, compromise or balance was wrong and to seek an improvement.

The role of leadership

The way leadership was enacted in these organizations was usually perceived as a crucial factor. As the Chief Executive of Astra Zeneca remarked when commenting on the importance of achieving the appropriate move away from the stultifying forces of control and budgets, 'So where does innovation take place? How do you get creativity? How do you get to the edge? My job here is more to keep pushing in that direction. And that's a very atypical role for a senior manager'. As we have noted, this distinction between leaders who protected the organizational status quo and leaders who were prepared to radically reform the organization regularly in order to avoid the build up of conservatism was one of the most important distinctions of all.

Within this less structured more empowered world, however, some degree of patterning and regularity was required and processes supplied this. Processes, when properly (that is clearly but minimally) defined, establish relationships, dependencies and responsibilities between people and functions. However, they must not be too restrictive.

Conclusions

Our objective in this line of enquiry concerning innovation has been, through a knowledge and understanding of managers' meanings and theories of innovation, to reveal some clues as to why some organizations seem to have a persistent problem with innovation while others seem able to enjoy sustained records of innovation. The study and understanding of managers' perceptions is a critically important area of study not least because the study revealed that organizational structures, functioning and performance are a *consequence of managers' assumptions, knowledge, paradigms, mindsets and values*.

We found that managers laid very considerable stress on the nature, role and contribution of the leader(s) of the organization. Other research has also suggested the importance of the top team role in innovation (see, for example, Cummings 1965; Hage and Dewar 1973; Kimberley and Evanisko 1981). However, what previous research has not emphasized, or recognized sufficiently, is the way in which and the extent to which managers' interpretations shape the whole constellation of factors which, in turn, govern innovative performance.

Leadership was defined as centrally significant in both 'types' of organizational approaches to innovation. In the one, the leader defends the organization against the dangers of innovation and protects the status quo against change. In the other approach to innovation, the leader leads the charge, on behalf of innovation against the status quo. The role of the leader is to find the dividing line 'between chaos and order, to achieve balance by periodically smashing the organization and ensuring flatter structures and a strong sense of direction'. Organizational cultures vary with the two very different types and missions of leadership. In the poor innovators, these cultures are conservative, stressing the values of the present and the past, wary of innovation and change, stressing danger over opportunity, seeing the organization as the ultimate authority and the individual as passive and powerless. In the effective innovators, cultures stress change, emphasize the significance of the individual against the organization and stress enterprise and energy rather than compliance and obedience.

Managers echoed the importance of the 'ambidextrous organization' (Tushman and O'Reilly 1996); the tension between managing the business for today (exploitation) and preparing it for tomorrow (exploration) (March 1991); and the inherent problems of innovating in well-established firms (Dougherty 1996; Markides 2002; and Van de Ven 1986). It is not possible to tell how far our managers were informed by these and other authorities. And it doesn't actually matter, because the important point is not the provenance of their ideas but the application. The important point is that from our managers' point of view, these ideas of balance and the fine dividing line were central to their understanding of what they were trying to achieve. They found these ideas useful not only in understanding what was happening, but also in informing what they were trying to do in their organizations.

If the individual creative hero is perceived to be the solution then organizations may allow considerable freedom to particular individuals. Conversely, the rational, planned perspective results in the orderly linear approach to research and development. A third belief system results in an attempt to create a culture of experimentation and 'play'.

Crucially, it can be hypothesized that the largest proportion of managers across the country are likely to be located in organizations which do not have a track record of significant and sustained innovation. Our findings suggest that if and when managers in these settings do become attracted to the idea of innovation (or are instructed to embrace it) they will tend to champion one or other of the models to which they happen to have been exposed. Thus, within mainstream organizations with a new top-down edict to 'be innovative' one finds managers variously urging or assuming that this implies the establishment of an R&D unit or alternatively a liberal culture. The middle band is thus caught between competing models of innovation. Our recommendation is that those senior managers seeking, with serious intent, for greater organizational innovation need to attend not only to the idea of 'creativity', but also need to surface and examine the *different* kinds of ways through which 'innovation' can occur, and to hold healthy, open and informed debate about which approach is to be preferred in a given situation. They need also to be prepared to surface and debate their various implicit assumptions among themselves and not just with external researchers and consultants.

Perceptions and beliefs about innovation influence the allocation of resources. They influence the organization of innovative activity – including, for example, the extent to which innovation is allocated to a select few or is regarded as a diffused responsibility. There are implications also for the way R&D is organized – indeed whether there will actually be any R&D and if so on what scale. Competing perceptions affect whether information and forward plans are kept secret or are shared across organizational boundaries and thus they influence the degree of collaboration with suppliers, customers and competitors.

So, to summarize the practical implications. The preceding analyses reveal that there are a range of perceptions and cognitions which are displayed by managers. They also reveal that these are frequently *patterned*. In other words, within particular organizations it is common to uncover a predominating language and logic which carries the coded signals and the accepted stance towards innovation. This has a powerful influence on behaviour irrespective of 'official' pronouncements. The first practical implication therefore for any managers who are serious about innovation is to recognize the pervasive influence of such cognitive boundaries. Only when this is done can the search for possible alternatives be commenced.

Practitioners would also be well advised to take special note of the finding that the organizations capable of sustained innovation exploited the ability and willingness of managers to engage in open and honest debate. Conversely, the organizations less effective in innovating tended to discourage or even stifle such debate. The healthy, open discussion included dialogue about how their organization defined, valued and managed innovation. This in itself was an important step towards improving innovation performance. This occurred not only because the identification and resolution of possible obstacles in how innovation was defined and managed could be drawn into the open but also through the constant analysis of the adequacy of the balance between tight and loose organizational structures and cultures.

Clarification of understandings about the nature of innovation in a particular organization can also help in the strategy formulation process. Managers can debate their current, compared with their desired, exposure to new markets, new customers and new technologies. And there can be discussion and therefore analysis about the varied risks and competency requirements associated with these. Innovation ultimately results from managerial perceptions of the need for change, the perception of the opportunity to change and the perceptions about the way to change. Perceptions, beliefs and assumptions are thus vital aspects to be understood.

The overall conclusion for the practitioner is that organizations can benefit if perceptions and beliefs about innovation are clarified, made explicit and made subject to debate and challenge. This open discussion would also purposively explore and map the range of views and perceptions that are characteristic and prevalent within the organization. It may come as a surprise to uncover, as we did in a number of the case organizations, that there may be a resigned acceptance that innovation is not 'really' a *serious* objective. Other, competing, conservative, 'realist' stances may crowd it out. In these instances executives were seeking to cope with the dilemma by evading it.

7

Dilemmas and paradoxes of managers' knowledge

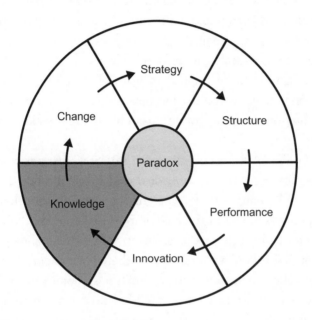

Figure 7.1 The six paradoxes – knowledge.

In this chapter we attend to the fifth of the Six Paradoxes. Earlier, we examined the dilemmas and paradoxes relating to business models and strategies and in other chapters we have explored aspects of these in areas such as performance management and innovation. Now, in this chapter we want to step back in order to 'get behind' strategic thinking in order to probe the knowledge and assumptions which inform and underpin strategizing and the construction of business models.

As Porter and Ketels have detected, the knowledge bases of executive decision making require attention: 'Why do so many companies fail to have a strategy? Why do managers avoid making strategic choices? Or, having made them in the past, why do managers often let strategies decay and blur?'

(Porter and Ketels 2003). In other words, why do senior managers – who are, one assumes, normally intelligent, experienced and committed to the success of their business – make decisions which are detrimental to their overriding objectives? Why don't they see the crisis approaching? Why do they fail to drop obsolete strategies and develop smart new ones? Is it possible that in some ways the successes of the past restricts the ability to develop new objectives and new organizations for new times?

This paradox has been noted many times by many observers of organizations: senior managers, responsible for the performance and direction of a business may appear unable to respond adequately to changing circumstances; they appear to be trapped in ways of thinking and assumptions which may once have served the business well but which now are at odds with prevailing or emerging conditions. This is the paradox addressed by this chapter.

Johnson (1987; 1988) in a classic analysis of how organizational strategies are developed explores the reasons for the inability of a board in a poorly performing retail company to develop and support necessary changes to the company's business model in the face of increased competition and declining demand for its historic products. He attributes this inability to the fact that the board's thinking was limited by a shared 'paradigm'. This paradigm is the set of beliefs and assumptions, which is so dominant and pervasive and historic that it is taken for granted by those who share and operate within the paradigm. It is discernible in the stories and explanations of the managers, and it plays a central role in the interpretation of environmental stimuli and configuration of organizationally relevant strategic responses. 'The paradigm is a … set of beliefs about the organization and the way it is or should be, and since it is taken for granted and not problematic, may be difficult to surface as a coherent statement' (Johnson 1988: 84–5).

These claims we believe are enormously important. The possibility is that the senior team of an organization may hold sets of shared beliefs and assumptions which are held very strongly but are so taken for granted that executives hardly know they hold them. Furthermore, these limiting assumptions may influence what and how the team sees, understands and analyses the business environment and so influences what and how the board thinks about and chooses for its strategic responses. This chapter thus addresses some central and critical paradoxes that emerge from the nature and implications of senior managers' knowledge.

'Senior managers' are defined here as those managers who have and take responsibility for shaping the two key determinants of organizational performance – the strategic objectives and direction of the business and the capability of the organization to achieve these objectives. The relevant 'knowledge' held by these managers consists of the assumptions, beliefs and convictions which these managers hold which shape their thinking about and decisions on issues of organizational direction and design. Managers' knowledge is central to an understanding of the role of paradox in organizational dynamics and destiny. Furthermore, organizational success can become dependent upon long established, tried and tested recipes, knowledge of the world, of the organization's products, processes, clients and markets which facilitate efficient deployment of existing skills but limit seeing or learning new methods.

What is known, assumed and believed can become barriers to exploration, to recognition of the importance of unknowing and unlearning. Valentin (2002) notes that complacency may derive from history: 'past successes and ideological rigidities can foster dysfunctional inertia and mindsets'. Likewise, Tushman and O'Reilly (1996) note how established norms obstruct change. Managers not uncommonly become personally committed to established routines (Lant 2002).

There are numerous versions of the central paradox that can centre on the knowledge managers hold which structures their strategic thinking. As we have seen, one is to focus on the 'path dependency' of organizations – the ways in which historic and embedded organizational structures, processes, routines and structures of knowledge and ways of thinking influence the direction of organizational development or even limit the possibility of such development. So, organizations' futures can be limited or influenced by their histories. 'Path dependency' is itself a dilemma and a paradox. On the positive side, a firm is protected from new entrants because the capability to benefit from a technological trajectory may be dependent on prior knowledge gained by engagement at an earlier stage of the curve; on the negative side those insider firms benefiting from path dependency risk being so attached to the trajectory that they are less prone to the acquisition of external knowledge which lies outside that 'path'.

Another version of this paradox is that success breeds failure: established and tested organizational ways of thinking and ways of doing which have underpinned organizational success sooner or later, especially under changing circumstances will lose their relevance and advantage and if senior managers are too committed to these organizational recipes they may find it hard to recognize that they are no longer working or be unable to think outside them.

Finally, as the discussion below will illustrate, managers' knowledge can influence their ability to develop new knowledge. In other words, what managers know can limit what they can learn. How they know the world and their organization and the links between the two can limit their ability to understand changes in the world and how their organization needs to change with them. This picks-up again on our theme of the importance of 'framing' and 'reframing'.

The central role and importance of organizational knowledge for competitive performance is asserted widely and frequently. Yet knowledge has been studied in limited and incomplete ways, and definitions of knowledge in organizations have been restricted to operational knowledge at the expense of a recognition or analysis of the nature and role of strategic level knowledge. The focus in this chapter is the knowledge of executive managers – the nature, implications and differentiating features of the knowledge held by the executive members of top management teams and the role of this knowledge in informing and underpinning executives' judgement in key strategic areas. This knowledge is examined with reference to its positioning along two dimensions – the degree of its tacitness versus explicitness and the degree to which it is differentiated or consensus-based. In this chapter we develop a framework based on these dimensions and we employ this framework to illuminate the nature of organizational knowledge and to illuminate executive thinking and decisions about issues of strategy and organizational capability.

Fads, fashions and prevailing assumptions

'Business' and 'organization' are inherently uncertain. There are no universally established and agreed ways of doing things – no single simple model (what to do) or model of business (how to do it). Nor are there agreed and established connections between different strategies and different organizational forms. It is true that at any time and place, certain assumptions and beliefs are more dominant than others – in recent years, ideas of maximizing shareholder value, or of downsizing, or of talent management have variously predominated.

When organizational downsizing was at its peak and was seen as a test of modernity, courage and competence of top teams Budros (1997) studied the reasons and consequences of downsizing. He found that firms nearly always claimed that technical, economic performance pressures triggered the downsizing: that it was a rational and inevitable response to competitive, profitability pressures. However, many writers have noted that there is an important difference between the formal strategy that managers espouse and claim publicly and the assumptions and values that lie behind these claims. In the case of downsizing, the reality, Budros claims on the basis of a number of studies, is that downsizings 'generally have deleterious organizational (financial) and human consequences …' (1997: 244). Rather than showing adherence to the norms of good rational management, downsizing actually 'violates norms of economic rationality when attention turns to the consequences of their actions' (1997: 245).

Why then did they do it? Budros explains executives' enthusiasm for downsizing by reference to executives' commitment to prevailing values and ways of thinking – the powerful social rules or 'myths' that specify prevailing conceptions of acceptable organizing principles, without demonstrating empirically the economic rationality of the principles. Executives feel pressed to '… adopt practices that are compatible with rationalised institutional myths even when the practitioners are inefficient economically and that adopters are rewarded with enhanced social legitimacy and ultimately survival prospects' (1997: 245).

However, none of this refutes the argument that organizational forms and strategies are (a) chosen by executives (however imperfectly and irrationally) and (b) that these choices are based on executives' convictions and assumptions about what their business must do to succeed and what it needs to be like to achieve these aims. Indeed, the Budros analysis shows the importance of the convictions and assumptions held by executives.

The function of the executive is to make decisions about key issues of strategy and organizational capability. These decisions in the face of inherent uncertainty and incomplete and flawed data are based on executives' judgement of how best to make sense of the world and how to achieve their organization's purposes. And these judgements are based on their 'patterns of belief about their situation and its potentialities' (Grinyer and Spender

1979: 115). Executive judgement on key organizational issues is based on their knowledge of, and beliefs about, what strategies are available, what are appropriate for the organization and which strategies are best for different environmental conditions, or are best suited to different strategies.

The nature and quality of the assumptions and knowledge which underpin and inform strategic thinking are critical to the quality of organizational strategy and capability. Business strategies are developed not in response to managers' objective knowledge of the world 'but in response to managers' perceptions as seen through the lenses which are coloured by their beliefs and political interests' (Fahey and Narayanan 1989: 362). Some businesses fail 'not because resources or systems needed to cope effectively with the real external environment cannot be acquired or implemented economically and expeditiously, but because various behavioural factors impair strategic problem-sensing or effective strategy development and implementation' (Valentin 2002: 41). Similarly, recent interest in organizations as sources of shared cognitive schema show how these schema structure perceptions, values and beliefs. Organizations are knowledge-defining entities.

Research has described the ways in which managers' shared knowledge of the external world (markets, competition and industrial structure) are influenced by entrenched and organizationally generated schemas (Gioia 1986; Reger 1990; Calori et al. 1992; Sparrow 1994; Gioia et al. 1994; Weick 1995). This research supports the conclusion that managers learn to see and know the world in terms of simplified and established frameworks. This can also be functional. It serves to focus and minimize data-processing time and can be very efficient. However, these same routines may become restrictive and counter-productive under new circumstances.

The ability of executives to be reflexive about and be capable of moving beyond existing competences and established knowledge is critical. Global competitive battles 'have demonstrated the need for an expanded paradigm to understand how competitive advantage is achieved ... Winners in the global market-place have been firms that can demonstrate timely responsiveness and rapid and flexible product innovation, coupled with the management capability to effectively co-ordinate and redeploy internal and external competences'. Strategic management in such circumstances have a key role to play in 'adapting, integrating, and reconfiguring internal and external organizational skills, resources, and functional competences to match the requirements of that changing environment' (Teece et al. 2002: 183).

Following this brief review of the cognitive literature we now want to dig a little deeper into one aspect of these kinds of findings – the nature of executives' knowledge.

Developing strategy: the role of executives' knowledge and thinking

The assumptions and beliefs managers share play an important part in senior strategic level decisions by influencing the 'socio-cognitive processes in strategic management'. These are processes through which executives seek to acquire, store, share and act upon 'information, knowledge and beliefs concerning those issue that have an ultimate bearing on the longer-term direction of the organization as a whole' (Hodgkinson and Sparrow 2002: 6).

Managers' cognitive structures influence what they see and what sense they make of what they see. Managers use 'templates' to simplify, to organize and to make sense of their environment. Their thinking and decisions on key issues such as strategy and organization are influenced by the assumptions, beliefs and models which they hold separately and collectively. The cognitive perspective focuses on the knowledge structures that underpin thinking and decisions about strategy – especially the ways in which senior managers define, classify and respond to definitions of the external environment.

The cognitive approach focuses on 'shared' knowledge structures, and while this does not necessarily imply that within any organizations there is consensus around these matters, it is a likely inference that there may well be common patterns. In fact, the issue of the degree of consensus/difference within the top team on the knowledge underpinning organizational thinking is important – and one we develop later in this chapter.

Understanding, knowing and finally acting upon the world involves a number of connected but separate processes. Two are particularly important – identifying, collecting and classifying data – the way the world is 'represented' or 'mapped' – and the ways in which these data once categorized are understood and explained and acted upon. This second stage, although closely related to the first involves a movement from classification to what could be called 'theory'. And theory involves commitment to and use of 'working models'.

Managers' shared knowledge of the external world (markets, competition and industrial structure) is influenced by entrenched, shared, organizationally generated and disseminated schemas. But, offsetting the efficiencies which these can produce, the more successful organizations become, 'the more likely they are to have a large repertoire of structures and systems which discourage innovation while encouraging tinkering' (Van de Ven 1986: 596).

There is a risk when trying to explain and account for senior managers' thinking and decisions that an over rational model of decision making is used – an 'over socialized' conception of strategy-making which sees it as a property of, and a straightforward 'response' of executives to external pressures, an approach which overlooks the crucial role of executives shared assumptions and beliefs. Strategy-making is actually influenced by 'shared understandings, cultural rules, languages and procedures; how managers in practice use these forms of knowledge cannot simply be 'read off' mechanically from the knowledge systems themselves. Managers are not '... simple automata, but ... artful interpreters of practices ... actors may be creative agents; they are potentially reflexive enough and their social systems open and plural enough to free their activity from mindless reproduction of initial conditions' (Whittington 2006: 615).

The processes which determine managers' decisions on strategic issues consist of what Whittington calls 'practices': 'shared routines of behaviour, including traditions, norms and procedures for thinking and acting' (Whittington 2006: 619). Like all organizational processes involving the identification of problems, options and the choice of solutions, these processes require 'skills and tools' (Whittington 2002: 119). And these tools include assumptions, values and views about how the organization works and what needs to be done to make it work differently.

So, understanding strategic choices and decisions requires an understanding of the 'internal organizational goings-on that give rise to a particular strategic choice rather than on the macro-causal factors determining strategic success' (Chia and Holt 2006: 636). This draws attention not only to the need to identify and understand the 'practices' (forms of knowledge and ways of thinking) which underpin strategic thinking and decision making but also the need to clarify how and when and by whom strategy is developed. Understanding how managers actually 'do strategy' means attending to the ways in which strategies can emerge as a consequence of a patterned consistence of actions notwithstanding – but also not assuming, a lack of explicit intention (Chia and Holt 2006).

Why are executives' ideas powerful?

The importance of managers' shared assumptions and beliefs which under-pin their decision making lies not only in the existence of these shared assumptions but in their power – their dominance which in some cases puts these assumptions beyond debate so they become 'facts of life'. How is this dominance explained? How can we explain the relationship between power and knowledge in discussion and decisions on organizational strategy and design? What managers know is influenced by the play of power and author-ity – which, at any period, makes certain sorts of ideas powerful, pervasive and in one sense perceived therefore as 'true'. Decisions on organizational strategies and change are underpinned in explicit and subtle and possibly tacit ways by pervasive and powerful bodies of ideas, assumptions and beliefs. These exist in the larger society, which gives them authority and the appeal and truth. These ideas are often so dominant as to be taken-for-granted and seen as part of a 'natural order' which tacitly or explicitly offer 'the power of truth, the potency of rationality and the promises of effectivity' (Miller and Rose 1993: 51).

The ideas which structure and underpin executives' thinking on organi-zational decisions are significant in their implications and reflect the signifi-cance of their origins – their power comes from their truth which may appear as self-evident. Tacit knowledge is not knowledge of a different type from explicit knowledge: it is just knowledge that is less communicable – or less communicated – and less articulated. It is similar to the notion of taken-for-granted knowledge and assumptions – knowledge that is so much part of the 'natural order' that those who hold the knowledge are hardly aware of what they know and assume (Polanyi 1966: 4).

It is important to identify and analyse the actual bodies of knowledge held by senior managers – the actual 'paradigms', assumptions, beliefs and theories. In this volume, Chapter 6 on innovation does this in some detail, drawing on research and consultancy carried out by the authors. However, in this chapter the focus is less on the content nature of knowledge held by managers and more on the features of this knowledge – features which, we believe in themselves have significant impact on the ability of the top team to recognize what they know and the possible limitations of what they know, and their ability to respond positively to new challenges and circumstances.

These key features comprise two sets of alternatives:

(1) Is the knowledge explicit and obvious or is it implicit and therefore held almost unconsciously?
(2) Is the knowledge shared, or do executives hold different sets of assumptions and paradigms?

Tacit knowledge and explicit knowledge; consensual knowledge and differentiated knowledge

The first distinction is between tacit and explicit knowledge. That knowledge can be tacit may now be accepted almost as a truism but it remains highly significant especially for the type of knowledge addressed by our study. Tacit knowledge raises the possibility that executives may have strong feelings about a particular proposal – their own or another's – and yet not recognize, or fully recognize, the assumptions and beliefs they hold which colour their interpretations of the proposal.

Nonaka and Takeuchi (1995) have argued that tacit knowledge consisting of technical knowledge and of beliefs and schemata needs to be converted into explicit knowledge. This notion of tacit knowledge in some ways comes close to what writers such as Berger and Luckmann (1967) have called the social construction of reality – at least in its emphasis on being taken for granted and tacit. However, Nonaka and Takeuchi's definition of tacit knowledge introduces a new dimension: that this knowledge is positive, useful and functional in terms of the organization's aims and priorities. This assumption is questionable.

The other key polarity is that between consensual and differentiated knowledge. Whether executives share the same assumptions and beliefs about strategy and capability or hold different sets of underpinning logics is highly significant to the dynamics of the top team, the nature and quality of decision making and very possibly ultimately to the performance of the organization.

Knowledge in organizations is often differentiated. These differences in ways of seeing the organization, its structure and the outside world reflect organizational differences and reveal differences in interest and power. It is misleading to assume *a priori* that organizational knowledge is unified. Grant has suggested that a key feature of an organization's ability to create value from knowledge is its capacity to aggregate knowledge – the 'ability to add new knowledge to existing knowledge' (Grant 1996: 111). This ability is unquestionably valuable (see Teece *et al.* 2002) and indeed can be a major source of innovation when the combination reconfigures an established system or arrangement to link together existing elements in new ways.

However, it cannot be assumed that knowledge can always be aggregated, not only because this requires a common language or framework such as that supplied by business planning frameworks, management competences, accountancy systems and standards and so on, but more fundamentally because some organizational knowledge – and especially knowledge about core organizational issues of purpose, structure, markets, customers competitors, mission, etc. – is differentiated even oppositional. It cannot be added together because each set of knowledge rejects and seeks to undermine the other, sometimes vigorously and vehemently.

Differences in what differently situated members of organizations know and what they know about arise naturally within organizations which are hierarchical, power systems where power and benefits are distributed unequally. Differences in organizational circumstances, location, power position and benefits underlie differences in interpretive knowledge frameworks and knowledge and are expressed in differences in and struggles over knowledge and over the respective status (or authority) of knowledge. An approach to knowledge in organizations must incorporate this possibility. As Giddens has remarked, 'Any sociological theory which treats such phenomena as "incidental" or "secondary and derived" and not as structurally intrinsic to power differentials is blatantly inadequate' (Giddens 1984: 264).

A major tradition of analysis of organizations focuses on organizations as sites of contention and conflict where power and knowledge are deployed to achieve or maintain dominance – or to critique and reduce it. 'Organizations are ... arenas in which coalitions with different interests and capacities for influence vie for dominance' (Palmer et al. 1993: 103). Differences in interests and organizational location and situation relate to differences in knowledge – ways of seeing the organization and its purposes which are expressed through different sectional viewpoints and interpretative frameworks. As Greenwood and Hinings (1996: 1033) note, 'much of the work on differentiation and conflict in organizations ... shows how technical boundaries between departments and sections are reinforced and buttressed by cognitive boundaries'.

In conflicts related to knowledge, groups will seek to impose their view of reality. And they will seek to develop and disseminate knowledge which legitimizes their position and their view of the organization's priorities. They will seek to undermine or rule as invalid, dangerous or worse, rival views. They will seek legitimacy by claiming consistency with accepted or proposed sources of moral authority: the founding fathers, the original charter, or the organization's accepted prime purpose. However, power is inherent in knowledge itself. The process whereby a particular body of knowledge establishes dominance within an organization is not necessarily a result of its correspondence with any objective truth.

Executive team thinking about and formulation of, corporate strategies and organizational structures is informed significantly by the models and theories of organization and strategy which are held by members of senior teams. These theories inform both what senior managers propose for the business – strategically and organizationally – and how they react to other's proposals. They inform and potentially limit all stages of the strategic process (definitions of the environment, environmental scanning, data analysis, the identification of acceptable strategic possibilities). Yet, despite their critical role the underpinning theories and convictions are all too frequently left implicit and unexplored.[1]

---

[1]The research project on which this chapter is based was an ESRC-funded project which focused on executive teams. Ten organizations were studied drawn from a variety of sectors including retail, construction, business services, health care, facilities management, banking and pharmaceuticals. Three mutually-reinforcing methods were used: in-depth one to one interviews with each member of the respective executive teams; direct observation of management meetings of all kinds including executive board meetings; and scrutiny of secondary sources including, most notably, executive board agendas and minutes plus internal company reports. The observations of meetings allowed insight into the naturally-occurring conversations of directors and senior managers and facilitated the observation of non-verbal signals passing interactively between them.

Findings about executive managers' strategic knowledge

Senior teams must be able to recognize, evaluate and make sense of the implications of different and possibly competing conceptions held by members about what their organization should be doing and what they should be like in order to attain required goals. This helps to overcome what is otherwise an important but sometimes puzzling phenomenon: that senior managers seem unable to develop new strategies and directions for their business or to find new and improved ways of organizing their business to improve its efficiency. One certainty amidst the uncertainties facing businesses is that sooner or later the business model will be ill-suited for purpose under changed circumstances. What brought success will sooner or later begin to result in failure. Yet executives frequently find it hard not only to recognize the growing signs of failure, but also more seriously find it hard to trace any performance shortfall to the accepted business model.

The knowledge of executives which underpins their views on strategies and capability can be located on two axes (see Table 7.1). It is the core argument of this chapter that the four positions generated by the interplay of these axes have significant implications for the nature and processes of senior decision making on these matters. Each type carries its own implications.

The two cross-cutting dimensions give rise to four types of knowledge states. By this we mean the types of conditions which characterize the ways

Table 7.1 Four types of executive knowledge states.

	Tacit	Explicit
Consensual	Type 1: Common, submerged/ unexplored understandings	Type 3: Negotiated action
Differentiated	Type 2: Divergent, submerged/unexplored conflicts	Type 4: Manifest conflict

in which executives can deploy their knowledge. Thus, under Type 1 conditions, executives face circumstances where they have few opportunities to
scrutinize and challenge their colleagues' knowledge base or to have their
own assumptions challenged. Moreover, because there is broad consensus
the team can act in unison and goodwill tends to prevail. Under Type 2
conditions, their knowledge of business and their business models also
remain relatively unexamined and unchallenged but they are conscious that
differences exist. Where these circumstances obtain suspicion is fuelled that
difference can be attributed to malfeasance or stupidity. Under Type 3 conditions, knowledge is displayed more openly and consensus is reached
through negotiation. Under Type 4 conditions, knowledge is also made
explicit but the evident differences leads to manifest conflict which may for
various reasons – as discussed below – be difficult to handle constructively.
In the section which follows we elaborate these types and we give examples
of their operation and consequences.

Type 1: common unexplored understandings

Executives in organizations with a common but unexplored understanding
about most, or all, key strategic issues drew heavily upon their shared tacit
knowledge. This generated easy, familiar and deep levels of agreement –
often of long standing – about what the business was doing and had been
doing and should do and what it needed to be like in order to pursue its
proper and historic role and objectives. These assumptions usually centred
on a distinctive normative model of organization, customer proposition and
employment relations.

The retail company example

In one of the retail companies, the top team operated with a high level of
tacit consensus. This was based on a series of shared but largely unsurfaced
well-established historic assumptions. These were largely unstated except by
general references to a shared and taken-for-granted set of business and
organizational 'principles', 'values' and models. These were hallowed and
given authority by history and by the intentions of the founders (who were
often quoted as a way to legitimate a preferred stance). There was frequent
reference to 'our way of doing things'. This was often played as a kind of
trump card to de-legitimate alternative proposals.

In the retailer, executives had a real pride in the business model and their model of business but neither was fully stated explicitly. There was a conviction that with respect to strategy and organization the business was different and distinctive (which was true but probably not as true as executives thought). At the time of the research this historic consensus was beginning to come under pressure as performance problems became more and more evident. This proved to be a fascinating moment from a knowledge research point of view because it provoked some unusual reactions among the executives. A number of them preferred to try to ignore the negative market and financial signals. The performance indicators which would have focused attention on the fundamental issues were often marginalized. Instead, alternative less threatening and diverting issues were attended to – reorganizations, restatements of values, new store openings and so on.

Eventually, other executives alarmed by the growing evidence and by the lack of forthright action or sense of urgency began to question the common understanding. The erstwhile consensus which had been reassuring and which had served to reduce conflict and disagreement was beginning to be seen as problematic. This was not only because it now seemed possible that it was less distinctive than previously thought, but also because it now seemed that it might no longer be effective for employees or customers, and also because it tended to exclude other options.

However, because these retail executives shared so many assumptions and beliefs, they found it hard not only to think about new possibilities, but even to envisage ways in which such innovations could be generated. At this stage the executives almost literally did not know what to do. In the event, the new circumstances (declining performance, significantly increased competitive pressure, indications of disquiet within the business, problems around senior succession) were addressed initially by two types of activity. On the one hand, there was a piecemeal introduction of modern management processes (development and training, cautious and limited executive team building initiatives, performance management, supply chain redesign) which did not constitute a significant change in the assumptions underlying either business model or model of business and therefore were broadly acceptable to all members of the top team. The other initiative was to revive and refresh and re-emphasize the historic values and unique features of the organization through the relaunch of the business' values and the communication of these throughout the business. In short, a major strategy was to surface, revive and reassert the historic assumptions and models. This initiative could be seen, in terms of the model used here, as an attempt to make the tacit model more explicit.

The tacit consensus of this top team raised some interesting features. First, since the top team was not used to identifying, exploring and accepting differences in view point, they had found difficulty in managing difference, disagreement and conflict. They had a problem in distinguishing healthy difference from conflict. Disagreement was seen as potential conflict partly because they were not used to disagreement and secondly because they were not sure of and wary about, where it might lead.

Secondly, they had difficulty discussing and making decisions about strategy and organizational change. Partly this was because they had not had practice in having these discussions since previously key strategy and capability issues, when they arose which was rarely, had been resolved simply by applying the historic models. However, partly it was also because they saw strategy and capability issues as resolved by the application of the historic models. So strategy issues were – or historically, had been – resolved simply by invoking the accepted and taken-for-granted models. Also, because of this historic lack of attention to strategy issues, the organization had not developed the necessary structures to discuss and develop strategy. The top team collectively was unsure about its responsibilities for the development of strategies. Equally, individual members told us that they did not feel a responsibility for setting and monitoring strategy. As a result, governance issues were ambiguous and confused and the top team spent time addressing issues which were either in the distant future, or in the near past. Also, members of the top team had not developed the confidence and knowledge and experience to engage in debates about strategy – even if they saw these as legitimate or as part of their responsibilities as members of the top team.

When, as a result of external performance pressures, the top team were forced to acknowledge the need for a discussion of issues of both strategy and organizational capability, a third issue arose which troubled them. On one level, it looked little different from the same issue facing any business: what should we do, how should we change? But, it had an added dimension since these questions were not, and in their view could not be, answered simply in terms of market opportunities and their organizational requirements. For this organization, with its deep-seated, tacit, taken-for-granted assumptions about strategy and capability, any decision on these issues had to be 'legitimate'. This was a favourite term of the chairman when discussions about future directions were occasionally, initiated. Not only were the discussions themselves questioned, their outcomes were assessed in terms of whether they were true to the historic models of the business. This raised a serious, persuasive and as yet unresolved dilemma: should the business try to compete with the competition by being like them or by being different from them (and thus true to its tacit models)?

Towards the end of our research involvement, the tacit model was beginning to be surfaced and made explicit (although the issues discussed above about attitudes towards and responsibilities for strategic discussions and decision making persisted) not least because a major component of the top team's response to competitive and organizational pressures was to launch a business-wide programme for clarifying, 'refreshing' and publicizing the historic differentiating core values of the organization and attempting to 'hard-wire' these into key personnel processes and decisions: competences, promotion, training and so on.

Organizations where the top team share strong tacit assumptions find it easy to generate commitment, but this could be at the expense of the quality of analysis. Under these circumstances, options are limited by the dominance of the historic model and the possibility of path dependency is strong. Those who advocate a review of the historic model, or who advocate a break with it, face questions about legitimacy. Change if it is possible at all probably raises two difficulties. First, it occurs only within the tight constraints of the original model – that is, as incremental revitalization. Or, because the top team has little experience of analysis and assessment of options for strategy and organization, there is a tendency to embrace too quickly and too uncritically new alternatives.

Type 2: divergent, submerged/unexplored conflicts

In other organizations we researched, executives worked on the basis of divergent knowledge bases and divergent interpretive schemas. These differences were important enough: but what made them even more important was that the existence, cause and consequences of these radically different cosmologies about how to manage at a strategic level co-existed in a tacit, implicit, un-surfaced and unexplored way. Managers found it difficult to understand why others took such radically different (and in their view misguided) approaches to a whole range of issues which they saw as critical to the success of the organization. Because the underlying assumptions and logics which informed and generated the fundamental differences were tacit, managers explained these differences in often personalized ways. This tendency fuelled suspicion and mistrust. The conflict was displaced from root issues and translated into arguments about the personal shortcomings and the merits of very specific initiatives and proposals.

The retail bank example

The senior team of one of the banks was committed to a strategy of innovation and was committed to ensuring the organization was geared up to achieve this strategy by encouraging innovation, a core strategic value. Members of the top team differed radically but implicitly in what they meant by innovation and in their view of the necessary organizational arrangements to achieve it. There were two positions, discussed below. The two key features of the assumptions about strategy and capability held by members of the top team – that they were different but tacit – were displayed by the evident frustration felt by each camp about the views and actions of the other. There was an inability of each group to understand the position and rationale of the other. The result was a situation of considerable conflict, mistrust, disappointment and frustration. However, these emotions were not expressed directly; there were few efforts made (until after the research was completed) to understand the origins of the divergent approaches in different theories of business.

The conflict between the two groups centred on the symptoms of the different models – actions taken or proposed by each side – not on the theories which informed these different positions. One group was guarded and conditional in their approach to innovation and saw it as risky, and at times irresponsible. They saw the sort of organization necessary to achieve innovation as formal, structured and controlling, containing many safeguards against the dangers of innovation: for example an elaborate and comprehensive innovation management system to filter out unworkable ideas. Innovation was defined by this group as a specialist function which needed to be tightly controlled by the market-facing product businesses. The necessary organizational culture was and should be deferential, hierarchical, cautious and compliant. The role of leadership was to preserve the business against the risks of unnecessary change and from unsuccessful and expensive innovation; to ensure that any permitted innovation did not threaten and could be subsumed by, the organization and its historic features and strengths.

In these circumstances, while a range of assumptions and theories about business models and models of business co-existed within the top team, these models were not brought forward for explicit examination. Those who tried to surface differences were defined as poor team players. People disagreed – often passionately – but didn't understand why they disagreed and may not even have fully recognized or understood the theory which guided their own and certainly others' convictions.

The existence of tacitly different sets of assumptions underpinning views on strategy and capability produced a number of consequences in these types of organizations. First, diversity of views tend not to be positive in these circumstances because when disagreements occur neither side can understand the provenance of, or grounds for, the proposals for the other. They lack a common language and they lack a way of discussing that they lacked this language. In these sorts of cases differences become moralized and personalized.

Secondly, disagreement – because it is masked and distorted – creates mistrust and alienation. It tends to result in groups being even less able to communicate with each other.

Thirdly, the issues at stake can be fundamental and in these cases it is crucial that a way be found to surface and assess the differences which exist within the top team. However, since the source of the differences is usually unacknowledged this debate does not normally take place. Each side simply explains the attitudes of the other by reference to stereotypes: 'old-fashioned', 'traditional', 'reactionary', 'irresponsible', 'lacking understanding of our distinctive proposition' and so on.

Type 3: negotiated action

Executive knowledge under Type 3 situations is characterized by consensus around an explicitly stated knowledge of strategy and of business. In these cases – often characteristic of small to medium businesses where the original owner/entrepreneur's vision of strategic and organization (and the links between the two) has generated success – all members of the top team are committed to this clear philosophy.

The biotech firm example

This was a medium sized firm based in a science park in the English Mid-
lands. The senior executives comprised a mix of many of the founding scientists and some newly recruited professional managers. The objectives and
values of the firm were clearly stated and much discussed. There was a very
open culture and a great deal of sharing of knowledge about projects. It was
often remarked that the organizational culture was still very much like an
academic laboratory where there was a common quest and excitement about
the discovery and application of knowledge.

One or two professional managers who had attempted to impose too
divergent a business philosophy upon the firm had been persuaded to move
on. There was a resistance to too much formality and the founders and their
surrounding team were not easily impressed by management systems. In
place of systems there was a strong emphasis on recruiting and retaining
highly talented biologists and biochemists. The organization structure was
very flat and most staff had the opportunity to influence the decision making
of the company.

There are some inherent dilemmas which characterize this third type
based on the consensus/explicit model. First, because there is just one model
senior staff in these situations are often unable to think of alternate ways of
achieving their ends. For example, if values are placed so centrally as in the
pharmaceutical case, then management tends to be defined negatively.
Hence, all issues of growth and development have to be resolved by normative methods. In other words, the dominant model limits the ability to think
of other models. It also stymies the ability to think of alternative ways of
achieving the same ends.

Secondly, where there is a dominant single model accepted by all members
of the top team, there is a tendency to inhibit creative and divergent thinking. Decision making becomes easy – possibly too easy. As long as the model
brings success, all is well, but when new ways of working are required these
types of top teams may have difficulty in identifying or objectively assessing
proposals which are radically at odds with the historic models. They may
also have difficulty dealing with difference and disagreement. The usual
response to dissent is either to convert the dissenters or to remove them.
When a situation arises that requires strategic management to reconfigure
internal and external organizational skills, resources and functional compe-

tences to match the requirements of a changing environment executives in explicit/consensual situations are likely to face a huge difficulty.

Finally, as in religious groups, the commitment of top teams to an explicit and dominant organizational/business model is often associated with a charismatic founder/entrepreneur who individually or through/with the top team develops the model. This makes for a series of possible problems for such organizations when the founder finally leaves – issues of succession, problems associated with the inevitable institutionalization of charisma and the possibility that, post the exit of the founders, disputes will break out about the status and legitimacy and relevance of the original model.

Type 4: manifest conflict

In this type of executive team, knowledge is stated explicitly and multiple formulations come into conflict. This type (different views and approaches to organization and business) is in theory the most functional and healthy of the four. The existence of differences allows the possibility of innovation and the analysis of different models and scenarios theoretically opens up the possibility of calm and objective search for the most useful model. Difference, diversity and disagreement are legitimate and explicit in this model. Openness to new possibilities, freedom from historic recipes and the ability to think outside historic restraints should all be highly possible under these circumstances.

The logistics company example

In LogiCo only one member of the top team had spent his entire career in the organization. All the others had joined in the past couple of years from outside, and each from very different types of firms. Each of these firms of origin was highly successful and each therefore represented a viable, plausible, model. Moreover, their firms of origin had clear, explicit and dominant business models. These newly recruited senior executives brought with them their experiences of these successful ways of doing business. Indeed, their recruitment was impelled partly because of the experience they brought, from these competitors, of alternative models.

For this company, which was at the time of the research undergoing a performance crisis, this wealth of detailed knowledge of alternative business models was at once both liberating and confusing. Previously, the company had operated with an explicit and consensual business model, which was strongly historically based with clear normative elements. However, performance issues had caused the top team to conclude that new models were necessary – hence the recruitment of executives from outside bringing with them clear but very different models and experience.

However, even though, as already noted, this type in some respects seems to offer the most favourable of options, there can, nonetheless, be problems. A multiplicity of models can create a level of uncertainty and ambiguity that creates difficulty. There are too many choices and too few ways (and not enough time) to choose between them. Executives need to make decisions about key issues facing their business. However, as Brunsson and Olsen (2002) have noted, for decisions to initiate action, they require not only analysis but also motivation and commitment, especially when the consequences of the decision are very great, as they are for strategic and organizational decisions. Under these circumstances, executives certainly need to assess options, but they also need to create an agreed way forward and there is evidence that focusing for too long on the complexities and choices of decision making can evoke uncertainty and hesitation.

Executives face two pressures: to make the right choices and to mobilize the team and the organization to get things done. Achieving the appropriate balance between thorough discussions of differences and the underlying models, and mobilizing and motivating coherent and consensual teams is difficult. Although the explicit/difference model supplies fertile ground for the identification and analysis of different options it also raises the risk that if there is excess of choices this makes decision making difficult and mobilization behind a choice especially problematical.

Conclusions

The main objective of this chapter has been to illuminate the paradox identified by Porter – and many others: how to explain that those entrusted with the stewardship of businesses may fail to recognize changes in their business's environment, fail to see or address the deficiencies of their businesses strategy or organization and fail to change direction or capability in effective ways, in time. The paradox arises because of the possibility that it is not simply the complexity of the issues that causes executives difficulty but in some way that their membership of the organization and the sets of working assumptions and ideas they have developed and used (successfully) during their stewardship of the business obstructs their ability to design and implement necessary change. This chapter has addressed this issue by highlighting some key and significant features of the *knowledge* managers use and assume when making key strategic decisions.

This requires a focus on knowledge at the strategic rather than operational level and a view of knowledge as *theoretical* knowledge – the underlying sets of assumptions and beliefs that generate the understanding and interpretation that underpins judgement, or 'propositional statements'. (Tsoukas and Vladimirou 2001: 983). This form (or view) of knowledge, was, as Tsoukas and Mylonopoulos (2004) point out, anticipated many years ago by Daniel Bell when he remarked that in the post-industrial society what is decisive for the organization is 'the centrality of theoretical knowledge that ... can be used to illuminate many different and varied areas of experience' (Bell 1974: 20).

Executives' decisions on issues of strategy and capability are informed and justified by their views of what is best and how to achieve it – their propositional knowledge about their organization and its efficiency. Although strategy and change are presented frequently as if they are a direct and unmediated response to changing environmental circumstances, they are in fact a result of management choice and judgement (Brunsson and Olsen 2002: 215).

This chapter has developed and employed a new taxonomy in the categorization and analysis of knowledge of members of top, strategy-making teams. Rather than looking at the content of executives' assumptions and beliefs we have focused on two key features of this knowledge because these key features play a part in influencing executives' ability to know what they know and reflect on, assess and when necessary change and move beyond their assumptions and beliefs.

This framework comprises four categories based on the cross-relationship of two key distinctions. One of these distinctions – tacit/explicit – is a familiar one but it has not previously been applied to strategic level knowledge. Polanyi (1966) notes that skills in the use of tools, including intellectual tools, can become so taken for granted that we no longer realize we are using them. The other distinction: consensus/differentiated, although familiar from the organizational literature, is less common within the knowledge/strategy literature.

The research reported in this chapter confirms not only that senior managers rely upon knowledge which underpins and informs their views on what their organization should (and should not) seek to achieve, and on how their organization should be structured to achieve these purposes, but also suggests that the two key distinctions: tacit/explicit and consensual/differentiated, when combined, are useful for understanding how senior managers think about and make decisions on key issues of business strategy and organization (and for how they see the linkages between these). This analysis of senior management strategic thinking has noted the obstacles to innovative thinking; the vulnerability to path dependency and other barriers to clear, open and well-based strategic thinking. We have noted the strategic errors which such obstacles generate. This research helps us understand both the nature of these obstacles, the sources of the ability of strategic management to achieve the sorts of radical reconfiguration of strategy, organization and competences defined by Teece *et al.* (2002) and others as the source of competitive advantage. The research suggests that the nature and quality of top team thinking is shaped by the features of the knowledge which underpins it.

Since issues of organizational structure and performance are important for senior members, differences in views on how or when the organization should be changed will be held intensely, and since organizations frequently involve and invoke values in their structure objectives and dynamics, will be defined in moralized terms as well as in terms of efficiency. If, as Tsoukas and Mylonopoulos (2004) argue, organizational knowledge can be a *dynamic capability* leading to continuous organizational development, then the analysis of the knowledge underpinning key strategic decisions and the ways in which this knowledge is tacit, explicit, consensual or differentiated, is critical to an understanding of the possibility of executives achieving this capability.

8

Dilemmas and paradoxes of organizational change

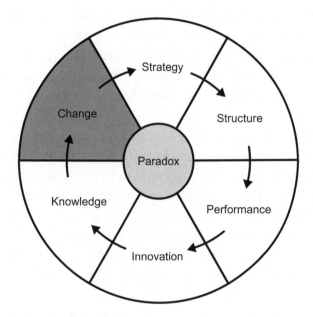

Figure 8.1 The six paradoxes – change.

If we come here today and there's no trouble tomorrow, we haven't done our jobs!

(Anita Roddick)[1]

Introduction

Change is central to the concerns of this book in two different yet related ways. First, managers' typical response to the recognition of the existence or possibility of paradox is very often to initiate a programme of

[1]Roddick, A. (2000) 'Taking it personally', 1 November, *Geographical* magazine. London: Royal Geographical Society. Cited by Tate (2009).

organizational change. The manager's prevailing logic in so doing is usually
to 'resolve' the paradoxes often by emphasizing one of the polarities which
underpins the paradox. We have seen many examples of this throughout
this book. In Chapter 4 we explored a selection of new organizational forms,
one of the features of which was that they were seen frequently by managers
as ways to handle or avoid the paradoxes which accompany organizational
structures. And in Chapter 5 we explored new approaches to the management of performance. Performance management techniques usually have as
their objective an attempt to solve the perennial (and in our view inherent
and integral) paradoxes that accompany managers' attempts to manage
people in ways which maximize their contribution to the organization and
their sense of commitment to the organization through some mix of control
and/or commitment.

So, organizational change is central to managers' responses to paradox,
and for this reason it requires attention here. However, there is another and
more fundamental reason for our attention to organizational change and
that is that change itself is characterized by paradox. In a sense this should
not be surprising since all other aspects of organization are prone to paradox.
Because paradox is central to organizational structures and processes, then
we would expect paradox to characterize processes of organizational change
– especially when these processes are inspired by attempts to escape from or
solve the implications of paradox.

Organizational change is a dominant and constant feature of organizational
life. This is so at least partly because change is seen as a way of resolving
fundamental tensions and polarities (the sources of paradox). But, as will be
discussed in this chapter, much organizational change depends frequently on
a polarized conception of organizational forms and organizational processes
which are characterized in terms of starkly defined oppositions. So, projects
of organizational change which are attempts to resolve paradox (which
depend on oppositions) end up deploying conceptions of alternative organizational forms or processes which in themselves are inherently oppositional.
As the discussion of the work of du Gay and Alvesson in Chapter 3 suggested,
the reasons for this are clear: by attributing exaggerated deficiencies and
weaknesses to the rejected organizational option (for example, bureaucracy
and centralization) the designers of change are able to enhance the attra-
ctiveness of the opposed preferred option. So much so, that the rejected
polarity is 'ruled out' automatically just as the preferred option is 'ruled in',

and discussion or advocacy of the rejected polarity becomes almost unthinkable, since it has become almost literally indefensible and undiscussable.

However, the cost of this form of analysis and argument – which is deployed in order to generate support for the proposed change – is the perpetuation of the notion of polarity itself which underlies the need for change (as managers see it). So, ironically, by seeking to resolve paradox and its implications, programmes of change which depend on caricatured and (often) highly morally-contrasted polarities actually *reinforce* the zero-sum forms of thinking which represent failed ways of understanding and exploiting paradox. For example, managers and consultants contend that change is necessary to ensure movement away from the dysfunctions of bureaucracy and towards new forms of organization (see Chapter 4) and this is of course a classic polarization. But, by insisting on this either/or way of defining alternative organizational structures they undermine debate; by allocating so much value to one pole at the expense of the other they fail to acknowledge that both poles have advantages and disadvantages and they rule out discussion of the possibilities (and advantages) of a hybrid or ambidextrous form of organization of the kinds discussed in Chapter 4.

In fact, despite the claims and criticisms of the proponents of the antibureaucracy form of organization, empirically it is clear that both forms continue to co-exist and that both have strengths and weaknesses even under current circumstances (where we are told, the anti-bureaucratic form is required by new competitive and environmental pressures). The claim that bureaucracy has been superseded is empirically doubtful. It remains the most common form of organization and even its alternative – the decentralized autonomous strategic business units rely on the continuation of bureaucratic arrangements.

However, despite questions about the consequences of change or the assumptions underpinning it, there is little doubt about its prevalence. Surveys of managers show that 60% of UK managers report a major restructuring of their organization (Worrall and Cooper 2009).

The literature on organizational change reveals a puzzle – a puzzle which in our view originates in the paradoxes at the heart of change: on the one hand, it is claimed that the successful design and management of change – especially when this achieves the type of change known as 'transformational', or the 'learning' or 'adaptive' organization – represents a major source of sustainable competitive advantage (Pettigrew and Whipp, 1991;

Hamel and Prahalad 1992). However, on the other, it is claimed that most change programmes fail (Beer *et al.* 1990). How can we explain the fact that change is pervasive, that it could confer competitive advantage but that it frequently fails to do so? What are the reasons for this failure? The explanation lies, we argue, in the inherently paradoxical nature of organizational change itself.

Senior managers are often unsure about what to change and how. They face a number of dilemmas: they are probably wary of change – if they are sensible – sensing what research confirms, that most change projects fail both to introduce the planned change and to achieve the desired benefits. They *may* want to be faster, more flexible and responsive and more customer focused; they want to develop new organizational forms and reposition or even dismantle their organizational boundaries, but even if they do they don't know how to achieve these goals and they are likely to experience trouble in seeking to achieve them. One major difficulty they face is in separating out the necessary analysis of the problems and the challenges the organization faces – how to identify and address the various aspects of the organization that can impact on performance and how to relate these elements of organizational capacity to desired organizational objectives and strategies – from the plethora of advice, prescription and change packages on offer from management consultants.

The nature and sources of change paradoxes

Although senior managers understandably want their organizational change to be problem-centric rather than solution-centric, it can sometimes seem easier to accept an off-the-shelf package from outside experts. But, if you can buy a change package so can everyone else; and these off-the-shelf packages may not only damage some important features of the organization (see below) but buying a package will do little to develop the internal capability of the organization to design and manage change. Buying a change package means that this key capability is, in effect, outsourced. And if organizational change is fashion driven, conforming to the assumption and prescriptions that are powerful and pervasive at the time – then in a sense the change is not a change at all, for organizations that follow the prevailing truths are simply complying with the status quo and thus following the trend, thus changing but not changing.

The source of the paradoxes associated with designing and managing change can be traced to four key issues which are addressed in this chapter:

- the knowledge and role of managers;
- the nature of organizations;
- the objectives of organizational change projects;
- the paradoxes that surround change itself.

The knowledge and role of managers

Many accounts and analyses of change – or the pervasive exhortations of consultants on the importance of change – overlook or underestimate the critical role of senior managers in the design and management of change and also underestimate the problems and dilemmas that managers face when handling their responsibilities for change. The change literature is unbalanced, being predominantly concerned less with analysis and more with prescription, more with operational issues than with issues of strategy and more with matters of implementation than of design. However, in this chapter we shift the focus from issues of the management of change to the processes of executive decision making surrounding change design.

Managers, especially senior managers, play an active and key role in the decisions on organizational change; their judgement and analysis are crucial. Yet, most accounts of change tend to assume a somewhat reactive, passive role for managers, stressing their subordination to larger social forces and movements. Management is defined (implicitly) as carriers or relays in the transmission and application of ideas that are generated outside the organization.

This tendency to underestimate the roles and responsibilities of managers for the design of change is revealed in accounts of the role of management consultants who are seen as responsible for creating powerful bodies of received truths – change movements such as BPR, outsourcing and delayering – which then become normal or modern. These programmes of change become defined as core elements of the modern organization, unquestioned solutions to certain sorts of organizational problems. Thus, as Brunnson and Olsen (2002) argue, change becomes 'institutionalized' – established by and through extra organizational forces – as necessary and modern.

However, this emphasis on institutionalized change – on the fads and fashions of organizational change which define prevailing regimes and which in turn define the nature of modern organizations – while drawing attention to the pressures organizations face to comply to prevailing truths also contributes to a conception of the role of management in change. This is a conception which, we argue, needs to be challenged not only because it is empirically questionable, but also because we wish to encourage managers to see their roles as more active and critical than these accounts of institutionalized change usually suggest.

By defining managers simply as relays of powerful and pervasive ideas from outside the organization, they are, in effect, defined as subordinate to these larger social forces. The implication is that they are cast as passively applying dominant ideas and exhortations and thus lose the capacity for intervention and choice. And this results in the neglect not only of managers' roles in change, but also of the ways in which they actively seek to understand how their organization works, the problems their organization faces and the best ways to adapt it to new and changing circumstances. Managers are not automata; at their best they are artful and creative agents seeking actively to make sense of their organizations and the business environments in which they compete to manage the relationships between their businesses and their environments. Change is central to these responsibilities.

The difficulties leaders and managers face in fulfilling these responsibilities stems in part from the way past 'solutions' become embedded in current operations which in turn form ongoing sets of assumptions and working knowledge. Whole series of potential 'choices' are in fact evaded because they are routinely 'taken' through implicit choice in the form of ongoing organizational procedures and forms. This is one space which interim managers can occupy sometimes to great effect. They can bring whole new sets of ideas which break away from past practices. They tend, however, to be used mainly in turnaround situations when the optimal time for internally-driven change has already been missed.

The nature of organizations

Some years ago, John Child noted that organizational structures and strategies can only be understood in terms of the 'processes whereby strategic decisions are made which directs attention onto the degree of choice which can be exercised in respect of organizational design' (Child 1972: 2). This chapter explores these choices and the constraints which impact on them.

Many of those who encourage organizational change or who within organizations seek to achieve it, fail to recognize that effecting change is inherently difficult. Organizations aren't usually designed to change; they are designed to do things quickly and efficiently with minimal need for reflection and modification. So, inevitably, they normally find change difficult.

A particular paradox is that organizations' difficulties with change often arise not from weaknesses but from strengths. As was argued in Chapter 5, organizations are designed to be highly effective at doing things – making and delivering goods and services. However, being good at doing things is not the same as being good at thinking about what and how they are doing things or about how to change these established processes. Indeed, the very achievement of high speed, high quality, operational efficiencies means that thinking and behaviour become almost unconscious and hence routinized. However, this makes it difficult for managers to rise above these established patterns and ways of thinking or to think outside these historic mindsets and established procedures.

So, the track record and successes of most organizations do not easily or often lead to a competence at designing and changing organizations. Recent research into innovation in organizations (see Chapter 5) confirms the view that organizational efficiency at *exploiting* processes, products and technologies is at odds with the ability to *explore* new processes products and technologies. And the same applies to the ability to change which is, in its way, a form of innovation. Most organizations are poor at thinking about new things to do or new ways of doing what they do: precisely *because* they are good at what they do. This is what Argyris calls 'trained incapacity'.

This point about the inherent conservatism of organizations is a somewhat different point from that made in Chapter 7 – that managers' assumptions and theories are likely to influence how they approach issues of organizational strategy and change. The point here is that organizations *per se* are prone to *inherently* limited thinking; decisions taken in organizations are systematically prone to irrationality. It is normal.

The objectives of organizational change projects

In their classic book A *Behavioural Theory of The Firm* (1958) March and Simon contend that organizational choice takes place in response to a problem, uses standard operating rules and involves identifying an alterna-tive that is acceptable from the point of view of evoked goals. Thus, 'the variables that affect choice are those that influence the definition of a problem within the organization, those that influence the standard decision rules and those that affect the order of consideration of alternatives. The standard decision rules are affected primarily by the past experience of the organization and the past record of organizational slack. The order in which alternatives are considered depends on the part of the organization in which the decision is being made and past experiences in considering alternatives' (March and Simon 1958: 64). In short, they argue, organizational decision making is characterized by quasi resolution of conflict. This results in the persistence of unaddressed and unresolved latent conflicts. It means the avoidance of uncertainty especially when too much uncertainty and unpre-dictability are likely. It also means that search routines that simply revisit areas and solutions that have worked before. And it involves a particular form of 'organizational learning' – organizations learn to attend to some parts of the environment and not to others.

Brunnson and Olsen describe these aspects of organizational functioning especially well. In organizations, 'Behaviour is determined by culturally conditioned rules which manifest themselves in certain routines for action and which give meaning to these actions. They reflect relatively stable values, interests, opinions, expectations and resources'. They go on to say that every organization has a history, and in the course of time it 'evolves its own accepted ideas about what work is important and what results are "good", and about how such results can be achieved. Some ways of thinking and behaving come to be seen as self-evident, thus excluding other inter-pretations and behaviour ... Structures and processes also acquire an *intrinsic value* and cease to be regarded simply as a way of achieving the variable objectives of the leaders' (1993: 214, our emphasis).

These comments on how organizations work and on the relationship between how they work and how they change, suggests that understanding how organizations change requires an understanding of how they operate in general. And this, in turn, raises the question of how we understand and perceive organizations and thus how we understand how they work. As was noted in Chapter 1, there are (at least) two ways of looking at organizations. One way is to see them as rational, systematic, unitary entities – machines or systems designed to achieve explicit goals. According to this view, change occurs when goals must be amended (because, for example, of environmental challenges or opportunities or because of inefficiencies in achieving goals or subgoals) and when organizations must be adapted to new objectives or to new and improved standards of effectiveness and efficiency. Organizational structures will be designed monitored and assessed in terms of their adequacy in contributing to the achievement of organizational goals. This is an attractive and in some ways a sensible approach: but it is as much an aspiration as a reality.

A second way to view organizations is to see them as emerging and adapting to circumstances spontaneously and naturally without formal management intervention. In this view, organizations are not simply instruments; they are also cultural entities, pluralistic and political societies where different points of view, different objectives and different ways of seeing things (especially the organization and its structures and processes and goals) co-exist with different degrees of authority.

In fact, as well as viewing these perspectives as different ways of *seeing* organizations one can also regard them as different *aspects* of the organization – as two ways of understanding and as two co-existing logics or ways of thinking and existing within the organization. So, we suggest, organizations are in fact not like either of these models; they are like both simultaneously. Managers themselves live within both logics, and seek to manage within both and to handle the interactions between both. To be effective, they must not only try to work within the rational logic (organization as a method to achieve organizational goals), but they must also recognize and work within the alternative approach, the alternative reality.

This is especially important with respect to change. Managers must seek to design and handle change as if the organization were simply a means to achieve shared goals. However, their attempts to change will fail if they do not recognize and engage with the political, cultural, emergent and informal aspects of the organization within which they work – that is, they need to accept the importance of *both polarities*, not simply stress one at the expense of the other. If managers are to be able to maximize their organization's potential for rational change, they have to accept the existence and role of powerful irrational forces. Later in this chapter we address some of these with respect to the nature and origins of change.

Another reason for the uncertain outcome of change projects is that senior managers in organizations find it difficult to identify what needs to be changed and how. This problem is often bound up with the features of the organization that need to be changed. Some of the features of an organization that need to be changed may also make the identification of these problems, and their solution, difficult and even dangerous.

There are many examples of this. Senior managers may be unwilling to recognize a problem if is associated with decisions for which they are responsible; core strengths of the organization may become firmly routinized (which aids operational efficiencies) but under changed circumstances be less appropriate (and very hard to change). Mind sets can easily develop especially if they are beneficial and successful but sooner or later act as corporate blinkers: ultimately nothing fails like success. Organizational success recipes which have always worked well in the past may begin to fail under changed circumstances. But, this kind of failure may be hard to recognize for senior managers who are deeply committed to established ways of seeing (and responding to) the competitive environment.

The paradoxes of change processes

A final problem we will explore in this chapter is that organizations are not only inherently conservative they are also inherently complex and problematic – that is, they comprise a number of contradictions which cannot be solved. There are some fundamental tensions that all organizations face and which, with a limited range of options, they try to resolve but which always persist and are fundamentally insoluble in that any solution solves some difficulties but generates others.

Some obvious examples have already been discussed in this book: centralization versus decentralization, the tensions between exploration and exploitation, or between control and empowerment of staff, or using an internal labour market versus recruiting externally. In each case, the underlying problem cannot be solved. Take centralization/decentralization: recently consultants have been recommending decentralization as a major source of competitive advantage: attack centralization and bureaucracy, liberate the product businesses to act autonomously and entrepreneurially within their separate markets, break the shackles of central office, make businesses accountable only for performance. And of course there is something in all of this: making people accountable for performance rather than for obedience does make sense. However, while decentralization solves some problems it creates others: corporate synergies go by the board; cross-selling suffers, silo mentalities (a term unknown in the old centralized days) flourish, patterns of cooperation communication and collaboration suffer, staff development, training and innovation are all put at risk and the long term is sacrificed for the short term and so on.

This has implications for change. It means that the beguiling blandishments of the consultants need to be viewed with caution; it means that achieving a balance between old and new, between the twin ends of the polarities is more important than an over enthusiastic and naïve commitment to one or the other (which will soon have to be tempered by a move back – probably under a new name like 'shared services' – to the rejected pole).

Seeking to unravel the problems that organizations seem to have in designing and managing change, leads us to the inherent conservatism of organizations. It also leads to the central role of management in the decision-making processes that underpin decisions on organizational change. Chapter 7 has already argued that senior managers' knowledge plays a central part in executive thinking; this also applies to their thinking on issues of organizational change.

In the next section we discuss the various rationales that underpin organizational change. Under what circumstances should organizations change? What are the purposes of organizational change?

Why change? The relationship between organizational capacity and organizational strategy

We find that the first and most common reason for managers to initiate organizational change programmes is that they judge that organizational *capacity* – which consists of structures, roles, skills, systems, values and processes – is not geared up to support the achievement of organizational *purposes*. Thus, when managers believe that the organization is not able to do properly what they want it to do effectively and efficiently they seek to initiate change. We know from research, experience and observation that organizations differ – in their structures, systems, values and skills base. We also know that different strategic objectives require different types of organization. If you want to develop an organization capable of radical innovation it is going to look (or it should look) very different from an organization that is focused on price as a competitive differentiator (for the organizational features required to support innovation see Storey and Salaman 2004).

According to the rational view of organizations, organizational structures, processes, cultures and competences should all work together to support the achievement of the organization's objectives (and indeed to ensure the formulation of sensible objectives and intelligent strategies). However, very often (especially under changing circumstances) they do not, or the extent to which they do so is insufficient to meet the competitive pressures they face. This means that the efficiency and effectiveness of these various elements of organizational capacity require adjustment (or replacement).

In various workshops which we have run for senior managers we have found it remarkable how easily managers can identify features of their organization which are unhelpful to, or are even actively obstructive of, the achievement of what the organization is ostensibly trying to achieve. It is especially remarkable how prepared they are to tolerate this gap between performance and requirements. We have often asked why do they so readily tolerate organizational features which they themselves acknowledge are dysfunctional?

There are two possible problems. First, the various elements of the organization that together build what we call 'organizational capacity' may not support each other. So, for example, certain sorts of people may be recruited but then, as they are not trained properly or paid properly or developed and managed properly, they leave. Or, managers may be exhorted to focus on quality or to be innovative but the performance management system pays little regard to such behaviour.

But, however well or badly integrated the separate elements of organizational capacity may be, the second issue is: how well do the separate elements of the organization's capacity support the achievement of the organization's goals? In a series of workshops we ran on this issue with particular regard to the achievement of innovation we found that in a number of organizations which were ostensibly and explicitly focused on innovation as a major organizational priority, managers found no trouble at all in identifying numerous aspects of the ways the organization was structured and run which in their view fundamentally blocked the encouragement of innovation. The investigation of the adequacy of the relationship between organizational capacity and organizational objectives is the most important area of analysis and rarely fails to uncover many important areas for change. However, recognizing the shortfall between organizational capacity and necessary levels of performance against old or new objectives is one thing. Knowing *what to change and how* is more difficult, partly for the reasons identified earlier about managers' theories of organization and their role in influencing senior management decision making; and partly because of the inherent conservatism of organizational decision making.

However, it is not only what managers know that can get in the way; it is also what they do not know. They do not know (because there are no established and tested certainties in these matters) how to change the various elements of the organization in order to impact organizational performance. Of course, if an organization is competing on price it is obvious that a major factor in considering organizational change will be the importance of reducing costs. However, if the cost of reducing costs is that employees are further disengaged, or suppliers' margins are further squeezed or internal activities are now outsourced, in the long term any of these change may produce perverse and unanticipated consequences. Often changes which seem at one time to be so obviously sensible and right as to be almost beyond question, look very different when a full assessment of their consequences is made. For example, what could be more obviously sensible than to pay people by their results and so tie performance measures to variations in pay? Yet, as Chapter 5 has shown, such initiatives have been shown to have negative consequences, undermining group work and collaboration, overlooking those elements of cooperation and commitment which are essential to good performance. There are always non-contractual bases to contracts. These measures only seem 'right' in terms of a particular (and time-restricted) notion of the worker and his or her motivation and attitude to work. They rely on a particular and contestable theory of how organizations work.

Another problem is that not only is it sometimes far from obvious how a particular business strategy could be supported organizationally (for example, what would an innovative organization look like?), but also aspects of the existing organization limit the ability or willingness of the organization to move in the required direction. Chapter 7 illustrates this predicament. The managers of contract cleaning companies we tried to help may have recognized the possibility and the advantages of moving to the provision of value-added services to clients, but their existing structures and competences made the move itself very difficult indeed. And the example of EngCon suggests that if a business is to take innovation and talent management seriously, it requires a radically different type of organization.

Why change? Basic systems

Although it is true that it is not possible to say what an organization should look like – how it should be structured, its leadership, skills, etc. – until you know what it is trying to achieve, (i.e. an organization's structures and systems must be aligned with or relative to, the organization's purposes) nevertheless, there are some things which have a significant impact on performance no matter what the organization is trying to achieve. There are some best practice measures which are universally beneficial. Research unequivocally shows that these simple and rather obvious measures really make a difference – whether we are dealing with a trendy boutique or a steel mill. These measures are: good communications, systematic selection and training, team work and performance management systems. This is hardly surprising: good communications must be better than no or poor communications, systematic selection better than haphazard selection. However, the point is not trivial because often, even sophisticated enterprises still do not have the basic elements in place and in such cases the first thing they should do we would normally say is install them. A recent study of the performance of UK hospitals showed that these measures saved lives. The performance of hospitals is measured by – among other indicators – mortality rates. There is a positive relationship between the incidence of these housekeeping measures and mortality rates.

Even large, successful and relatively sophisticated modern organizations may lack some of the basic elements of modern management systems. But, introducing modern systems into organizations which lack them can be complex – when organizations lack key features such as performance management or systematic training it is not always enough simply to design a framework and set of processes and then install them. Often the absence of the features is not simply accidental – it reflects the background and culture of the organization. For example, we worked with the executive board of a retail organization in which performance management in any systematic sense was largely absent at upper and middle levels. A new incoming HR Director wanted to install 'modern systems'. However, as we discovered, simply trying to bolt on a performance management system to an organization which is systemically unsympathetic and unused to performance management may not work. The underlying factors which predispose managers *not* to manage performance remained and they continued to influence how people behaved. It was found that these underlying factors had to be addressed and resolved first. Hence, in this case, although a performance management system was introduced, it was found that senior managers not only lacked the skill to implement it (which was relatively easily solved), they were also unused to behaving in ways consistent with the view of management inherent in the performance management approach: clear role responsibilities, seeing the manager as a developer, being able to 'let go' of authority and so on. In consequence, the first year of the new performance management system was difficult. It took another year to address these latter set of underpinning issues before the value of the new performance management system took effect.

Why change? Core competences

There are two ways of relating organizational capacity to organizational strategy. You can try to adapt the organization to improve its 'fit' with the current or – more likely – the new, strategy, or you can build strategy around the things the organization is good at – the organizational strengths. As a number of analysts have pointed out, organizations do not differ greatly in their ability to obtain tangible resources – staff, finance, plant, technology, etc. Yet performances differ markedly. The difference then must be explained not by differential access to resources, but by the way organizations *use* these resources – their internal competences, processes and routines.

The first approach to organizational improvement starts with analysis of the market and identifies market opportunities and gaps and then rebuilds the organization to support the new strategy. However, the approach we are discussing here reverses this sequence and starts with the identification of organizational strengths and builds strategy around real organizational abilities. Of course, both ultimately come to the same place: finding a balance between a strategy that is sensible and worthwhile in terms of analysis of the market and its dynamics, and the organizational capacity to achieve this.

The idea that strategy can be built around an organization's intangible resources – its core competences – is now well established and the concept itself is by now a familiar one. However, from the point of view of our concern with organizational change there are some important and practical implications of this approach.

First, it is important to be clear and sure that what managers insist are the organization's core competences actually survive the three critical tests: is the organization truly better at this activity that its competitors? Is this superiority sustainable? And do customers value this ability in the sense that they are prepared to pay for it? If a claimed competence fails any of these tests it is not a core competence. We researched one organization – an airline – where managers were justifiably proud of the airline's safety record which was a result, they claimed, of the strength of the engineering and maintenance departments, of the values of the organization and its management systems and staff morale. All true. However, this wasn't a core competence because safety is not a factor that drives customer behaviour. Safety is a threshold factor, not a differentiator. If an airline doesn't have a good safety record most customers don't even consider it: having a good safety record qualifies an airline to be regarded as a viable option, no more.

Secondly, core competences can be developed and enhanced by change. However, they can also be damaged by short-sighted, off-the-shelf change packages which destroy the subtle, implicit bases of core competences. These may be the social capital of long-established habits of cooperation and collaboration; the tacit knowledge and judgement of experienced employees, high levels of commitment to quality and support for the development of recruits. All these can be destroyed by the introduction of packages which set up new boundaries between organizational units (strategic business units) or sweep away older, more expensive and experienced and knowledgeable staff through delayering. Or they may be damaged by attempts to define, measure and reward job performance which miss key ingredients of successful job performance (tying job performance indicators to payment). Those organizations that *do have* a strategically relevant core competence may thus allow it to become damaged through neglect, or through the imposition of off-the-shelf change programmes.

An international insurance company we worked with had a real strength in underwriting. They had a large number of highly experienced and knowledgeable underwriters, well managed and working in cooperative, multiskilled teams where they learned from each other and shared problems. This infrastructure was damaged as a new chief executive launched a radical change programme to 'modernize' the company. This involved de-layering which removed some of the older (and more experienced) staff who took their tacit knowledge with them. It involved a move to strategic business units which broke up the teams and removed cooperative and knowledge-sharing relationships and routines. It also included an emphasis on commercial values and 'customer-focus' which required underwriters to become sales staff, focusing on revenue at the expense of risk. This change programme alienated and confused staff and damaged morale. The result was a series of catastrophic underwriting decisions and the destruction of the organization's enviable core competence which then had to be painfully and incompletely rebuilt through formal training programmes.

Why change? The adaptive organization

The normal conception of change is that it is a method of moving from one state (A) to another state (B), such as, for example, from centralized and bureaucratic to decentralized and empowered. This is the sort of approach enshrined in Lewin's notion of unfreezing (the existing order) and freezing again (the new order). However, there is another view of change, based on the learning/adaptive organization. This is the one we have pursued successfully with a number of organizations. This approach is based on the idea that competitive advantage can accrue to the organization that is good at changing, that is quicker to see the need for change, better able to see how to change and better able to implement and embed the changes. The ability to design and manage change becomes, in itself, not only a source of competitive advantage but also something that characterizes the organization as a whole.

This is similar to, but much more than, the common executive aspiration (at least at the espoused level) that the organization should become more 'flexible'. The ambition to become an adaptive or learning organization implies that the organization as a whole becomes skilful at sensing when, where and how to change.

There are certainly some examples of organizations that have tried to move in this direction. Thus, Nick Land, managing partner of Ernst & Young UK, told us he wanted the firm to move from being centralized, technical and introverted, to being customer focused, responsive, empowered and adaptive. He wanted an organization that was able and willing to change. He devised a change process to encourage the firm to move towards a more adaptive form where change would become normal. And he sensed the key issue that such a project raised – something that applies in a general way to many change programmes – that the *process* of change is as important as the *content* of change. He realized that while he wanted to encourage Ernst & Young to be more adaptive and responsive to changing needs he could not design and roll out these changes from the centre – that would be directly contrary to what he wanted to achieve. He had to design a process whereby all members of the firm were involved in forums discussing and agreeing changes, so that the medium became the message, with the normal distinction between means and ends collapsed.

One reason to change therefore is, paradoxically, in order to become better at changing. The rewards of this sort of change – towards a more flexible and organic type of organization that is able to change constantly in an adaptive way rather than relying on the occasional massive transformational change – are considerable: 'Corporations will have to learn to reformulate strategy and realign their organizations continuously if they are to survive in an increasingly turbulent environment' (Beer and Eisenstat 1996: 598).

This idea that change could be designed to improve the ability of the organization to change has some interesting implications, particularly for senior managers. It means, for example, that the role of the executive includes a responsibility to encourage and lead 'creative destruction', unsettling the organization just as it begins to settle down after change. It means that the objective of change is to improve organizational ability to change and therefore the review and analysis of the organization's change capacity becomes a major priority. And it means that senior managers must develop the ability to recognize the existence, nature and historic limitations of the organization's established ways of doing things and its characteristic ways of thinking. From these they should try to selectively retain what is still valid but drop what is now obsolete.

Although many commentators stress the importance of being able to design and manage change well, fewer recognize that this is not a natural skill of senior managers and fewer still recognize that organizations may have to change in order to be better able to change. Simply by being intelligent, committed, competent senior managers of successful organizations, senior managers are not, as a result, likely to be competent at designing and managing change.

Indeed, one could argue that the competences of running an organization and changing an organization are often at odds, so much so that the experience of running an organization is likely to encourage ways of thinking and decision making that are in many ways unhelpful when designing radical organizational change. A key reason why *actual decision-making* varies from the normative rational model (as has been found by many studies) is not because managers aren't bright enough, or that they are subject to various psychological biases and distortions, or that they have too much or too little or the wrong sort of information, (some of which – at least – may be true) but because, as Brunsson notes, managers are *less concerned with analyses and decisions than they are with action*. 'Practitioners get things done, act and induce others to act' (1982: 110). Managers make decisions to initiate action but 'there exist both decisions without actions and actions without decisions' (Brunsson 1985: 111).

Managers are concerned with getting things done; and this means that they are concerned to ensure that the necessary preconditions for successful action are in place – clarifying expectations (the expectation among the decision takers that decisions will produce the right effects); ensuring motivation among the top team, ensuring the commitment of the top team to the action. But, as Brunsson points out, ensuring clear and decisive action to which all members of the board are enthusiastically and firmly committed and in which they all believe, is achieved by decision-making processes which break the rules of rational decision making.

So, organizations – and senior teams – have two responsibilities: to decide the right thing to do and to get it done: 'the one is not better than the other, but they serve different purposes and imply different norms' (Brunsson 1985). And Brunsson suggests that these two responsibilities are different and cannot be elided and require different ways of working and different logics and rationalities. Searching for lots of alternatives, estimating consequences thoroughly, fully evaluating alternatives and final choice making (all key elements of the rational decision-making approach) when carried out thoroughly and comprehensively can damage the key components of effective action – commitment, consensus, clarity and motivation by causing delay, creating distractions, undermining consensus and destroying enthusiasm.

This may be why designing organizational change is difficult: because senior managers must find a balance between two legitimate but countervailing impetuses – logics of analysis and decision making and logics of action. Both are crucial but over-emphasizing one at the expense of the other will lead to poor decisions energetically implemented, or sensible decisions unimplemented.

Why change? Strategic capacity

Organizational success is dependent on the ability of the organization to understand the competitive forces within which it operates and to exploit opportunities and avoid vulnerabilities through its business strategy and to develop, manage and mobilize its organizational resources to support its chosen strategy. So far we have dealt largely with the second of these factors – organizational capability. However, what about the organization's ability to develop strategy in the first place?

There is a wealth of research which shows that organizations' abilities to formulate strategy can be limited: this issue was discussed and illustrated by the case examples in earlier chapters. This is the final area that might require attention. Addressing this issue is extremely delicate. However, it is often the most important issue of all.

There is a range of factors that can impact on the quality of executive strategic thinking: structures, cultures (both cognitive and normative), group factors and dynamics. The most difficult task, however, is not so much the understanding of how these factors can give rise to biases and distortions, but the crafting of interventions to help senior managers recognize problems in their own thinking and decision making. This is difficult, because such interventions are likely to spark defensiveness (as Argyris terms it, 'circling their wagons') and so it is necessary to design interventions which avoid or ameliorate this risk. Secondly, the problems are likely to be deep-seated and embedded: otherwise they would probably have been resolved earlier.

Nevertheless, because of the critical importance of the quality of senior managers' thinking and strategy formulation (and its role in determining organizational performance) any change programme must have a strategy for addressing these issues.

Understanding the different aspects of the organization which impact on levels of organizational performance is central to any change intervention and these factors supply the agenda for the diagnostic phase of any change programme. However, diagnosis alone is not enough. Changes must also be designed and implemented. Designing change is, oddly, relatively straightforward: it follows pretty directly from the identified problem. Once you know what is wrong it is often not very hard to see what needs to be done. What is hard is stopping over enthusiastic managers and consultants from designing change before they know what is really wrong. But, designing a strategy for implementation: working with the organization to identify what is wrong, what needs to be done and how to do it, is more complex.

Recognizing the various and different ways in which organizational performance can be improved is the first essential step in designing change. However, changing organizations is also inherently problematic because of the numerous paradoxes that are associated with organizational change, and we now turn to an examination of these.

Key change problems and solutions

One major difficulty is separating out the necessary analysis of the problems the organization faces – how to identify and address the various aspects of the organization that can impact on performance – from the advice, prescription and change packages on offer. Although organizations may want their change to be problem-centric rather than solution-centric, it is sometimes easier to accept an off-the-shelf package from outside experts. This is usually the less good option. In order to have effectively managed organizational change, two things are necessary: a supply of problems and a supply of solutions. The trouble is that too often the problem is defined retrospectively in terms of available solutions. Misdiagnosing the organization's problems and installing inappropriate off-the-shelf change packages may have long-term negative consequences for the business. One specific danger is that the actual problems are not surfaced and resolved. Another is that an inappropriate change package may seriously damage some of the complex subtle strengths of the organization – staff loyalty, patterns of communication and cooperation, tacit underpinning knowledge and so on.

Key change problems: organizational capacity to change

It cannot be assumed that organizations are either inherently good at designing or implementing change. Indeed, there is reason to expect that they will not be good at changing themselves. Organizations aren't designed to change, they are designed to do things; so inevitably they find change difficult. Designing and managing change requires a certain set of skills. It requires knowledge, experience, theory, the ability to reflect on organizational matters and to diagnose organizational strengths and weaknesses. There is no reason to expect managers to have these attributes; in fact there is reason to expect them *not* to have them.

As we have noted, organizations are subtle, contradictory and complex entities – designed to be highly efficient at doing things and this means that thinking and behaviour become almost unconscious and hence very speedy. However, this makes it difficult for managers to be able to rise above and think outside of these established patterns and historic ways of thinking. Organizational age and size correlate negatively with innovation and change. Radical innovation within an industry usually comes from outside the industry. 'Established companies find it hard to innovate because of structural and cultural inertia, internal politics, complacency, fear of cannibalising existing products, fear of destroying existing competences, satisfaction with the status quo, and a general lack of incentive to abandon a certain present (which is profitable) for an uncertain future' (Markides 2002: 246). Moreover, the features of an organization that need to be changed may also make the identification of these problems, and their solution, difficult even dangerous. There are many examples of this. Senior managers may be unwilling to recognize a problem if it is associated with decisions for which they are responsible.

Key change problems: symptoms and sources

What are the objectives of change? Identifying the problems which need to be resolved through organizational changes within an organization is inherently difficult. It is, in our experience, a major area where support and guidance is necessary. The real problem with designing change is not designing the change but identifying the problem the change is intended to solve.

Often the problem with designing change is separating levels of problem. Things may obviously need to be changed, their ineffectiveness is so apparent. This is easy. But is it the core problem? Possibly not. In the army they used to say 'there are no bad soldiers, just bad officers'.

Often the core problem (particularly when the problem is intractable and persistent) is not addressing the problem but addressing its persistence.

Argyris quotes a Chief Executive as saying: 'In my opinion, the best sign of an incompetent executive or organization for that matter, is one who keeps producing consequences that he or she does not intend' (Argyris 2004: 82). This points to an important truth: organizational problems that require change are often hard to surface particularly when they are associated with the senior team and thus generate 'defensive routines' (which while designed to prevent embarrassment or threat also act to forestall the organization's ability to identify the identifying and addressing the source of the embarrassment or threat). Secondly, organizational issues that need to be changed arise not out of incompetence but out of strengths and skill – hence the notion of trained incompetence. Often the real issue that requires attention particularly with persistent problems is why does the problem persist? The issue that needs to be addressed is not the issue itself but why the power system finds it so hard to address and resolve the problem. What is the process that keeps producing consequences that are neither intended nor wanted?

Many apparent problems are really just symptoms. The real problem is not the apparent problem: low morale, waste levels, poor team-work, lack of a succession plan, etc., but the existence or persistence of the problem. Why do senior managers not identify and resolve the problem? The issue lies with the (lack of) willingness and/or ability of the executive team to face and resolve such issues.

For example, in a recent project the initial presenting issue brought to us was the perceived lack of senior management training and development. It was true that there was indeed such a lack at senior levels and what little there was, was haphazard and arbitrary and the processes of selecting people for programmes were opaque, confused, subjective and distrusted. However, this problem was obvious – to us and to the managers. So why hadn't something been done about it? This turned out to be the real problem. The answer was partly that the lack of succession planning was seen as 'normal': the senior managers had to survive through the same unsystematic 'sink or swim' approach. So, it was factually and culturally normal. But, secondly, and more significantly, by not having a structured, transparent and explicit succession system, senior managers preserved their right to make arbitrary and subjective (and changing) decisions about succession. If there were no formal successors and if candidates for succession were selected by senior managers according to their preferences, this meant that a large number of middle/senior managers could see themselves as possible successors and this encouraged attitudes and behaviour towards the decision makers (for example, deference) which senior managers found agreeable and useful.

But of course this attitude was hard to justify. So it was *undiscussable*; which meant that the real source of the problem – the thing that really needed to be changed – was the thing that was most hard to change.

Another example also relates to training and development interventions. These are designed to address perceived problems of management competences. However, a more important issue is often not so much how well managers do their jobs but the nature of the jobs themselves. In many cases the issue is not skills but roles: people (and organizational units) may not be clear about their responsibilities, they may not be held clearly accountable, and accountabilities themselves may not be clear. This is especially likely to occur when delegation has occurred both between managers and their reports and between business units and head offices. This interface is the fertile ground on which ambiguous expectations allow mixed messages to flourish.

A final milieu where these problems of finding the proper focus of change occur is around senior team 'behaviour'. These are perceived frequently as problematic. The solution is often to sponsor team-working interventions (or the use of MBTI or other psychometric instruments). However, the sources of the difficulties may not (or certainly not only) lie in the dynamics of the top team or the psychometric profiles of the members. They may also arise from the style and behaviour of the leader of the team – a far more difficult problem to address since he or she is usually the project sponsor, and from the role, objectives and structure of the board. Each of these means that managing change can be highly problematical.

Key change problems: changing how we change

Identifying what needs to be changed in an organization and how runs into another paradox. Organizations tend to try to resolve their difficulties by addressing them in ways which seem sensible, tried and tested, and rational and familiar. Existing values, ways of thinking and established knowledge or theories of organization held by senior managers limit how managers think about organization and change – and indeed, if they and when they think about it. The thing that needs to be changed (culture) also affects the *possibility* of change, the *things* that are changed and the *ways* that they are changed.

So, organizations address things that need to be changed in ways which are consistent with and reflect the thing that needs to be changed. If the problem is that senior teams have trouble having frank, open and honest discussions about sensitive issues of performance – for which ultimately they are responsible – they are likely to have trouble having frank and open discussions about not being able to have frank and open discussions. Likewise, senior teams that are characterized by conflict will probably experience conflict when they try to deal with the fact they constantly generate conflict. If an organization has a tradition of centralized, top-down, bureaucratic organization and wants to move to a more delegated, decentralized, autonomous empowered structure, it will be tempted to make the move in a top-down, centralized way with manuals and centralized communications and elaborate constraints on the delegated powers – 'just to make sure that things are done properly'.

Even when senior managers have recognized a problem that requires change it is not always obvious what changes are necessary to achieve the desired change. It is tempting to attribute the source of problems to available and pervasive solutions. So, problems of manager commitment or enthusiasm are seen in terms of culture change programmes; or problems of worker performance are defined in terms of performance management. Yet in both cases the real sources of the problem may be more complex and more multifaceted.

Key change problems: changing the organization or helping it learn to change?

Helping an organization to change is like helping it to learn. Indeed, the change process is very similar to the learning process and much ineffective change is ineffective because it is the result not of learning but of imitation or of imposition. However, if change is similar to learning then this has implications for how one can help an organization change or learn. You cannot help someone learn by telling them what to do: in this case they do not learn they simply obey or imitate. Nor can you help learning by doing it for them. To help someone learn means enabling and encouraging them to make the key diagnoses and decisions, and to monitor and sometimes support and steer and warn.

But what does it mean for an organization to learn? And how can an organization be helped to learn? The external, off-the-shelf package as we have noted, risks the avoidance of real learning. Learning is of two sorts and even when change is internally driven and designed it is more likely to support one – relatively superficial – sort of learning rather than the other, more fundamental, learning. Many authorities have argued that organizations, by their very nature, suffer from learning disabilities. Drawing on our previous discussion of Argyris's rich insights, we can again note that being good at 'single loop' learning – that is, good at solving specific problems based on accepted paradigms and systems – means that the organization is less good at 'double loop' learning, which requires that these premises and paradigms are identified, assessed and changed or replaced.

According to this view, double loop learning is the most important and the most difficult. Encouraging and enabling an organization to develop the capacity to learn in this way is important. However, there is a further paradox – if double loop learning is inherently difficult but also very important, it cannot be achieved only through externally-driven or supported programmes. The capacity to think and learn in a fundamental way about what the organization is doing and how it is doing it is arguably the most important source of competitive advantage.

The same applies to supporting organizational change: the key priority should be to enhance the capacity of the organization as a whole to design and manage change. The organizational capacity for change needs to be enhanced along with the ability of the senior team to ensure constant evolutionary change (in contrast to consultant-driven, episodic, change which can perversely, engender dependency).

Conclusions

Change is increasingly a normal and necessary feature of organizations as they struggle to avoid or handle or exploit the challenges of fast moving competition and rising customer expectations. And change is the way managers respond to the recognition of the impact of paradox: that their attempts to move the organization towards a future they desire may require a new stance on the polarized choices they think they face. These efforts to change organizations (new types of structure, new ways of managing performance, new ways of thinking about and positioning the boundary of the organization, new ways of working with suppliers, customers and even competitors) are attempts of various sorts to solve or avoid the constraints of paradox and the polarities on which paradox is based.

This chapter has argued that organizational change can itself reflect and generate paradox. The attempt to modify organization to solve paradox (for example, by outsourcing activities so that any problems associated with managing the activity in house are exported to a supplier outside the organization) generates new paradoxes and reflects existing ones. In the case of outsourcing, for example, by changing the status of the relationship between the user and supplier of the service/product from an organizational relationship to a contractual one, it soon becomes clear that however well written the service level agreement and however well drafted the contract (both activities requiring time expense and skill) the new contractual relationship, by defining very precisely what is expected, invariably omits aspects of the old organizational relationship which may have been unnoticed but were also valuable – tacit patterns of communication, cooperation, collaboration and commitment to shared ends. Ultimately, contract works because of shared trust; it does not replace it. When organizational relationships of cooperation are replaced by contractual ones, tacit aspects of the original relationship which were important but overlooked could well be omitted from the formally specified relationship.

Hence, change is necessary yet most change-programmes fail. This is because not only is change inherently problematic, generating its own paradoxes and problems, as discussed in this chapter, but in many cases the underlying approach to change reflects the type of polarized thinking examined throughout this book. And so, change programmes often fail to exploit paradox because they seek to solve it by imposing one polarity at the expense of the rejected and often vilified other. If chosen organizational means (change projects) fail to achieve their designated ends and frequently produce ends which are the opposite of these desired, one reason for this may not simply be that the wrong means have been selected, but that the wrong ends have been sought.

What is the solution to this conundrum: that change is required to exploit paradox but is not required to solve it? How can change take advantage of the possibilities of paradox without exacerbating its perverse consequences?

The answer is a further paradox: to adopt an approach to the management of paradox which seeks not to solve or neutralize paradox by selecting one polarity, but to seek to achieve both, or neither; and to change towards an organization where opposites co-exist, where hybridity and ambidexterity are the *intended* outcomes. This requires a new capability, one which we encourage leadership groups to acquire for the effective exploitation of paradox. That is the subject of our next, and final, chapter.

Part 3

CONCLUSIONS

In this final Part of the book we bring the strands together and we do so with a particular regard to the needs of leaders of, and leaders in, organizations. These are the people who ultimately carry the responsibility for, and indeed are in the best position to seek, the exploitation of the power of paradox.

We suggest that, in this age of uncertainty, dilemmas and paradoxes are especially evident and prevalent. The ultimate responsibility of leadership is to make sense of these and to handle them in a competent manner. This, we argue, demands a new mode of leadership. The management of dilemma and paradox is thus the essence of leadership today.

9

Implications for leaders of organizations

In the Preface to this book we quoted the words of Chris Argyris (1999: 92):

> If paradoxes are an important phenomenon for administrators ... why is it
> that the prominent theories of administration or organization do not have
> them as a central focus? What would it require to craft theories where paradox
> has a prime role?

In the intervening chapters, we have argued that organizational paradox
should be allocated a focal role in organizational analysis. We have argued
that managers should recognize the pervasiveness and significance of organizational paradox and complexity and begin to regard them not as incidental
or accidental but as systemic and indeed integral to the dynamics of organizing. And, furthermore, they should see them not as nuisances or aberra-
tions, as errors or problems which must be resolved by decisive management
action, but as creative opportunities to be welcomed, accepted and exploited.
To follow this advice requires, of course, a new way of thinking. In particular, it means that managers must overcome ingrained and accepted ways of
thinking – mindsets which may originate in managers' needs to gain commitment to their proposals by overstressing the negatives and risks associated
with rejected polarities (and thus gaining colleagues' acceptance and commitment) but which have the damaging effect of defining organizational
problems in terms of unhelpful polarities.

In this book we have sought to theorize paradox. Our interest is not solely academic (though we believe that our academic interest in the phenomenon brings to bear relevant and valuable bodies of research and literature); our interest in paradox comes from the many times we have found ourselves closely involved in, and indeed struggling with, paradoxes as we seek to support and guide managers as they try to understand their organization's predicaments, try to solve problems of design or seek to manage change. As the previous chapter showed, in these attempts we frequently found ourselves not only exposed to paradoxes, but also involved in them. We found managers who were apparently keenly aware of the need for radical change because of performance problems, or competitive pressures or radical changes in the nature and strength of competition, but when they designed changes we found that the way they designed change, and their change plans, were in fact designed in many ways to perpetuate the status quo. We found that managers would, in all apparent sincerity, discuss their serious organizational challenges, would (possibly with our help) recognize possible solutions and the changes that were required to roles, structures and top team dynamics – and yet these changes would not be implemented.

They would become caught up in a debilitating series of obstructions and prevarications. Managers wanted to change but didn't want to change; they wanted to discuss change but they didn't want to discuss how they would have to change. They were happy to discuss key organizational problems but not the fundamental organizational problems. Hence, while they recognized that change was required they were not prepared to address how they themselves and their shared knowledge, values and roles needed to be changed.

So, the first element of our argument is that organizations generate paradoxes because of their complexity and because they are characterized by a series of fundamental oppositions or tensions. The second element of our argument is that managers in organizations tend to respond to these in ways which, paradoxically, exacerbate their effects. The key interrelated points of the book are that paradox, such as the point that purposeful action often produces unanticipated opposite effects, is integral to organizations and that managers' reactions to these paradoxes misunderstand and therefore mishandle the effects and possibilities of these paradoxes. An unsuccessful response to paradox (which inherently implies a degree of failure of previous actions) is to regard the paradox as a nuisance and therefore to try to solve or eliminate it. For example, the attempt may be made to redesign organizational structures to allow greater delegation and autonomy to strategic business units and then to find that these autonomous units cease cooperating or communicating with each other, erect barriers between themselves, lose interest in corporate activities, lose interest in cross-selling opportunities, duplicate service staff and so on. Such consequences are then regarded not only as unhelpful and undesirable but more surprisingly and revealingly, as rather unexpected.

Since paradoxes are ubiquitous and inherent in organizations, the way managers perceive, conceptualize and respond to or handle these paradoxes is crucial. Much managerial and organizational decision making proceeds, and this in itself is another paradox, as though a rational solution or 'answer' can be found. In practice, and this is the defining feature of organizational paradox, we find that one 'answer' frequently produces another problem or question or generates a reaction which is the reverse of that intended. Rather than seeing this as a frustrating failure, or denying the evidence that the initiative has produced unanticipated and undesired effects, or responding by further amplification and application of the failing policy, our suggestion is that managers reframe this situation as a set of interesting challenges which require new ways of seeing the problem and as a result new solutions.

In short, we advocate that managers respond to evidence of paradox paradoxically. They should not try to resolve paradox by linear, straightforward, conventional management thinking such as clarifying options, assessing risk and benefits, and then selecting the 'best' option, but rather, think paradoxically about the dilemmas and polarities underpinning the paradox. There are many aspects to this. One is recognize that for certain problems there are no solutions; that all solutions have benefit and disbenefits; another is to reject the pressure to choose between polarized options and to have both – to choose both, or a hybrid, and to accept that there is no ultimate solution, no perfect way of organizing a perfect business model.

Dilemmas and paradoxes, as we have seen, are ubiquitous and inherent. And yet despite this, much managerial and organizational decision making proceeds (and this in itself is another paradox) as though a rational solution or 'answer' can be found. In practice, we find that one 'answer' frequently produces another problem or question. Rather than pretend this does not occur, and instead of seeking to find the solution through the application of more and more analysis and data, the existence of dilemma and paradox can be reframed as a set of interesting challenges. There is no ultimate solution, no theory of everything which would lead to mere duplication and lack of surprise, variety and challenge. This is the optimistic aspect of living with paradox – it carries continual challenge, novelty and excitement. There is no fear of a perpetual solution.

In Chapter 1 we argued that handling paradox successfully is essentially about learning to 'reframe' issues in new ways. In the intervening chapters we have illustrated how such reframing can occur. Instead of assuming that the objective is a tidy 'solution' one might recast the challenge as a way to *exploit the simultaneity of opposites*. This is ultimately an exercise in understanding problems in new creative ways. It is an exercise in thinking and understanding. This creativity in problem solving is thus much more than an unsatisfactory compromise – i.e. a partial loss on two fronts. Instead, it is having one's cake and eating it – a partial gain on two or more fronts. Likewise, it is a more intelligent answer than erratic switching and flip flopping from one side of dilemma to another. The metaphor of the see-saw used by Charles Handy is apt – the intelligent use and enjoyment of the see-saw derives from a harmonious exploitation of its mechanisms. Likewise, in riding a bicycle there is a practiced and accomplished management of competing forces – and their utilization for achieving momentum and speed.

We also argued that the prevalence of dilemma and paradox derives from the nature of organization and is exacerbated by the accelerating rate of change and thus the diminished periods when other things appear to remain equal. This constant push for change – from customers, suppliers and competitors offering substitute services as well as novelty variants – means that equilibrium is hard to maintain. Other forces, such as almost instantaneous communications across the globe, mean that ideas and information are in constant flow – there is seemingly no stable steady state. Lack of a continuing 'fit' becomes ever more noticeable.

We now offer a brief overview of the main themes in the preceding chapters and then move on to show cross-cutting connections. We conclude with pointing up some of the key lessons for leaders of organizations. We suggested that there are six main dilemmas and paradoxes relating to strategizing, structuring, performance managing, innovating, knowledge handling and changing.

Dilemmas and paradoxes of strategy and of business models

In this summary we bring together strategizing and knowledge handling (Chapters 3 and 7). We showed the ways in which management decision making is historically based; we revealed how management thinking is affected by what managers already 'know'. We explored the knowledge and assumptions underlying strategic thinking; the essential paradox here was that senior managers, responsible for the performance and direction of a business may appear unable to respond adequately to changing circumstances – they appear to be trapped in ways of thinking and assumptions which may once have served the business well but which now are at odds with prevailing or emerging conditions. Patterns and routines become part of the accepted 'paradigm', a set of beliefs and assumptions so dominant and pervasive that it is taken for granted by those who share and operate within it.

Our examination of managers' knowledge also led to a discussion of the 'path dependency' of organizations – the ways in which embedded organizational structures, processes and ways of thinking influence the direction of organizational development or even limit the possibility of such development. 'Path dependency' is itself a dilemma and a paradox. On the positive side, a firm is protected from new entrants because the capability to benefit from a technological trajectory may be dependent on prior knowledge gained by engagement at an earlier stage of the curve; on the negative side, those insider firms benefiting from path dependency risk being so attached to the trajectory that they are less prone to the acquisition of external knowledge which lies outside that 'path'.

The templates managers use to simplify, organize and make sense of their 'business world' are the heart of many of the core dilemmas. These shorthand cuts to making an infinitely complex world graspable and comprehensible also tend to make the choices seem too categorical – that is, either in this box or that. The dilemmas thus arise from these over-determined arrangements of the apparent options.

So, what managers know may hinder their ability to learn things beyond what they know. Knowing, however well based and thorough, inevitably means not knowing: it means relegating certain areas and possibilities to beyond the frameworks and assumptions of current knowledge. For certain areas and choices to be familiar must mean others are seen as strange .The problem is as often inside as it is outside: it lies in how we see the world. This was the paradox explored in Chapter 7: that what managers know creates barriers and impossibilities; and that therefore executive success depends on their moving beyond the convictions and assumptions that they, and their senior teams, hold. The key issue facing senior managers when designing strategy and ensuring organizational capability, the two responsibilities of senior executives, is not (or not only) what problems the business faces, for these are usually reasonably obvious; nor is it how to solve these problems, for if this isn't apparent already, high quality assistance is available from consultants and advisers. The real problem particularly for persistent problems is: why is the executive group unable to solve these problems? Why is it unable to design or implement solutions? And one answer to this question, we suggested, lies in aspects of executives' knowledge and thinking: the ways they see, conceptualize, understand and know the world they face, the world (or more seriously, the worlds they face) and the worlds they construct and create.

The implication for leaders, from our analysis of business models, is that they need to pay close regard to their own frames of reference. They need to be reflective about what they know, not simply knowing what they know, not simply holding this knowledge to be true, but capable of recognizing the assumptions and limits of what they know – even recognizing that what they are convinced is true and relevant may in fact be wrong. The hagiographic and ghosted autobiographies of today's heroic leaders emphasize how charismatic leaders are characterized to an unusual degree by extraordinary levels of self conviction: they know they are right, even when the world doubts them. However, Chapters 3 and 7 suggest another possibility: that conviction, sooner or later becomes dangerous. Mobilizing others requires conviction. But this strength can easily become a weakness if leaders are not able to realize the limitations of conviction and the advantages of doubt. Furthermore, when facing disagreements from others on key issues of strategy and organization they need to be capable not simply of disagreeing with others, but of surfacing and exploring the different assumptions and knowledge which underpin these differences.

The leader who assumes, and is encouraged to assume, that his or her authority rests on omniscience is flawed: not only because omniscience is impossible in a rapidly changing world, but it is also undesirable. Partly because only by recognizing, indeed demanding, that senior colleagues too have knowledge, is the possibility of error decreased and the possibility of better quality and creative solutions improved. Also, as we suggested, knowledge can limit options as well as open them. Existing and prevailing knowledge can limit organizational development. The role of leaders therefore is to encourage reflection on, and debate about, existing assumptions and knowledge to allow for the possibility of new solutions that are not path dependent.

More than this, leaders have to attend not only to the question about what to do, and which path to take, but they also have to face the additional dilemmas of how to get it done and have it accepted and supported. And this is where the risk arises that managers may seek to gain commitment by simplifying, polarizing and over evaluating the options available. Leaders who aspire to exploit the power of paradox of course still need to construct mutual commitments, endorse proposed actions and express confidence in success, but not at the expense of a grossly simplified conception of options, not at the cost of a total rejection of alternatives in order to gain commitment to the preferred option.

We revealed the ways in which executives' conceptualizations of business models impact on the manner in which directors react to, and try to develop, strategies to meet new threats and opportunities, and the ways existing structures and arrangements may limit how executives think or act. The construction engineering consultants case (EngCon) showed how senior managers had a clear conception of the organizational arrangements necessary for their competitive success: the firm had to be able to attract recruit, develop, motivate, retain and deploy the talents and creativity of talented staff. It suggests that these managers were aware of and sought to exploit (not solve or avoid) paradox, in a number of ways. The leaders of EngCon were aware that there are ways to manage the classic paradox: the tension between the need to control and to motivate, to inspire and encourage creativity and innovation through a series of explicit organizational principles, and the need to ensure surveillance and control – through mechanisms that would not be experienced as obstructive. EngCon's executives show a pathway to develop a form of organization that not only liberates staff, but also ensures control through self-motivation and encouragement and through a variety of control mechanisms working at personal, peer, small group and organizational levels, all supported by normative and financial control.

Secondly, the executives were explicitly aware that EngCon had to be small and big simultaneously. The Chief Executive noted that innovation was closely related to organizational size and to the process and characteristics of small organizations. Since innovation was crucial, EngCon had to retain the core principles of small firms (small working groups, flat hierarchy, close and easy contact with senior management, involvement of senor management in the work, etc.), even though EngCon was growing and would grow further.

The cleaning contractors' case revealed a different set of lessons for leaders who seek to exploit the power of paradox. Here, the issue was less *how* to develop value-adding strategies and capabilities; instead, the lessons relate to a sharp realization of the difficulties that arise for firms in escaping from the historic and existing mindsets, systems, structures and competences. The crucial lesson is for leaders to begin the hard task of 'unlearning'. This means helping to relinquish and possibly renounce the existing and possibly, so far successful, business model. This will be the one to which nearly all senior members of the organization owe their success and possibly their status and identity. Leading a path away from it will often be very hard indeed – as it was in this case.

We thus agree with Brunsson's observation that managers have a tendency, when assessing options and making key choices, to exaggerate the positive qualities of the preferred option and overstate the weaknesses of the rejected option. This seems to be associated with the importance they attach to achieving commitment and reducing uncertainties. This kind of focus on gaining commitment to proposed action, in contradistinction to *decision rationality* which stresses the rather different aspects of systematic decision making, leads towards the simplifying of choices. The full range of options may be disguised and reduced in order to minimize uncertainty and gain commitment. Leaders may lean towards proposals which they believe will attract wide support. One way to dress the proposals to achieve this may be to simplify to a degree which misleads. It emphasizes the 'broad principles' rather than the detail. This may succeed initially but possibly at the cost of a sense of betrayal and disillusionment in the medium term. Such attempts to emphasize certainty and conviction in a context where the reality is replete with complexity, uncertainty and ambiguity, thus present the leader with a series of interconnected dilemmas.

Dilemmas and paradoxes of organizing

With regard to organizational design, we noted that while the 'end of bureaucracy' has been heralded many times, there appears to be evidence that successful organizations are operating with dual forms – i.e. introducing new flexible and agile features while also maintaining the stabilizing and controlling advantages of more traditional forms. Rules and procedures often became ends in themselves. These unanticipated consequences and 'dysfunctions' of bureaucracy made it the *bete noir* of the proponents of enterprise. However, the key dilemma is that organizations abandoning the planning, coordinating and direction-setting mechanisms of traditional forms of organizing also remove the stabilizing dimensions of organizational form that are at a premium during periods of uncertainty. Hence, leaders and managers have to learn to manage the tensions arising from the duality of these forms and principles. Different approaches can be compatible. An admix of the principles of hierarchy, market and trust leads to some interesting and novel forms which demonstrate the power of working with paradox.

Dilemmas and paradoxes of performance management

We noted dilemmas and paradoxes concerned with performance management. Some form of performance management is almost invariably thought to be required in every organization. However, this intent is beset with dilemmas about which of the many performance management and control devices to utilize. And these dilemmas are compounded by the paradox that such devices and interventions can result in unintended consequences and can provoke behaviour contrary to that intended.

We noted that of the various 'factors of production', the human factor is the most open ended and uncertain. While physical materials can be bought in known quantities and grades, the 'purchase' of labour power is always subject to a degree of open endedness. Effort and initiative can be withheld in numerous ways; people can be 'busy' but essentially unproductive. In order to seek to manage performance various control devices have been deployed over many years. Direct control using an 'overseer' is one of the more basic methods. But, it can lead to resentment and conflict and it is also costly.

Hence, various 'indirect' methods have been used such as payment for performance. If people are paid purely by the hour – or any other unit of time – the employer may fear that insufficient effort will be offered. If, on the other hand, payment is by the piece, the employer may fear that quality will be compromised as the employee seeks to maximize pay by turning out large quantities irrespective of quality. To overcome this tendency, regimes of inspection were introduced. But again, inspectors are essentially unproductive and so these labour inspection regimes have their own unforeseen and unintended consequences.

Multiple forms of performance management may be used in combination. It will be recalled how the car substitute vehicle scheme worked with a performance management mix of direct supervision from team leaders and payment by results for the staff members initiating the phone calls. The consequence of this regime was high labour turnover. Business models dependent on more enduring and committed forms of work input might find this approach counterproductive. Approaches to performance management that ignore its essentially paradoxical nature – for example, that employees have to be directed and controlled and monitored and motivated to behave in ways that cannot be fully specified, run the risks described by Edward Deming. He asked: 'What do targets accomplish? Nothing? Wrong: their accomplishment is negative. Management by numerical goal is an attempt to manage without knowledge of what to do. This is what makes it so attractive to bad managers' (1986: 44). This is one problem. However, there is a converse: managerial over specification of how jobs are to be done runs the risk of both de-motivating and of missing more creative solutions.

Dilemmas of innovation

We noted that would-be innovators in senior management positions face a number of dilemmas. First, there was Christensen's now classic dilemma that the much vaunted adage that it is necessary to 'listen to customers', can be fatally misleading. Consistently, when asked about their preferences for future developments, established customers would report that they wanted cheaper and upgraded versions of existing products or existing products with minor improvements. Meanwhile, new entrants would be undercutting the lead product with novel products that established customers would initially deny they sought. Yet, ignoring customers' expressed wishes and resorting to an insular approach can be equally dangerous.

A second dilemma for innovators is that radical innovation can be especially difficult for established firms to achieve. While incremental innovation reinforces the nature and dominance of existing organizational arrangements and competences, radical innovation normally challenges these. It undermines the established pattern of strengths and routines. Established firms enjoy many advantages – they have resources, a customer base, a distribution network, a supply chain and so on. However, by the same token, radical innovation threatens all of this because it usually involves new ways of thinking and acting which are outside of the established channels. Moreover, it requires competences and processes which are radical departures from existing organizational arrangements. We noted how such firms fail 'because they cannot play two games at once'.

One of the most pervasive and constantly recurring of managerial dilemmas is whether to seek a market or an organizational solution to a problem or opportunity: for example, whether to outsource or insource an activity or service. An important answer to this question in recent times has been to seek collaborative and partnership arrangements which seem to offer a way to preserve elements of both without opting entirely for one or the other. These partnerships may take various forms such as joint ventures, strategic alliances and inter-organizational networks. These forms of solution appear to offer a means to pursue innovation while continuing to maintain the core business; we noted the tension between these two at various points in the book. Collaboration in these various modes can reduce the risk inevitably associated with innovation by distributing it. Moreover, it can help surmount the competence limitations of an organization by the addition of other complementary competences.

Drawing on our research across a large number of organizations which had declared a 'commitment' to innovation we showed how, in practice, we found perceptions about the role of innovation to be *patterned*. In other words, within particular organizations we uncovered a predominating language and logic which carries the coded signals and the accepted stance towards innovation. This had a powerful influence on behaviour irrespective of 'official' pronouncements. It influenced the allocation of resources and the extent to which innovation is allocated to a select few or is regarded as a diffused responsibility. Competing perceptions determined whether information and forward plans were kept secret or were shared across organizational boundaries and thus they influence the degree of collaboration with suppliers, customers and competitors. A practical implication therefore for leaders who are serious about innovation is to recognize the pervasive influence of such cognitive boundaries. Only when this is done can the search for possible alternatives be commenced.

Leaders are also advised to take special note of the finding that the organizations capable of sustained innovation exploited the ability and willingness of managers to engage in open and honest debate. Conversely, the organizations less effective in innovating tended to discourage and even stifle such debate. The healthy, open discussion included dialogue about how their organization defined, valued and managed innovation. This in itself was an important step towards improving innovation performance.

Clarification of understanding about the nature of innovation in a particular organization can also help in the strategy formulation process. Leaders can debate their current, compared with their desired, exposure to new markets, new customers and new technologies. And there can be discussion and therefore analysis about the varied risks and competency requirements associated with these. Innovation ultimately results from managerial perceptions of the need for change, the perception of the opportunity to change and the perceptions about the way to change. Perceptions, beliefs and assumptions are thus vital aspects to be understood.

Leadership groups can usefully promote ways to ensure that perceptions and beliefs about innovation are clarified, made explicit and made subject to debate and challenge. This open discussion would also purposively explore and map the range of views and perceptions that are characteristic and prevalent within the organization.

The paradoxes of change

In Chapter 8 we noted that the processes of organizational change are not only inherently paradoxical in that they are subject to their own complexities and possibilities of unanticipated and undesired effects (one of which was that although there is a great deal of change much of it produces little fundamental change and may even be designed to preserve the status quo), but also that while organizational change is often seen as a necessary response to paradox, it may also perpetuate or even exacerbate paradox. One reason for this is that managers, in order to generate commitment and enthusiasm, may exaggerate and simplify the available options (ruling one in and ruling the rejected one out) and thus perpetuate the very form of analysis that underpins the situation they are trying to change from. The effective response to paradox is indeed to design change. However, the type of change and the approach to change will need to be modified in line with the suggestions proposed in this book – to embrace, not to resolve, paradox.

Cross-cutting applications and a summary of lessons for leaders

Although we have summarized the key points in topic form above, the themes, in practice, interrelate. The management of innovation has been one major theme and we devoted a chapter to it in its own right. But in addition, it is inextricably linked with the major themes found in the other chapters. For instance, we regard innovation as an intellectual, cognitive process. Accordingly, the way in which managers approach their business strategy, and their model of business, influences crucially their orientations to innovation. We reported on our different research projects which bear on this theme in the chapters on strategy, innovation, organizing and knowledge. The influence is two-way. Managers' cognitions, we tried to show, shape choices made about types of organizational form. Conversely, aspects of organization in turn encourage or discourage innovation. They do this by influencing how managers and leaders think, and what they are induced to think about.

Similarly, the dilemmas concerning performance management were also found to have their roots in underlying assumptions about how business organizations work. Traditional thinking was based on the engineering of incentive and disincentive systems that were designed to promote efficiency and profitability by appealing to workers' self interest. This meant rewarding, or disciplining, workers based on an essentially economics-based notion of behaviour. However, an alternative set of assumptions based in psychology, sociology and political science stresses instead the importance of managerial leadership and cooperation among employees.

We also noted a close association between the issue of managerial approaches to innovation and the strategic thinking related to the problem of 'strategic persistence' in mature firms (Lant and Milliken 1992). Persistence with a strategy is, we tried to demonstrate, ultimately a product of managerial interpretations.

A related issue is the frequently perceived conflict between three activities: work, learning and innovation. Drawing on the work of Seely Brown and Duguid, we went in active search of the interplay and interdependence between work, learning and innovation. By focusing on practice it can be shown how learning forms a bridge between 'working' and 'innovating'. Communities of practice can be important loci of practical activity which combines elements of all three. Another lesson for leaders of organizations and leaders in organizations is to seek out opportunities to promote such communities or the conditions under which they can emerge and flourish. But, this has to be done in subtle ways. We noted that organizations usually depend upon significant amounts of informal activity. Paradoxically, normal 'organizational' interventions serve to restrict activity to pre-given frames. These tend to restrict and even stifle the value of much informal work or at best drive it underground. Thus, as Brown and Duguid have also found, these often very valuable forms of knowledge and practice become even less visible to the organization as a whole. As a result, subsequent reorganizations and/ or official changes to practice are likely to 'disrupt what they do not notice'. Thus, the gap between espoused and actual practice may then become simply too large for the informal organization to bridge. Dysfunctionality is likely to result from this vicious circle of control and reaction. The lesson for leaders here is that, in certain circumstances at least, they should consider reframing their view of organization not as a pyramid but, in order to tap into that healthy combination of working, learning and innovating, to reimagine their enterprises as a 'community of communities'.

Our research revealed and illustrated that organizational arrangements across each segment of business – strategy, performance management, innovation and so on – the sources of strength in some circumstances can be sources of restraint in others. Operating efficiencies once achieved can serve to act as constraints when a significant shift of strategy requires radically new structures and processes. These are the essential dilemmas and paradoxes of business models. We agree with Stacey (2000) who observed that:

> The idea that paradoxes must be solved and the tension they cause must be
> released to be successful is part of the paradigm that equates success with the

dynamics of stability, regularity and predictability. The notion that paradoxes can never be resolved only endlessly rearranged, leads to a view of organizational dynamics couched in terms of continuing tension generating behaviour patterns that are irregular, unstable and unpredictable, but lead to creative novelty.

The overall lesson for leaders is that they can benefit from an overall realization of the nature of paradox and synthesis that extends across all of these areas. Synthesis can be thought of as the conscious and deliberate utilization of opposites. It is different from compromise in that it seeks to exploit the strengths of each pole whereas compromise suggests sacrificing some of the strengths of each.

If top teams want to improve their decision making, then, rather than spend inordinate amounts of time on psychological profiling and team building, they might try to focus more on the techniques of effective decision making. These include clarifying desired outcomes (not accepting broad labels such as 'growth' as a sufficient guide as such loose terminology can lead to artificial disputes); providing a range of options which go beyond 'accept or reject' options; clarifying the pros and cons of different alternatives; and during the discussion seek to construct 'new' options which preserve some of the best elements of some of the already discussed options (Frisch 2008).

'Management' is, in essence, the art of practical *action*. This means the wider global and national forces have to be transmuted in local contexts. As a result, the principles which made sense in the abstract become complicated and contradictory when implemented alongside other principled choices. Managerial knowledge is developed through action, trial and error and experience. It develops through and requires simultaneity of learning and acting; it is a situated practice. However, too much reliance on the apparent self-evident 'commonsense' of this practical learning can deflect managers and leaders from a realization that the emergent patterns of thought and the learned and half-learned applications of management theory disguise a whole set of underlying constructs and cognitions. One of our purposes in writing this book was to draw together multiple research projects conducted over many years in order to open up an awareness of the diversity of cognitive models and practical options. However, the former can often impede access to the latter – as we have shown in many parts of the book with case examples.

Finally, we have also tried to show how exploiting paradox can be, and surely is, a *leadership* opportunity and duty. This book ultimately is not simply or solely about paradox: it is about leadership, and its stance on leadership is that complex paradoxical entities such as organizations, especially when operating in times of such dynamic change, require a new form of leadership – leaders who reject the claims of traditional 'heroic' leadership (omniscient, passionate, conviction-driven, total certainty) and replace these with the recognition of the need for doubt, balance, ambivalence, ambiguity and recombination of ideas. The paradoxical nature of managing business and organizations can be an exciting, challenging and liberating experience. But it needs a new form of leadership. If leaders are to embrace and exploit paradox they must begin to behave paradoxically themselves. For many leaders this would require a radical break with established behaviour and prevailing conceptions of leadership.

The conventional image of the leader describes a person full of conviction and optimism about what to do and how to do it, a person who, having chosen the way forward is full of confidence about the direction chosen, a person who requires total commitment to the direction and organizational purpose, a person for whom a paradox would be a negative indication – a sign of a failure, of ineffectiveness, of unclear and improper leadership. But, *leaders who exploit paradox* temper conviction with doubt, they temper commitment with hesitation; their conviction is qualified by recognition of other possibilities – including the recognition that all strategies have strengths and weaknesses; they accept that all strategies ultimately fail – often because of the very nature which originally made them successful.

These leaders recognize the power of paradox and see their role not as defending their existing arrangements (which they had probably helped design) but as seeking to destroy or challenge the very status quo they had constructed. They see that all models of organizations – including those that are so pervasive and powerful that they pass for received truth in any chosen period – fail to do justice to the complexity of organizations, and they recognize the inadequacy of any model of organization as a source of organizational description or prescription. The paradoxically-intelligent leader manages to balance generating commitment with allowing and valuing doubt; seeks to solve problems by questioning conceptions of the problem; and is most anxious when others begin to be most satisfied. As one manager in our innovation project commented: the secret of the management of innovation is to seek a balance between the opposed forces of the organic and mechanistic approaches to organization – exploitation and efficiency and exploration and innovation, but never *to be satisfied that this balance has been achieved!* The secret here is residual doubt and dissatisfaction. The opposite, one might think, of conviction leadership. There is no final answer to the many tensions of organizing noted throughout this book but finding appropriate ways to combine elements of each in a judicious way is a skill which can be developed.

We suggest that, in this age of uncertainty, dilemmas and paradoxes are especially evident and prevalent. The ultimate responsibility of leadership is to make sense of these and to handle them in a competent manner. This, we argue, demands a new mode of leadership. The management of dilemma and paradox is thus the essence of leadership today.

As Quinn (1988: 88) observes:

> Just as organizations are usually not without tensions neither are managers. There are no clear maps for problem detection or solution. Many diverse kinds of behaviors are expected and these are, at a minimum, distant, at a maximum competing ... [an insightful framework] allows for the dynamic tensions that can sometimes be at the heart of managerial life. It allows for the fact that behaviours may change. A manager may engage in a set of behaviours reflecting one set of values at one point and in an entirely different set of values at another point.

The ultimate power of paradox derives from its liberating potential. While it draws attention to what might be seen as a negative message that no 'solution' is sustainable, its optimistic side is energizing: new opportunities of a surprising kind are possible when paradox is accepted and its potential realized.

References

Preface

Argyris, C. (1999). *On Organizational Learning*. Oxford: Blackwell.

Handy, C. (1994). *The Age of Paradox*. Boston, MA: Harvard Business School Press.

Thompson, M.P. (1988). 'Being, thought and action', in R.E. Quinn and J.P. Campbell (eds), *Paradox and Transformation*. Cambridge, Mass., Ballinger.

Chapter 1

Abernathy, W. (1978). *The Productivity Dilemma*. Baltimore: John Hopkins University Press.

Anand, B. (2008). 'The value of a broader product portfolio', *Harvard Business Review* January: 20–1.

Bouchikhi, H. (1998). 'Living with and building on complexity: a constructivist perspective on organizations', *Organization* 5(2): 217–32.

Brunsson, N. (1985). *The Irrational Organization: Irrationality as a Basis for Action and Change*. Chichester/New York: John Wiley & Sons, Ltd.

Child, J. and Faulkner, D. (1998). *Strategies of Cooperation*. Oxford: Oxford University Press.

Clegg, S.R. and Vieira da Cunha and Pina, M. (2002). 'Management paradoxes: a relational view', *Human Relations* 55(5): 483–503.

De Wit, R. and Meyer, R. (1999). *Strategy Synthesis: resolving Strategy Paradoxes to Create Competitive Advantage*. London: International Thomson.

Eisenstat, R.A. (2008). 'The Uncompromising Leader', *Harvard Business Review* July–August.

Liker, J. and Hoseus, M. (2008). *Toyota Culture*. New York: McGraw-Hill.

Leonard-Barton, D. (1992). 'Core capabilities and core rigidities: a paradox in managing new product development', *Strategic Management Journal* 13: 111–26.

MacDuffie, J.P. (2008). 'Disciplined processes and innovation at Toyota', Academy of Management, Anaheim, Los Angeles.

March, J.G. and Olsen, J.P. (1976). *Ambiguity and Choice in Organizations*. Oslo: Universitetsforlaget.

Moyer, D. (2008). 'Strategy paradox', *Harvard Business Review* June: 144.

Osono, E., Shimizu, N., *et al.* (2008). *Extreme Toyota: Radical Contradictions That Drive Success at the World's Best Manufacturer*. New York: John Wiley & Sons, Inc.

Prahalad, C.K. and Krishnan, M.S. (2008). *The New Age of Innovation: Driving Co-Created Value Through Global Networks*. New York: McGraw-Hill.

Quinn, R.E. (1988). *Beyond Rational Management: Mastering the Paradoxes and Competing Demands of High Performance*. San Francisco: Jossey-Bass.

Raynor, M.E. (2007). *The Strategy Paradox: Why Committing to Success Leads to Failure (And What To Do About IT)*. New York: Currency.

Senge, P. (2007). *The Fifth Discipline: The Art and Practice of the Learning Organization*. New York: Doubleday.

Wasserman, N. (2008). 'The founder's dilemma', *Harvard Business Review* **86**(2): 102–9.

Chapter 2

Argyris, C. (1999). *On Organizational Learning*. Oxford: Blackwell.

Ashkenas, R., Ulrich, D., Jick, T. and Kerr, S. (1995). *The Boundaryless Organization*. San Francisco: Jossey-Bass.

Bartunek, J.M. (1988). 'The dynamics of reframing', in K.S. Cameron and R.E. Quinn, *Paradox and Transformation: Toward a Theory of Change in Organizations and Management*. Cambridge, Mass.: Ballinger.

Beardsley, S., Johnson, B., *et al.* (2006). 'Competitive advantage from better interactions', *McKinsey Quarterly* 2: 52–63.

Benner, M.J. and Tushman, M. (2003). 'Exploitation, exploration and process management: The productivity dilemma revisited', *Academy of Management Review* 28(2): 238–56.

Brown, S.L. and Eisenhardt, K.M. (1998). *Competing on the Edge: Strategy as Structured Chaos*. Boston: Harvard Business School Press.

Cameron, K.S. and Quinn, R.E. (1988). 'Organizational paradox and transformation', in R.E Quinn and K.S. Cameron (eds), *Paradox and Transformation: Toward a Theory of Change in Organizations and Management*. Cambridge, Mass.: Ballinger.

Child, J. and McGrath, R.G. (2001). 'Organizations unfettered: organizational form in an information intensive economy', *Academy of Management Journal* 44: 1135–48.

Critchley, B. and Casey, D. (1989). 'Organizations Get Stuck Too', *Leadership and Organization Development Journal*, 10(4).

De Vries, K. (1995). *Organizatioal Paradoxes: Clinical Approaches to Management*. London: Routledge.

Eisenhardt, K. and Martin, J. (2000). 'Dynamic capabilties: what are they?' *Strategic Management Journal* 21: 1105–21.

Eisenhardt, K.M. (2000). 'Paradox, spirals, ambivalence: the new language of change and pluralism', *Academy of Management Review* 25(4): 703–5.

Eisenhardt, K.M. and Westcott, B.J. (1988). 'Paradoxical demands and the creation of excellence: The case of Just-in-Time Manufacturing', in R.E. Quinn and K.S Cameron (eds), *Paradox and Transformation: Toward a Theory of Change in Organizations and Management*. Cambridge, Mass.: Ballinger.

Evans, P. and Doz, Y. (1992). 'Dualities: a paradigm for human resource and organizational development in complex multinationals', in V. Pucik, Tichy, N. and Barnett, C., *Globalizing*

Management: Creating and Leading the Competitive Organization. New York: John Wiley & Sons, Inc.

Evans, P., Pucik, V., *et al.* (2002). *The Global Challenge: Frameworks for International Human Resource Management.* New York: McGraw-Hill / Irwin.

Ford, J.D. and Backoff, R.W. (1988). 'Organizational change in and out of dualities and paradox', in R.E. Quinn and K.S. Cameron (eds), *Paradox and Transformation: Toward a Theory of Change in Organizations and Management.* Cambridge, Mass.: Ballinger.

Galunic, D.C. and Eisenhardt, K.M. (2001). 'Architectural innovation and modular corporate forms', *Academy of Management Journal* **44**: 1229–49.

Graetz, F. and Smith. A.C.T. (2007). 'The role of dualities in arbitrating continuity and change in forms of organizing', *International Journal of Management Reviews* **9**(4): 1–16.

Gupta, A.K., Smith, K.G., *et al.* (2006). 'The interplay between exploration and exploitation', *Academy of Management Journal* **49**(4): 693–706.

Hampden-Turner, C. (1990a). *Charting the Corporate Mind: From Dilemma to Strategy.* Oxford: Blackwell.

Hampden-Turner, C. (1990b). *Corporate Culture: From Vicious to Virtuous Circles.* London: Economist Books.

Hedburg, B.L.T., Nystrom, P.C. and Starbuck, W. (1976). Camping on seesaws: prescripions for a self-desgning organization', *Administrative Sceince Quarterly* **21**: 41–65.

Kimberley, J.R. (1988). 'Reframing and organizational change', in R.E. Quinn and K.S. Cameron (eds), *Paradox and Transformation: Toward a Theory of Change in Organizations and Management.* Cambridge, Mass.: Ballinger.

Lewis, M.W. (2000). 'Exploring paradox: Toward a more comprehensive guide', *Academy of Management Review* **25**(4): 760–76.

Miller, G.L. (1992). *Managerial Dilemmas: The Political Economy of Hierarchy.* Cambridge, Mass.: Cambridge University Press.

Murninghan, J.K. and Conlon, D.E. (1991). 'The dynamics of intense work groups: A study of British string quartets', *Administrative Science Quarterly* **36**: 165–86.

O'Reilly, C.A. and Tushman, M.L. (2004). 'The ambidextrous organization', *Harvard Business Review* April: 74–81.

Orlikowski, W.J. (1996). 'Improvising organizational transformation over time: A situated change perspective', *Information Systems Research* **7**: 63–92.

Palmer, I., Benveniste, J., *et al.* (2007). 'New organizational forms: towards a generative dialogue', *Organization Studies* **28**(12): 1829–47.

Pascale, R. (1991). *Managing on the Edge.* Harmondsworth: Penguin.

Pettigrew, A.M. and Fenton, E.M. (2000). '*Complexities and dualities in innovative forms of organizing*', in A.M. Pettigrew and E.M. Fenton, *The Innovating Organization.* London: Sage.

Quinn, R.E. (1988). *Beyond Rational Management: Mastering the Paradoxes and Competing Demands of High Performance.* San Francisco: Jossey-Bass.

Sterman, J.D., Repenenning, N.P., *et al.* (1997). 'Unanticiapted side-effects of successful quality programs: Exploring a paradox of of organizational improvement', *Management Science* **43**: 503–21.

Teece, D.J., Pisano, G., *et al.* (1997). 'Dynamic capabilities and strategic management', *Strategic Management Journal* **18**(7): 509–33.

Van de Ven, A.H. and Poole, S.M. (1988) 'Paradoxical requirements for a theory of social change' , in R.E Quinn and K.S. Cameron (eds), *Paradox and Transformation: Toward a Theory of Change in Organizations and Management,* Cambridge, Mass.: Ballinger.

Vince, R. and Broussine, M. (1996). Paradox, defense and attachment: accessing and working with emotions and relations underlying organizational change', *Organization Studies* **17**: 1–21.

Chapter 3

Argyris, C. (1999). On Organizational Learning. Oxford: Blackwell.
Brunsson, N. (1985). The Irrational Organization: Irrationality as a Basis for Action and Change. Chichester/New York, John Wiley & Sons, Ltd/Inc.
Brunsson, N. and Olsen, J.P. (2002). The Reforming Organization. London: Routledge.
Du Gay, P. (2003). 'The tyranny of the epochal: change, epochalism and organizational reform', Organization 10: 663–84.
March, J.G. (1991). 'Exploration and exploitation in organizational learning', Organization Science 2(1): 71–87.
Wilensky, H.L. (1967) Organizational Intelligence, New York: Basic Books.

Chapter 4

Adler, P. (2001). 'Markets, hierarchy and trust: the knowledge economy and the future of capitalism', Organization Science 12(2): 215–34.
Adler, P. (2003). 'Making the HR outsourcing decision', MIT Sloan Management Review Fall: 53–60.
Ashkenas, R., Ulrich, D., Jick, T. and Kerr, S. (1995). The Boundaryless Organization, San Francisco: Jossey-Bass.
Bourdieu, P. (1977). Outline of a Theory of Practice. Cambridge: Cambridge University Press.
Bourdieu, P. (1990). The Logic of Practice. Cambridge: Polity Press.
Child, J. (2005). Organization: Contemporary Principles and Practice. Chichester: John Wiley & Sons, Ltd.
Clegg, S. (1990). Modern Organzations: Organization Studies in a Postmodern World. London: Sage.
Courpasson, D. (2000). 'Managerial strategies of domination: power in soft bureaucracies', Organization Studies 21(1): 141–62.
Davidow, W.H. and Malone, M.S. (1992). The Virtual Corporation: Structuring and Revitalizing the Corporation for the 21st Century. New York.: Harper Business.
Dunford, R., Palmer, I., Benveniste, J. and Crawford, J. (2007) 'Co-existence of "old" and "new" organizational practices: Transitory phenomena or enduring feature?' Asia Pacific Journal of Human Resources 45: 24–43.
Edwards, R. (1979). Contested Terrain: The Transformation of the Workplace in the Twentieth Century. London: Heinemann.
Elfring, T.H.W. (2007). 'Networking by entrepreneurs: patterns of tie-formation in emerging organizations', Organization Studies 28(12): 1849–72.
Galbraith, J.R. (2002). 'Organizing to deliver solutions', Organizational Dynamics 31(2): 194–207.
Gouldner, A. (1954). Patterns of Industrial Bureaucracy. New York: The Free Press.
Graetz, F. and Smith, A.C.T. (2007). 'The role of dualities in arbitrating continuity and change in forms of organizing', International Journal of Management Reviews 9(4): 1–16.
Hamel, G. and Prahalad, C.K. (1992) Competing for the Future. Boston: Harvard Business School Press.

Hammer, M. (1996). *Beyond Reengineering*. London: Harper-Collins.

Hammer, M. and Champy, J. (1992). *Reengineering the Corporation*. London: Harper-Collins.

Improvement & Development Agency (2008). *Think Family, Think Commuity: The Role of Directors with Joint Responsibilities for Children's and Adult Services*. London: Improvement & Develoment Agency.

Kirkman, B.L. and Rosen, B. (2004). 'The impact of team empowerment on virtual team performance: The moderatig role of face to face interaction', *Academy of Management Journal* 47(2): 175–92.

Littler, C.R. and Innes, P. (2004). 'The paradox of managerial downsizing', *Organisation Studies* 25(7): 1159–84.

MacCormack, A. and Forbath, T. (2008). 'Learning the fine art of global collaboration', *Harvard Business Review* 86(1).

March, J.G. and Simon, H.A. (1958). *Organizations*. New York: John Wiley & Sons, Inc.

McNulty, T. and Ferlie, E. (2002). *Re-engineering Healthcare: The Complexities of Organizational Transformation*. Oxford: Oxford University Press.

Merton, R. (1957). *Social Theory and Social Structure*. Chicago: Free Press.

Nonaka, I. and Takeuchi, H. (1995) *The Knowledge-Creating Company: How Japanese Companies Create the Dynamics of Innovation*. Oxford: Oxford University Press.

O'Reilly, C.A. and Tushman, M.L. (2004). 'The ambidextrous organization', *Harvard Business Review* April: 74–81.

Palmer, I., Benveniste, J., *et al.* (2007). 'New organizational forms: towards a generative dialogue', *Organization Studies* 28(12): 1829–47.

Palmer, I. and Dunford, R. (2002) 'Out with the old and in with the new? The relationship between traditional and new organizational practices' *International Journal of Organizational Analysis* 10: 209–25.

Pascale, R. (1991). *Managing on the Edge*. Harmondsworth: Penguin.

Pascale, R.T. (1999). 'Surfing the edge of chaos', *Sloan Management Review*: 83–94.

Quinn, J.B. (1992) *Intelligent Enterprise*. New York: Free Press.

Reagons, R. and McEvily, A. (2003). 'Network structure and knowledge transfer: the effects of cohesion and range', *Administrative Sceince Quarterly* 48: 240–67.

Reed, M. (1999). 'From the iron cage to the gaze? The Dynamics of organizational control in late modernity', *Regulation in Organizations*. G. Morgan and L. Engwall. London: Routledge.

Schilling, M. and Steensma, H.K. (2001). 'The use of modular organizational forms: an industry level analysis', *Academy of Management Journal* 44: 1149–68.

Selznick, P. (1966). *TVA and the Grass Roots*. Berkerley: University of California Press.

Senge, P. (2007) *The Fifth Discipline: The Art and Practice of the Learning Organization*. New York: Doubleday.

Snow, C. and Miles, R. (1992). 'Managing 21st century network organizations', *Organizational Dynamics* 20: 5–20.

Stinchcombe, A. (1986). 'Contracts as hierarchical documents', *Organizational Theory and Project Management*. Stinchcombe, A., Heimer, C. Oslo: Norwegian University Press.

Storey, J. (2002). 'What are the general manager issues in supply chain management?' *Journal of General Management* 27(4): 65–79.

Storey, J. and Salaman, G. (2005). *Managers of Innovation: Insights into Making Innovation Happen*. Oxford: Blackwell.

Wenger, E. (1998). *Communities of Practice*. Cambridge: Cambridge University Press.

Chapter 5

Alchian, A. and Demsetz, H. (1972) 'Production, information costs, and economic organization. *American Economic Review* **62**: 777–95.

Argyris, C. (1952). *The Impact of Budgets on People*. Ithaca, NY: School of Business & Public Administration, Cornell University.

Baird, I., Post, J., et al. (1990). *Management: Functions and Responsibility*. New York: Harper & Row.

Barnard, C. (1937). *The Functions of the Executive*. Cambridge, Mass.: Harvard University Press.

Barney, G. (1992). *The Management of Organizations*. Boston: Houghton Mifflin.

Burns, T. and Stalker, G.M. (1968). *The Management of Innovation*. London: Tavistock.

Child, J. (1977). *Organization: A Guide to Problems and Practice*. London: Harper & Row.

Clegg, S. (1990). *Modern Organzations: Organization Studies in a Postmodern World*. London: Sage.

Edwards, R. (1979). *Contested Terrain: The Transformation of the Workplace in the Twentieth Century*. London: Heinemann.

Eisenhardt, K.M. and Westcott, B.J. (1988). 'Paradoxical demands and the creation of excellence: The case of Just-in-Time Manufacturing', in R.E. Quinn and K.S Cameron (eds), *Paradox and Transformation: Toward a Theory of Change in Organizations and Management*. Cambridge, Mass.: Ballinger.

Fayol, H. (1916). *General and Industrial Management*. New York: Pitman.

Fox, A. (1966). 'Managerial ideology and industrial relations', *British Journal of Industrial Relations* **4**.

Harvey, D. (1989). *The Condition of Postmodernity*. Oxford: Blackwell.

Hayek, F. (1948). *Individualism and Economic Order*. Chicago: University of Chicago Press.

Hofstede, G. (1968). *The Game of Budget Control*. London: Tavistock.

Johnson, P. and Gill, J. (1993). *Management Control and Organizational Behaviour*. London: Paul Chapman.

Katz, D.R. (1978). *The Big Store: Inside the Crisis and Revolution at Sears*. New York: Penguin Books.

Kinnie, N., Purcell, J. and Hutchinson, S. (2000). '"Fun and surveillance": the paradox of high commitment management in call centres', *International Journal of Human Resource Management* **11**(5): 967–85.

Knights, D. and McCabe, D. (1998). What happens when the phone goes wild? Staff, stress and spaces for escape in a BPR telephone banking work regime', *Journal of Management Studies* **35**(2): 163–94.

Koontz, H. and Weirich, H. (1988). *Management* (9th edn) Singapore: McGraw-Hill.

Korczynski, M. (2001). 'The contradictions of service work: call centre as customer-oriented bureaucracy', in A. Sturdy, I. Grugulis and H. Wilmott (eds), *Customer Service: Empowerment and Entrapment.*, London: Palgrave: 79–102.

Lawler, E.E. (1987). 'Pay for performance: a motivational analysis', in H.G. Nalbantian, *Incentives, Cooperation and Risk Sharing*. Totowa, N.J: Rowman & Littlefield.

Miller, G.L. (1992). *Managerial Dilemmas: The Political Economy of Hierarchy*. Cambridge, Mass.: Cambridge University Press.

Piore, M. and Sabel, C. (1984). *The Second Industrial Divide*. New York: Basic Books.

Robbins, S.P. (1988). *Management: Concepts and Applications*. Englewood Cliffs, NJ: Prentice Hall.

Smith, A. (1976). *An Inquiry into the the Nature and Causes of the Wealth of Nations* (first pub. 1776). Chicago: Benton.

Storey, J., Edwards, P.K. and Sisson, K. (1997). *Managers in the Making*. London: Sage.
Tannenbaum, A.S. (1962). 'Control in organizations: individual adjustments and organizational performance', *Administrative Science Quarterly* 2: 236–57.

Chapter 6

Argyris, C. (1985). *Strategy, Change and Defensive Routines*. Marshfield, MA: Pitman.
Brown, J.S. and Duguid, P. (1992). 'Organizational learning and communities-of-practice: towards a unified view of working, learning and innovation', *Organizational Science* 2: 40–57.
Christensen, C. (1997). *The Innovators Dilemma*. Boston: Mass: Harvard Business School Press.
Cohen, W.M. and Levinthal, D. (1990). 'Absorptive capacity: a new perspective on learning and innovation', *Administrative Science Quarterly* 35: 128–52.
Cummings, L. (1965). 'Organizational climates for creativity', *Academy of Management Journal* 8: 220–7.
Dougherty, D. (1992). 'A practice-centered model of organizational renewal through product innovation', *Strategic Management Journal* 13: 77–92.
Dougherty, D. (1994). 'The illegitimacy of successful product innovation in established firms', *Organization Science* 5: 200–18.
Dougherty, D. (1996). 'Organizing for innovation', in S. Clegg, C. Hardy and W.R. Nord, *Handbook of Organization Studies*. London: Sage: 424-439.
Freeman, C. and L. Soete (1997). *The Economics of Industrial Innovation* (3rd edn). London: Pinter.
Hage, J. and Dewar, R. (1973). 'Elite values versus organizational structure in predicting innovation', *Administrative Science Quarterly* 18: 279–90.
Henderson, R.M. and Clark, K. (1990). 'Architectural innovation: the reconfiguration of existing product technologies and the failure of established firms', *Administrative Science Quarterly* 35: 9–30.
Kanter, R.M. (1983). *The Changemasters: Corporate Entrepreneurs at Work*. New York: Routledge.
Kimberley, J.R. and Evanisko, M. (1981). 'Organizational innovation: the influence of individual, organizational and contextual factors on hospital; adoption of technological and administrative innovations', *Academy of Management Journal* 24: 689–713.
Lant, T. K. (2002). 'Organizational cognition and interpretation', in J.A.C. Baum (ed.), *The Blackwell Companion to Organizations*, Oxford: Blackwell: 344–62.
Lant, T.K. and Milliken, F.J. (1992). 'The role of managerial learning and interpretation in strategic persistence and reorientation: an empirical exploration', *Strategic Management Journal* 13(8): 585–608.
Lefebvre, L., Mason, R., *et al.* (1997). 'The influence prism in SMEs: the power of CEOs' perceptions of technology policy and its organizational impacts', *Management Science* 43(6): 856–78.
Leonard-Barton, D. (1992). 'Core capabilities and core rigidities: a paradox in managing new product development', *Strategic Management Journal* 13: 111–26.
March, J.G. (1991). 'Exploration and exploitation in organisational learning', *Organisation Science* 2(1): 71–87.
Markides, C. (2002). 'Strategic innovation in established companies', *Strategy for Business*. M. Mazzucato. London: Sage.
Milliken, F.J. and Lant, T.K. (1991). 'The effect of an organization's recent performance history on strategic persistence and change: The role of managerial interpretations',

in P. Shrivastava, *Advances in Strategic Management*, Vol 7. Greenwich, CT: JAI Press.

Mintzberg, H. and Waters, J.A. (1982). 'Strategy in an entrepreneurial firm', *Academy of Management Journal* 25(3): 465–500.

Moch, M.K. and Morse, E.V. (1977). 'Size, centralization and organizational adoption of innovation', *American Sociological Review* 42(10): 716–25.

Pavitt, K. (1991). 'Key characteristics of the large innovating firm', *British Journal of Management* 2(1): 41–50.

Prahalad, C.K. and Krishnan, M.S. (2008). *The New Age of Innovation: Driving Co-Created Value Through Global Networks*. New York: McGraw-Hill.

Schumpeter, J. (1934). *The Theory of Economic Development*. Cambridge, MA: Harvard Business School Press.

Schumpeter, J. (1942). *Capitalism, Socialism and Democracy*. New York: Harper & Row.

Teece, D. J., Pisano, G. and Shuen, A. (2002). 'Dynamics, capabilities and strategic management', in M. Mazzucato, *Strategy in Business*. London: Sage.

Tushman, M.L. and Anderson, P. (1986). 'Technological discontinuities and organizational environments', *Administrative Science Quarterly* 31: 439–65.

Tushman, M.L. and O'Reilly, C.A. (1996). *Winning Through Innovation: A Practical Guide to Leading Organizational Change and Renewal*. Boston: Harvard Business School Press.

Valentin, E.K. (2002). 'Anatomy of a fatal business strategy', *Decision Making for Business*, J.G. Salaman. London: Sage.

Van de Ven, A. (1986). 'Central problems in the management of innovation', *Management Science* 32: 591–607.

von Hippel, E. (1994). 'Sticky information and the locus of problem solving: implications for innovation', *Management Science* 40: 429–39.

von Hippel, E., Churchill, J., *et al.* (1998). *Breakthrough Products and Services with Lead User Research*. Oxford: Oxford University Press.

Chapter 7

Bell, D. (1974). *The Coming of Post-Industrial Society: A Venture in Social Forecasting*. London: Heinemann.

Berger, P. and Luckmann, T. (1967). *The Social Construction of Reality*. London: Penguin.

Brunsson, N. and Olsen, J.P. (2002). *The Reforming Organization*. London: Routledge.

Budros, A. (1997). 'The new capitalism and organisational rationality: the adoption of downsizing programs 1979–1994', *Social Forces* 76(1): 229–49.

Calori, R., Johnson G. and Sarnin, A. (1992). 'French and British top managers' understanding of the structures and dynamics of their industries: a cognitive analysis', *British Journal of Management* 3(2): 61–78.

Chia, R. and Holt, R. (2006). 'Strategy as practical coping: a Heideggerian perspective', *Organization Studies* 27(5): 636–55.

Fahey, I. and Narayanan, V.K. (1989). 'Linking changes in revealed causal maps and environmental change: an empirical study', *Journal Of Management Studies* 26(4): 361–78.

Giddens, A. (1984). *The Constitution of Society: Outline of a Theory of Structuration*. Cambridge: Polity.

Gioia, D.A. (1986). 'Symbols, scripts and sensemaking: creating meaning in the organizational experience', in H.P. Sims and D.A. Gioia, *The Thinking Organization*. San Francisco: Jossey-Bass.

Gioia, D.A., Thomas, J.B., Clark, S.M. and Chittipeddi, K. (1994). 'Symbolism and strategic change in academia: the dynamics of sensemaking and influence', *Organization Science* 5(3): 363–83.

Grant, R.M. (1996). 'Toward a knowledge-based theory of the firm' *Strategic Management Journal* 17: 109–22.

Greenwood, R. and Hinings, C.R. (1996). 'Understanding radical organizational change: bringing together the old and the new institutionalism', *Academy of Management Review* 21(4): 1022–54.

Grinyer, P. and Spender, J.C. (1979). *Turnaround: Managerial Recipes for Strategic Success: the Fall and Rise of the Newton Chambers Group.* London: Associated Business Press.

Henderson, R.M. and Clark, K. (1990). 'Architectural innovation: the reconfiguration of existing product technologies and the failure of established firms', *Administrative Science Quarterly* 35: 9–30.

Hodgkinson, G. and Sparrow, P. (2002). *The Competent Organization.* Buckingham: Open University Press.

Johnson, G. (1987). *Strategic Change and the Strategy Process.* Oxford: Blackwell.

Johnson, G. (1988). 'Rethinking incrementalism', *Strategic Management Journal* 9(1): 75–91.

Lant, T.K. (2002). 'Organizational cognition and interpretation', in J.A.C. Baum, *The Blackwell Companion to Organizations.* Oxford: Blackwell: 344–62.

Miller, P. and Rose, N. (1993). 'Governing economic life', in M. Gane and T. Johnson (eds), *Foucault's New Domains*, London: Routledge: 75–106.

Nonaka, I. and Takeuchi, H. (1995). *The Knowledge-Creating Company: How Japanese Companies Create the Dynamics of Innovation.* Oxford: Oxford University Press.

Palmer, D.A., Devereaux Jennings, P. and Xueguang Zhou (1993) 'Late adoption of the multidivisional form by large U.S. corporations: institutional, political, and economic accounts', *Administrative Science Quarterly*, Vol. 38.

Polanyi, M. (1966). *The Tacit Dimension.* New York: Doubleday.

Porter, M. and Ketels, C. (2003). *UK Competitiveness: Moving to the Next Stage.* London: DTI/ESRC.

Reger, R.K. (1990). 'Managerial thought structures and competitive positioning', in A.S. Huff, *Mapping Strategic Thought.* Chichester: John Wiley & Sons, Ltd.

Sparrow, P. (1994). 'The psychology of strategic management: emerging themes of diversity and cognition', *International Review of Industrial and Organizational Psychology* 9: 147–81.

Teece, D. J., Pisano, G. and Shuen, A. (2002). 'Dynamics, capabilities and strategic management', in M. Mazzucato, *Strategy in Business.* London: Sage.

Tsoukas, H. and Mylonopoulos, N. (2004). 'Introduction: knowledge construction and creation in organizations', *British Journal of Management* 15 (Special Issue): S1–S8.

Tsoukas, H. and Vladimirou, E. (2001). 'What is organizational knowledge?' *Journal of Management Studies* 38(7): 973–93.

Tushman, M.L. and O'Reilly, C.A. (1996). *Winning Through Innovation: A practical Guide to Leading Organizational Change and Renewal.* Boston: Harvard Business School Press.

Valentin, E.K. (2002). 'Anatomy of a fatal business strategy', in J.G. Salaman, *Decision Making for Business.* London: Sage.

Van de Ven, A. (1986). 'Central problems in the management of innovation', *Management Science* 32: 591–607.

Weick, K.W. (1995). *Sensemaking in Organizations.* Newbury Park, CA: Sage.

Whittington, R. (2002). 'Practice perspectives on strategy: unifying and developing a field', Working Paper Said Business School.

Whittington, R. (2006). 'Completing the practice turn in strategy research', *Organization Studies* 27(5): 613–34.

Chapter 8

Argyris, C. (2004). *Reasons and Rationalizations: The Limits to Organizational Knowledge*. Oxford: Oxford University Press.

Beer, M. and Eisenstat, R.A. (1996). 'Developing an organisation capable of implementing strategy and learning.' *Human Relations* **49**(5): 597–619.

Beer, M., Eisenstadt, R. and Spector, B. (1990). 'Why change programs don't produce change', *Harvard Business Review*, November/December: 158–66.

Beer, M. and Nohria, N. (2000). 'Cracking the code of change', *Harvard Business Review* May–June: 133–41.

Brunsson, N. (1982). 'The irrationality of action and action irrationality: decisions, ideologies and organizational actions', *Journal of Management Studies* **19**(1).

Brunsson, N. (1985). *The Irrational Organization: Irrationality as a Basis for Action and Change*. Chichester/New York: John Wiley & Sons, Ltd/Inc.

Brunsson, N. and Olsen, J.P. (2002). *The Reforming Organization*. London: Routledge.

Child, J. (1972). 'Organizational structure, environment and performance: the role of strategic choice'. *Sociology*, **6**(1): 1–22.

Hamel, G. and Prahalad, C.K. (1992). *Competing for the Future*. Boston: Harvard Business School Press.

March, J. G. (1991). 'Exploration and exploitation in organisational learning', *Organisation Science* **2**(1): 71–87.

March, J.G. and Simon, H.A. (1958). *Organizations*. New York: John Wiley & Sons, Inc.

Markides, C. (2002). 'Strategic Innovation in Established Companies', in M. Mazzucato (ed.), *Strategy for Business*. London: Sage.

Pettigrew, A. and Whipp, R. (1991). *Managing Change for Competitive Success*. Oxford: Blackwell.

Storey, J. and Salaman, G. (2004). *Managers of Innovation*. Oxford: Blackwell.

Tate, W. (2009) *The for Search Leadership*. London: Ashgate.

Worrall, L. and Cooper, C.L. (2009) 'The effect of organizational change on managers' experience of their working lives', in J. Storey, P. Wright and D. Ulrich (eds), *The Routledge Companion to Strategic Human Resource Management*. London/New York: Routledge.

Chapter 9

Adler, P. (2001). 'Markets, hierarchy and trust: the knowledge economy and the future of capitalism', *Organization Science* **12**(2): 215–34.

Argyris, C. (1999). *On Organizational Learning*. Oxford: Blackwell.

Deming, W.E. (1986). *Out of Crisis: Quality, Productivity and Competitive Position*. Cambridge: Cambridge University Press.

Frisch, B. (2008). 'When teams can't decide', *Harvard Business Review* November: 121–6.

Lant, T.K. and Milliken, F.J. (1992). 'The role of managerial learning and interpretation in strategic persistence and reorientation: an empirical exploration', *Strategic Management Journal* **13**(8): 585–608.

Quinn, R.E. (1988). *Beyond Rational Management: Mastering the Paradoxes and Competing Demands of High Performance*. San Francisco: Jossey-Bass.

Stacey, R. (2000). *Strategic Management and Organizational Dynamics: The Challenge of Complexity*. (3rd edn) Harlow: Pearson Education.

Index

Index compiled by Terry Halliday
(HallidayTerence@aol.com)